PORTFOLIOS FOR INTERIOR DESIGNERS

A Guide to Portfolios, Creative Resumes, and the Job Search

Maureen Mitton

WILEY

John Wiley & Sons, Inc.

Library of Congress Cataloging-in-Publication Data:

Mitton, Maureen.
 Portfolios for interior designers: a guide to portfolios, creative resumes, and the job search / Maureen Mitton.
 p. cm.
 Includes bibliographical references and index.
 ISBN 978-0-470-40816-2 (pbk.) ; ISBN 978-0-470-91340-6 (ebk); ISBN 978-0-470-91341-3 (ebk);
 ISBN 978-0-470-91342-0 (ebk)
 1. Interior decoration rendering. 2. Design services—Marketing. 3. Interior decoration—Vocational guidance. I. Title. II. Title: Guide to portfolios, creative resumes, and the job search.
 NK2113.5.M59 2010
 747.068'8—dc22
 2009049256

Printed in the United States of America

10 9 8 7 6 5 4 3 2

To my mother, who bought me a portfolio (and a blue wool suit) so that I would finally stop waiting tables and hanging out at the beach. And to my father, who thought nothing of driving across the country—any country—to see what was on the other side.

CONTENTS

ACKNOWLEDGMENTS

This book would not be even remotely possible without the many generous people who contributed the wonderful work that graces its pages. I have thoroughly enjoyed the process of looking at work by so many talented and helpful people. If time and space allowed, I would write a paragraph about each contributor; instead, a simple list will have to suffice.

A special thank-you to Ambica Prakash and Bob Atwell, who both contributed major chapter content. Bill Wikrent at the University of Wisconsin-Stout provided excellent technical information on a number of topics. As usual, the staff at Wiley has been wonderful, thank you to Paul Drougas, Sadie Abuhoff, and David Sassian. Andrew Miller seems to have taken my confusing sentences and made them into real paragraphs, for that I am very thankful.

I do thank all of you from the bottom of my heart.

Contributors list, in order of appearance:

(Schools and educators have been listed at the request of the contributor.)

Jim Taft

Melissa Brewer

Nicole Banaszewski

Laura Purcell

Shelley Pecha

Mollie Drabik

Sharon M. Stickney

Hannah M. Sparks

Jennifer Irey, Iowa State University. Instructor: Cigdem Akkurt.

Camilla Stine

Alvin & Company Inc

Catherine Popp, The Illinois Institute of Art-Schaumburg. Instructor: Suzann Nordstrom.

Pina Zangaro

Elizabeth Kruse

Jordan Breedlove

Jaime Schreiner, Iowa State University. Instructor: Cigdem Akkurt.

Denis Belenko

Katie Carlson

Ivan Trushin

Jennifer Leafblad

Hannah Roesler

Elizabeth Calka

Nathan Piper

Amy Stemper

Holly Sivula

Katie Goznian

Lindsay Lindner

Dustin Sparks

Julia Stephan

Lisa Schwennsen

Timothy Dolan

Carlin Traugott Cambell, Appalachian State University. Instructors: Timothy Dolan, Jeanne Mercer-Ballard.

Laura Van Der Sanden

Jennifer Pike, University of Cincinnati's College of Design, Architecture, Art & Planning (DAAP).

Amelia Treptow

Jennifer Williams, Florida State University. Instructor: Lisa Waxman.

Helen Woods

Katie Cantwell

Holly McWhorter

Julian Hensch

Clive Walters, Liverpool John Moores University

Katarzyna Borowy

Kyle Snyder

Molly Naparsteck

Dayna Beck, Westwood College

Emily Nettler

Thank you all again.

PART I

BUILDING BLOCKS

ONE

INTRODUCTION

The following quotes sum up key points in this book:

Design—*whether graphic, industrial, interior or architecture—is the process of taking unrelated parts and putting them together in an organized unit.* ▪

—ALEXANDER WHITE, *THE ELEMENTS OF GRAPHIC DESIGN: SPACE, UNITY, PAGE ARCHITECTURE, AND TYPE* (2002)

And:

Work your plan and plan your work. ▪

This book is intended as an aid in taking what are often seemingly unrelated elements and putting them together in an organized unit—and not being overwhelmed by the process (that's where having a plan worth working comes in).

Many students, graduates, and job seekers feel overwhelmed by the thought of putting together a portfolio: in representing your entire body of work, the portfolio can symbolize your fears about graduation, employment—even about a successful future. (No small issue there!) However, by breaking down the elements of portfolio development, you can, in fact, develop a plan that yields excellent results.

One key is to stay focused on the tasks at hand and not become overwhelmed by the future or by fear. Instead, focus on working through the process in a step-by-step manner as described in the following pages and symbolized in Figure 1-1.

PHOTOGRAPH BY JIM TAFF.

FIGURE 1-1 Imagining the job search and portfolio development process as a series of small and manageable steps will keep you from becoming overwhelmed. ■

The following chapters convey the ways in which the components of an interior designer's education, experience, and personal narrative can be put together in an organized manner. Additional information about the process and materials required for finding employment for interior designers is also included.

This book has a somewhat unusual organizational structure. The first section is devoted to the basic information required for the job search and for preparing the portfolio; the second section is devoted to examples. Much like a portfolio, the written components of this book are as succinct as possible, with the focus on the work and images.

OVERVIEW OF THE JOB SEARCH

For those of you who have not searched for and obtained a professional, full-time job previously, a bit of background about the process is included here. Put very briefly, the process can be seen as consisting of three phases:

> **≫ STANDARD FULL-TIME JOB SEARCH PROCESS PHASES***
>
> **Phase 1:** Preparation
>
> Self-assessment and development of a portfolio, resume, cover letter, and corollary items.
>
> **Phase 2:** Research and Distribution
>
> Researching potential employers and opportunities; the systematic distribution of the items prepared in phase one.
>
> **Phase 3:** The Interview and Offer
>
> Preparing for the interview, the interview and follow-up, receiving and accepting the offer.
>
> *Due to ongoing economic uncertainty, many first jobs are not full-time.

The process is, however, more complex than a short list might indicate, and there are many books devoted entirely to each phase mentioned. At specific times in your life, it may be worthwhile to do a serious study of any one of these items or phases. For example, self-assessment is incredibly important as you contemplate moving from one profession to another, or from one specialty area to another. Richard Nelson Bolles's *What Color Is Your Parachute* (2009) is an excellent resource for those involved in a job search, and it has quite a bit of content devoted to self-assessment for those considering career changes.

Remember the quote about working your plan and planning your work? Success with that concept starts right here. By working through the three phases listed above, you will be developing a plan that you can follow through on. Going through the first steps thoroughly will enable you to develop a clear understanding of what type of job you want or where you want to live; then you will have a plan worth working.

PHASE 1: PREPARATION

A serious self-assessment will help you identify your strengths and weaknesses, as well as the tasks that you find most enjoyable. Most readers of this book, however, have already made the decision to go into design after a previous period of assessment—as well as a huge investment of time and money. Rather than focusing on the type of personal assessment required as you contemplate career choices, this chapter will therefore consider ways of assessing your work, experience, and life story as you begin to prepare a portfolio and other job-search tools.

This type of limited self-assessment requires a careful evaluation of your education, the school or professional projects you've completed, your life experiences, as well as what brings meaning to your life. Think of it as a twofold process. You are assessing your strengths and experiences so that you can state them clearly in your resume and portfolio. And you are exploring what you like to do and what your goals are (project management? retail design? living in an urban setting?). The idea is to assess both what you can do well that makes you happy as well as how you can best demonstrate this to a potential employer.

FIGURE 1-2 Part of self-assessment leads to an understanding what type of living environment—rural or urban, for example—appeals to you. (This is a photograph of Chicago viewed from the Chicago River.) ■

FIGURE 1-3 Self-assessment also requires you to identify strengths, weaknesses, and things you enjoy doing. ■

The basic checklists that follow will help you with both types of assessments.

≫ SELF-ASSESSMENT: PREFERENCES AND INTERESTS LIST

List at least three types of design you enjoyed in school or in a previous job.

What are your geographic preferences? Are you drawn to a particular region, city, or state? Do you prefer an urban, suburban, or rural setting?

What is your firm size preference? Small firms tend to provide broader experience; large firms offer focused entry-level experience.

Consider stability: is financial or job security more important to you than working on exciting projects?

How much travel is acceptable to you?

How much money do you require? How little can you live on?

Consider time commitments: is a good deal of overtime acceptable or desired, or do you prefer more time off?

Where do you want to be in two years? In five years?

Experienced designers should consider what aspects of work they enjoyed or were successful with: project management, design, specification, client interaction, and so on. (List a minimum of five).

List five additional things that you want or that are not acceptable.

>> SELF-ASSESSMENT: STRENGTHS AND PROOF OF TALENTS, SKILLS, AND EXPERIENCE

How do I prove that I am worth hiring? (What must I include in the portfolio and resume?)

Best projects (see chapter 2, The Portfolio Inventory).

Best results on specific projects or experiences.

Job-related skills: software, programming, project management, specification writing, and so on. List at least ten.

Personal or self-management skills such as reliability, tolerance, and flexibility (these are part of who you are). List at least five.

Transferable skills (from seemingly unrelated work that might be used in design, such as the ability to lead meetings, work with clients, etc.). List five, if possible.

Specialized areas of knowledge (foreign languages, metric system use, building construction, etc.).

Specialized certifications such as Leadership in Energy and Environmental Design (LEED), National Council of Interior Design Qualification (NCIDQ), state certification or registration, and so on.

Unusual experiences that would set you apart in a positive way.

Specialized education such as a Council for Interior Design Accreditation (CIDA) accredited program, international study, or a minor or specialization in an allied field.

Organizational leadership experience (with a design association, as dorm management staff, or even as a camp counselor).

>> SELF-ASSESSMENT: DEAL BREAKERS

These are things that you are not willing to do or are not interested in. While these are worth identifying, do not be too quick to judge things that you have not experienced.

Project specialty/type of work: what type of project would you refuse to work on?

Values: what do you value that you are unwilling to compromise?

Type of firm or company (in-house designer, furniture dealership, etc.).

Are you able to work overtime and on weekends?

Are you able to travel?

Are you willing to relocate?

Where are you unwilling to live?

What is your absolute bottom line as far as salary?

These lists can be a start toward targeting your thoughts and focusing on your needs and desires. Understanding the answers to the questions in these lists will help you develop your resume and portfolio (phase 1, or preparation) and also aid with phase 2—research into your ideal firms and employers and how to contact them. Detailed information on resume writing and development, including help with skill identification, is provided in chapter 5; what is listed here is merely a beginning, meant to provide a jump start.

Portfolio development—the focus of this book—is another significant part of phase 1. The actual information for the planning and development of the portfolio can be found in the following chapter; that content has been treated separately for the sake of clarity—not because it should be seen as a separate phase.

PHASE 2: RESEARCH AND DISTRIBUTION

Research: Types and Sources

The purpose of this research is to develop a list of potential employers to which job-search materials can be distributed and to gain information about the type of work and projects potential employers are engaged in. Research therefore leads to both knowledge about possible job openings as well as background information about potential employers. The latter is important because it allows you to create customized cover letters and offers insight into a company's corporate culture.

There are two broad categories of resume distribution. The first is *targeted*. This means you find the exact firm—or type of firm—you wish to work for, and *target* your cover letter (and perhaps your resume as well) to each firm. Targeted distribution should also include some form of mini-portfolio or well-designed examples of your work. In some cases, the portfolio will also be edited to include specific projects targeted to an employer.

Broadcasting is another form of distribution in which cover letters, resumes, and samples of work are sent to a *broad* swath of employers. In such cases, less individualized editing is done to the resumes and cover letters. Broadcast resumes by nature are more generic; they are being cast wide, like a large net, in the hope of catching an employer. Nonetheless, a minimal amount of research should still be done about the firms to which broadcast resumes are sent so a project or type of work can be mentioned. (See chapter 5: Resumes and Related Correspondence.)

The decision about whether to broadcast or target resumes comes from answers to the questions in the individual self-assessment. When it is absolutely clear that a defined need creates a target, then research about that specific area should be conducted. For example, if the most important issue in a search is working near Denver, then research should be focused on appropriate employers in that area.

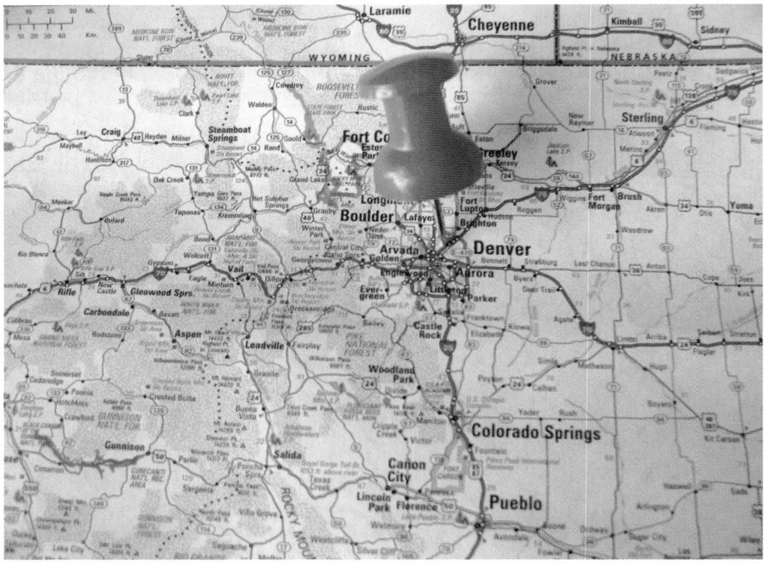

FIGURE 1-4 Self-assessment may identify a particular location or region as the focus of a job search. ■

Continuing with this example, you could pinpoint Denver and then research all of the potential employers within a 50-mile radius. If you are not planning to own an automobile, then you would target your research to employers in areas served by public transportation.

In some cases, the self-assessment will show that a design specialty—library design, for example—should be the focus of the research. Firms specializing in this type of work are uncommon, and specific periodicals and research into recently completed libraries will aid in this type of fact-finding.

While specific situations will vary, in most cases research will lead you to find out what kind of work potential employers do, where they are located, how they can be contacted, and perhaps even where to obtain more information about them. This information is not only helpful in providing the job seeker with a target but is also useful in creating cover letters with accurate references to the work of a specific potential employer. (See chapter 5 for information on cover letters.)

The research necessary for each job will vary greatly with the individual. Remember that research is not simply finding job openings; good research often involves finding out which firms do certain types of work or projects and then targeting those companies with targeted cover letters. In other words, research involves finding out who is doing what where and with whom. The following lists of sources for this type of research are just a starting point.

NATIONAL AND REGIONAL PUBLICATIONS

While not design specific, these publications can contain information about national and regional design-related business.

City business journals. Major metropolitan areas are served by Business Journals (main site: HTTP://WWW.BIZJOURNALS.COM). These tend to cover all businesses within an area, with construction, architecture, and design mentioned often and in special issues. Going back to the previous example, one could check the *Denver Business Journal* (HTTP://DENVER.BIZJOURNALS.COM/DENVER).

Local papers for cities and regions. Much like business journals, local papers cover construction, architecture, and design in special issues, and in sections on the home and business. The *New York Times*, *Chicago Tribune*, and *Los Angeles Times* tend to feature international and national design stories.

White pages and yellow pages. Online yellow pages (HTTP://YELLOWPAGES.AOL.COM) for each city are available. Searching for architecture, interior design, commercial interior design, and office furniture dealerships can prove helpful.

DESIGN ASSOCIATIONS

The following have helpful Web sites, magazines, and (in some cases) regional newsletters. It is worth looking at competition winners in addition to feature articles to find information on firms and specialties.

American Academy of Healthcare Interior Designers
HTTP://WWW.AAHID.ORG

American Society of Interior Designers (ASID)
The national magazine is ASID *Icon*
HTTP://WWW.ASID.ORG
HTTP://WWW.ASID.ORG/BCDEVELOPMENT/JOBS/BANK/DEFAULT.HTM

British Interior Design Association
HTTP://WWW.BIDA.ORG

The Center for Healthcare Design
HTTP://WWW.HEALTHDESIGN.ORG/BLOG

Chartered Society of Designers (CSD) (UK)
HTTP://WWW.CSD.ORG.UK

Design Council (UK)
HTTP://WWW.DESIGNCOUNCIL.ORG.UK/EN

Design Institute of Australia
HTTP://WWW.DIA.ORG.AU

The Hospitality Industry Network (NEWH)
NEWH Magazine
HTTP://WWW.NEWH.ORG

Interior Design Association Hong Kong
HTTP://WWW.HKIDA.COM

International Interior Design Association (IIDA)
The national magazine is *IIDA Perspective*
HTTP://WWW.IIDA.ORG
HTTP://WWW.IIDA.ORG/CONTENT.CFM/CAREERS

National Kitchen and Bath Association
HTTP://WWW.NKBA.ORG

Retail Design Institute (for chapter information, awards, etc.)
HTTP://WWW.RETAILDESIGNINSTITUTE.ORG
HTTP://WWW.RETAILDESIGNINSTITUTE.ORG/JOBS.PHP

DESIGN INDUSTRY PUBLICATIONS AND WEB SITES

American Institute of Architects (AIA) state and regional design magazines: State and regional chapters produce informative magazines that include articles on firms and often have lists of companies doing specialized work. To continue with the example given, *Architect Colorado*, AIA Colorado's quarterly magazine, would be the choice for research about design in Denver (HTTP://AIACOLORADO.ORG).

These publications and Web sites feature articles on projects and firms as well as annual design awards.

Contract magazine
HTTP://WWW.CONTRACTMAGAZINE.COM

Dezignaré
HTTP://WWW.DEZIGNARE.COM

HealthcareDesign magazine
HTTP://WWW.HEALTHCAREDESIGNMAGAZINE.
COM

Hospitality Design magazine
HTTP://WWW.HOSPITALITYDESIGN.COM

ID magazine
HTTP://WWW.ID-MAG.COM
The focus of this magazine is industrial design, but the annual design review includes environmental and furniture design categories.

Interior Design magazine
HTTP://WWW.INTERIORDESIGN.NET
Lists the top one hundred interior design giants and contains project and billing information about those firms.

Interior & Sources magazine.
HTTP://WWW.INTERIORSANDSOURCES.COM

International Facility Management Association (IFMA)
HTTP://WWW.IFMA.ORG

Metropolis magazine
HTTP://WWW.METROPOLISMAG.COM

ASSOCIATIONS AND PUBLICATIONS FOR ALLIED PROFESSIONS

The following publications and Web sites are not devoted specifically to design, but they occasionally run design-related articles and features.

The Associated General Contractors of America
HTTP://WWW.AGC.ORG

Hospitality Net (industry news section)
HTTP://WWW.HOSPITALITYNET.ORG

Library Leadership & Management Association (LLAMA)
HTTP://WWW.ALA.ORG/ALA/MGRPS/DIVS/
LLAMA/ABOUT/INDEX.CFM
Part of the American Library Association (http://www.ala.org); cosponsors of yearly design competitions.

National Association of Homebuilders
HTTP://WWW.NAHB.ORG

Nation's Restaurant News
HTTP://WWW.NRN.COM

Retail Traffic magazine
HTTP://RETAILTRAFFICMAG.COM

Networking

Formal networking is the systematic pursuit of new contacts and information. It's organized and planned. Networking is relational. A good networking relationship will be mutually beneficial to both parties. ▪

—Minnesota Department of Employment and Economic Development,
Creative Job Search (CJS) Online Guide (2009)

While the term *networking* has become a bit of a cliché, the concept of creating a network of linked contacts is quite worthwhile. A large percentage of jobs are gained by some form of networked relationship.

What most people seek to gain from networking is a series of contacts—that is, names of design professionals and potential employers. Some of these contacts may be helpful immediately, while others may prove helpful only years later.

Networking should be handled systematically. While your demeanor should be casual, the information you gather should be thoroughly organized. For example, at workshops, professional association meetings, and conferences, it is wise to make notes on the back of business cards you collect. Write down information that will remind you of the initial conversation or situation. The most organized networkers keep lists of contacts with phone numbers and dates and stay in touch by following up frequently (but not too often!).

According to the *CJS*, "**Networking isn't begging. In fact, you shouldn't be asking for a job; you should be seeking information that may lead to a job.**" It is imperative that you look at networking contacts as potential relationships, not as job sources.

Most social situations can be seen as networking opportunities; time at the gym, restaurants, and professional associations can all engender conversations about careers and contacts and may lead to good relationships that form a true career network over time. Some additional opportunities for networking are listed below.

≫ NETWORKING: OPPORTUNITIES

Design-related classes and workshops

Job and career fairs

Meetings of any professional organization (becoming a volunteer or an officer can provide the best opportunities)

Social organizations (anything from sports teams to local civic groups)

Trade shows

Specialized relationships
  Classmates

Professors

College alumni associations

Internet networking resources
  HTTP://WWW.LINKEDIN.COM
  HTTP://WWW.NETWORKINGFOR
  PROFESSIONALS.COM
  HTTP://PIPL.COM/DIRECTORY
  HTTP://WWW.SPOKE.COM
  HTTP://WWW.XING.COM
  HTTP://WWW.ZOOMINFO.COM

Keep a list with information about the people you meet and where you met them. Networking guidebooks often advise you to get in touch with contacts on a regular basis. Checking in with contacts occasionally is a good idea, but don't make a pest of yourself; use the experience to demonstrate your professionalism and levelheadedness.

Informational Interviews

Contacts in your network may lead to *informational interviews,* which are conducted as a means of getting feedback, advice, and guidance, rather than to obtain a specific job. When you contact the potential interviewer, specifically request such an interview, and be clear that you are seeking guidance and feedback rather than a job. Always offer to establish a short time frame (say, 15 to 30 minutes) for such appointments.

Informational interviews generally involve a very quick review of the portfolio as well as a few questions and answers. The interviewee should ask for advice about making improvements to the portfolio or resume and seeking additional design-related contacts. It is generally acceptable to ask to leave a resume—or to send a newly edited version with any suggested improvements at a later date.

Informational interviews straddle the phases between research and distribution. In many ways, you are seeking information for—researching—your job search. Yet it may also be the first time you have the chance to drop off a resume or to ask for additional information for future reference. Therefore, if you are offered an informational interview, go on it! And if your request for an informational interview is denied, don't take it personally; such things are usually a matter of time, and many professionals have little to spare.

Distribution

Distribution occurs when the employers located during the research phase are contacted and resumes and cover letters are distributed. Successful distribution requires a systematic and organized approach. Keeping accurate lists of what was sent, where it was sent, when it was sent, and any follow up that was done is highly recommended.

For designers, sending a resume and cover letter may not be enough; some type of visual content must be sent as well. (Design is, after all, visual work.) It may be in the form of a mini-portfolio, or a few letter-size sheets with project images on them. (More information on mini and sample portfolios can be found in chapters 2 and 7.)

Every situation is different. When a job opening is posted, you should send a cover letter (that includes a reference to the posting), a resume, and a mini-portfolio or examples of your work. When no job opening is posted, send the same items; however, in such cases, the cover letter must describe why you have a strong interest in working for that employer. (See chapters 5 and 6 for additional information on resumes and cover letters.)

The task of distribution is made easier after successful networking, when contacts can lead to productive information about openings and employers. However, in tight job markets, you may need to take drastic methods and distribute as much information as possible in the hope of gaining interviews. The following list contains information about additional options for distribution, as well as information about job openings.

JOB POSTINGS, LISTS, AND OPPORTUNITIES

On- and off-campus job fairs

Campus placement office

Design associations' job postings (see page 11)

Employment agencies and headhunters

General online job postings:
HTTP://WWW.AFTERCOLLEGE.COM
HTTP://WWW.BESTJOBSUSA.COM
HTTP://WWW.CAREERBUILDER.COM
HTTP://WWW.COLLEGECENTRAL.COM
HTTP://WWW.INDEED.COM

HTTP://WWW.JOB.COM
HTTP://WWW.JOB-HUNT.ORG
HTTP://JOBSEARCH.USAJOBS.GOV
HTTP://WWW.MONSTER.COM
HTTP://WWW.RILEYGUIDE.COM/JOBS.HTML
HTTP://WWW.SIMPLYHIRED.COM

Academic postings:

For interior design positions: http://www.idec.org

(See employment announcements.)

General academic positions: http://chronicle.com/jobs

PLACES TO UPLOAD PORTFOLIOS AND IMAGES
HTTP://WWW.CARBONMADE.COM
HTTP://WWW.COROFLOT.COM
HTTP://OTHERPEOPLESPIXELS.COM

PHASE 3: THE INTERVIEW AND OFFER

Being offered an interview is validation of your hard work conducting research and developing your resume and cover letter. Use this validation as a boost to feel positive rather than focusing on feeling nervous. This can be seen as the last part of the "plan your work and work your plan" quote; nothing should be left to chance.

In some situations, the first interview will be conducted by phone. This is often a screening interview conducted by a human resources professional or by a design manager. Questions asked in a phone interview are much like those asked at an in-person interview. If the phone interview goes well, a second interview may be scheduled; most often, these will be done in person. Some tips for interviewing are as follows.

>> INTERVIEW TIPS

Plan the trip to the interview in advance; know the best route and parking locations.

Arrive a few minutes early.

Dress appropriately.

Bring a notebook, a business card, a copy of your resume, and a leave-behind portfolio. (If you did not send one previously, this is a must do.)

Research: be informed about the type of work the employer does. If possible, familiarize yourself with actual projects.

Rehearse: practice dealing with your portfolio, shaking hands with your portfolio in one hand, and setting it down.

Use a firm handshake and maintain eye contact.

Do not make excuses for issues with any of the work in your portfolio. If a question comes up related to your work, answer it honestly but don't go on about negative aspects of projects or design work.

Provide positive examples to reflect your skills and attributes.

Keep answers to the point and aim for clarity.

Ask questions.

Listen—don't interrupt.

Be enthusiastic about your work and the work of the employer.

Try to relax: you've made it this far!

Thank the interviewer(s) and try to get a business card from each (these are new contacts in your network).

Some commonly asked questions are worth preparing for. One is, "Tell me about yourself." Think of your answer as a brief sales pitch. Prepare a short personal biography related to your professional life you can relate with clarity.

Interview questions about strengths and weaknesses are also common. Talking about strengths is relatively easy and is best done using concrete examples. For example, if organization is a strength, then give examples of times you have served as an organizer or things you have successfully organized.

Weaknesses are harder to discuss, and some answers to this question have become something of an urban legend over time. One standard response is that one's weaknesses are working too hard and caring too much about work, but such answers will likely be seen as a transparent attempt to avoid the question. A better option is to mention a weakness and discuss how you overcame it—perhaps you overcame shyness through your success at public speaking or organizational leadership, for example.

A list of additional commonly asked questions follows below.

» THE INTERVIEW: COMMONLY ASKED QUESTIONS

Why did you decide to be an interior designer?

Describe your education.

Describe your most rewarding college experience.

What have you learned from participation in extracurricular activities/ASID/college sports?

Why would you like to work for this company/firm/studio?

Why did you decide to apply for this job?

What is important to you in a job?

Give an example of a difficult decision you have made.

Give an example of how you solved a problem in the past.

Give an example of how you showed leadership in a previous situation.

What are your long-range career goals? What are you doing to achieve them?

Describe a work situation in which you were under a lot of pressure and how you handled it.

What do you anticipate might be your greatest problem with this job?

How do others describe you?

What will you do to be successful in this job?

What is your most memorable accomplishment?

Where do you see yourself in five years?

How are you qualified for this job?

Why should we hire you?

Why did you leave your last job?

You may also occasionally be asked your salary requirements (see page 18).

Your answers to these questions should illustrate your skills, creativity, strengths, and your ability to learn new things and contribute to the organization. Answering questions with polite confidence and enthusiasm will help to convey a good attitude.

The interview is also a time to get to know the firm and to get a sense of what working there would be like. Politely ask for a tour of the facilities and take a good look around to get a feeling for the corporate culture. The following is a list of questions that can be asked of employers in order to get to know more about the job and the company.

≫ QUESTIONS TO ASK EMPLOYERS

What qualities are you looking for in your new hires?

What are the responsibilities associated with this position?

With whom will I be working?

Who will be my supervisor (and what is his or her supervisory style)?

Can you describe typical first-year tasks and job assignments?

Can you describe a typical day on this job?

What is the history of this position?

Is there room for promotion should I exceed expectations?

How and when will my performance be evaluated on this job?

When do you plan to make the hiring decision?

The last step of any interview is writing and sending a thank-you note to those involved in the interview. This should be written immediately and sent as soon as possible. Information on thank-you notes and their content can be found in chapter 5.

If you learn the job has been given to someone else, let the employer know that you remain interested in the job (first choices occasionally do not accept jobs). Politely asking about future openings indicates your continued interest in the employer. If it seems appropriate, asking for feedback on the interview can be helpful at future interviews. While the feedback itself can be very disappointing, don't take it too personally; the fact that you were offered an interview is a huge compliment and something to be proud of.

Appendix 1 contains statements made by professionals that may prove helpful as you prepare for the interview.

The Offer: Salary and Negotiation

Salary is typically not discussed until there is an offer of employment. At the time of an offer there is, in some cases, a bit of negotiation about salary and benefits.

Employers may ask what your salary requirements are or, if you are already employed, what your current salary is. This is always a tricky situation, especially if the job is a good fit and other aspects

of it s   negotiation may force you to play a bit of cat and mouse. You can
alwa   around by asking, "What was the previous person's salary?"

One   against the salary offer and what the job has to offer
long term. Unfortunately, it is not uncommon for someone to accept a dream job and take
a part-time job in addition, just to make ends meet. The following is a list of considerations
regarding salary negotiations.

» SALARY CONSIDERATIONS

Research the cost of living in the area. Consider rent, parking fees, and other costs specific
to this area such as heating, cooling, goceries, and car insurance. Make a decision about
what you can reasonably accept.

Try to find the salary range for similar positions (consulting *Interior Design* magazine's Design
Giants Lists, and your network connections). The Bureau of Labor statistics may prove helpful in finding this information: [HTTP://WWW.BLS.GOV/OES/CURRENT/OES271025.HTM].

See also Coroflot's salary survey: HTTP://WWW.COROFLOT.COM/DESIGNSALARIES.

Consider long-term career benefits. Top-ranked firms and famous designers do not always
pay top salaries, but experience at such places can be a resume builder.

Consider benefits such as medical and dental insurance and profit sharing; these can be
worth a great deal of money.

If this is the job you want but not at the salary you need, be honest about that.

Review what you found in self-assessment and see how the offer relates to your findings.

Make a list of pros and cons regarding accepting the job at the salary offered. Discuss this
with someone whose opinion you value.

Reasonable requests for increased benefits, educational support, time off, and paid parking
may be considered in lieu of more money.

It is best to take some time to consider the offer rather than to accept it on the spot. Ask for
at least twenty-four hours to think things over and take time to ask questions and follow up
before accepting.

If the offer is less than you expected, discuss that fact—but not your feelings about it—
with your potential employer.

Being offered the same salary more than once may indicate that it is the top salary available.
It is reasonable to ask when a salary review might be possible if you accept a starting wage
lower than what you expected.

Saying no to a salary offer means saying no to the job: it is typically not a continuation of the
negotiation. This should be done in the most positive manner possible, as the employer may
eventually become a member of your network.

Internships, Contract, and Part-Time Positions

The terms *independent contractor, contractor,* and *contract position* refer to providing services for an employer without being an actual employee of that business. This type of position is technically self-employment and is also referred to as *consulting.* Firms often offer such positions when they are unable to commit to full-time employment or when they require services performed on an as-needed, rather than an ongoing, basis. The benefit to the employer is that there is no commitment to ongoing employment, and no benefits are provided.

In lean economic times, contracting employment is common, and such positions are often offered to entry-level designers as well as those with significant experience. Such offers have more to do with the state of the economy than with the individual. In some cases employers will offer design positions as contract-to-employee, meaning that after serving in a contract capacity for a stated period, the employees will move into full-time employment if they perform well.

Because independent contractors are self-employed, they are responsible for withholding their own taxes and paying self-employment (Social Security) and Medicare taxes. In the United States, the term *independent contractor* is a legal and tax-related term, requiring both the employer and the contractor to file specific income tax forms. There are also special legal requirements for contract work that should be reviewed by anyone considering such employment.

In most cases, independent contractors are not eligible for unemployment insurance, sick leave, or workers' compensation insurance. As a result, a great deal of responsibility falls on the contractor—and very little falls on the employer. Sometimes, however, employment agencies and temporary firms hire design professionals to serve as contract employees within other businesses; in such cases, benefits may be provided by the employment agency.

Contract positions can be sought in the same manner as full-time positions; the same steps of resume distribution and interviewing are involved. Because of the tax and benefit situation, contract employees should be well compensated: a contractor's wages should be at least two to three times higher than those of an hourly or salaried employee.

Part-time work is also offered to both entry-level and experienced designers. Often specialized projects, a tight economy, or the need to replace someone on medical leave will result in the need for part-time designers. This type of job is worth considering if you have other sources of income, you're motivated to work for the employer, or you need to work less than full time. The process for obtaining part-time work is much like the process described for seeking full-time employment.

Internship, cooperative education, practicum: these words can describe either volunteer or paid positions used to gain experience in your chosen field. Various colleges and universities use these terms to describe the concept of a student or recent graduate undergoing practical training within the profession.

Some universities require a paid internship, while others simply encourage them. In addition, some universities have highly engaged placement centers that aid in students obtaining internships, while others do little more than provide internship postings. Check with your school's placement or career center to determine what your current educational program has to offer.

The Interior Design Experience Program (IDEP) "is a monitored, documented experience program administered by the National Council for Interior Design Qualification (NCIDQ)," according to the NCIDQ Web site. Not a traditional internship per se, IDEP provides a structure for the transition between formal education and professional practice. IDEP also requires you to complete a specific number of hours under the supervision of an NCIDQ-qualified designer and to work with an outside mentor. Interested individuals can discuss the IDEP program with potential employers.

The information in this chapter has provided you with an overview of a manageable, step-by-step approach to the job search. The following chapters focus on the visual elements used by interior designers in that search: the portfolio, resume, cover letter, and related items.

REFERENCES

The references below contain works cited as well as recommended reading.

Bennett, Scott. 2005. *The Elements of Resume Style: Essential Rules and Eye-Opening Advice for Writing Resumes and Cover Letters that Work.* New York: AMACOM/American Management Association.

Berryman, Gregg. 1990. *Designing Creative Resumes.* Menlo Park, CA: Crisp.

Bolles, Richards. 2009. Job Hunter's Bible.com: Official Site for the Book *What Color Is Your Parachute?* HTTP://WWW.JOBHUNTERSBIBLE.COM.

————2009. *What Color Is Your Parachute?* Berkeley, CA: Ten Speed.

Updated every year. Career guidance and self-assessment are a focus.

Bostwick, Burdette. 1990. *Resume Writing.* New York: John Wiley & Sons.

Columbia State Community College. 2009. Career Services: Career Research Center. HTTP://WWW.COLUMBIASTATE.EDU/CAREER-RESOURCE-CENTER.

An excellent list of references and resources for self-assessment, career planning, and conducting a job search.

Coxford, Lola. 1995. *Resume Writing Made Easy.* Scottsdale, AZ: Gorsuch Scarisbrick.

Dezignaré Interior Design Collective. 2009. No Experience and Looking for Work. *Dezignaré* 2 (10). HTTP://WWW.DEZIGNARE.COM/NEWSLETTER/WORK.HTML.

A good resource for design students.

Emerson College. 2009. Career Services. HTTP://WWW.EMERSON.EDU/CAREER_SERVICES.

Farr, Michael. 2007. *Same-Day Resume.* Indianapolis, IN: JIST.

Fletcher, Kerry. 2009. eHow. How to Find a Job in Interior Design. HTTP://WWW.EHOW.COM/
    HOW_4679336_JOB-INTERIOR-DESIGN.HTML.

Marcus, John. 2003. *The Resume Makeover.* New York: McGraw-Hill.

Minnesota Department of Employment and Economic Development. 2009. *Creative Job Search
    (CJS) Online Guide.* HTTP://WWW.DEED.STATE.MN.US/CJS.

National Council for Interior Design Qualification. n.d. Interior Design Experience Program.
    What Is IDEP? HTTP://WWW.NCIDQ.ORG/IDEP/IDEPINTRO.HTM.

Piotrowski, Katy. 2008. *Career Coward's Guide to Resumes.* Indianapolis, IN: JIST.

Rutgers University Libraries. 2009. The Job Search Process. HTTP://WWW.LIBRARIES.RUTGERS.EDU/
    RUL/RR_GATEWAY/RESEARCH_GUIDES/CAREER/CAREER4.SHTML.

Wall Street Journal. 2009. Careers. HTTP://ONLINE.WSJ.COM/PUBLIC/PAGE/NEWS-CAREER-JOBS.HTML.

    A very helpful site with information about conducting a job search and other employment-
    related issues.

Whitcomb, Susan. 2007. *Resume Magic.* 3rd ed. Indianapolis, IN: JIST.

White, Alexander. 2002. *The Elements of Graphic Design: Space, Unity, Page Architecture, and
    Type.* New York: **Allworth.**

TWO

PORTFOLIO
DEVELOPMENT

Portfolio development is where Alexander White's "process of taking unrelated parts and putting them together in an organized unit" takes place. And that is very much the challenge of the portfolio—to put together a visually cohesive record of your educational and/or professional experiences. This requires meshing visual elements that may have no clear cohesion or seeking some means of connection for all the disparate parts of your experiences.

Yes, this task can seem overwhelming. And for that reason, many soon to-be-graduates—and working designers—put it off. That is a mistake! Rather than becoming overwhelmed, it's best to think of portfolio development as a progression of steps that allow you to identify a visual direction and then follow through on it.

Self-assessment is the first step in portfolio development. But in this case, the assessment has to do with identifying your own unique story, and using the portfolio to tell that story.

TELLING YOUR STORY, CREATING A PERSONAL NARRATIVE

The term *personal narrative* is typically used to describe a type of essay that tells a true story, as experienced by the writer. Often this involves writing about a personal experience and describing how it changed or influenced the writer. In portfolio development, the creation of such a narrative can be done with images, organization, composition, and other visual tools. It is typically not written—it is *shown*. (See Figures 2-1 and 2-2.)

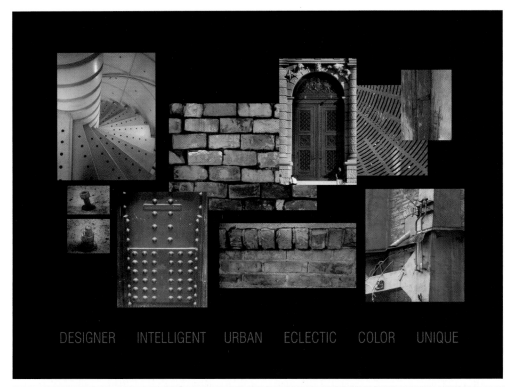

DESIGNER   INTELLIGENT   URBAN   ECLECTIC   COLOR   UNIQUE

MELISSA BREWER FINE ART STUDIO
CURRENT PAINTINGS | DRAWINGS | CERAMICS FOR PRIVATE COLLECTORS

BY MELISSA BREWER.

FIGURES 2-1 AND 2-2 An example of a portfolio with a clear personal visual narrative. This designer is telling her story through choices of imagery, composition, and color. Figure 2-1 illustrates the personal collage used to help develop the portfolio shown in 2-2. In addition to the visual imagery, the use of words at the bottom of the collage help set a direction in her choice of type. (More about type selection can be found in chapter 3.) ■

You tell your story—or relay your personal narrative—with the visual qualities of your portfolio and related items, such as your resume, stationery, and note cards. In order to tell your story, you must identify it. This can be done, in part, through the self-assessment list found in chapter 1.

While it is easy for some people to come up with a personal story and then make it visual, for others this can seem an overwhelming task. However, by selecting a series of visual images (and perhaps a few individual words), you can begin to develop a sense of direction for the portfolio. Selected images can be made into a collage or inspiration board, setting a visual direction for the portfolio. Figures 2-3 and 2-4 are examples of individual personal collages or inspiration boards. A visual narrative exercise tool can be found in appendix 2.

FIGURE 2-3 An example of a personal collage. ■

FIGURE 2-4 **An example of a personal collage.** ■

THE PORTFOLIO INVENTORY

Another important step in portfolio development is conducting an inventory of items for inclusion. This involves reviewing all student and/or professional work with the goal of selecting those projects that will create a successful portfolio. Toward that end, a portfolio inventory worksheet can be found in appendix 3.

In conducting a portfolio inventory, a number of things should be considered. Individuals whose goal is a very clear specialty area, such as hospitality design, must include high-quality projects directed at that target. This does not mean that only hospitality-related projects should be included: this is not always possible, and a portfolio should always demonstrate some range. Nonetheless, many items included in the portfolio should have a relationship to hospitality design, or show related strengths.

For those with a less focused design specialty in mind, elements included in the portfolio should reflect a range of project types, variety in the design solutions, and, in some cases, a range of stylistic approaches. Once again, a clear self-assessment will serve as an aid; those interested in a broad range of design opportunities must have a portfolio that reflects depth and breadth.

Interior design programs vary greatly in their focus and grounding. Programs may be research oriented, fine arts based, or related to interior architecture. Portfolios based on work done in these differing institutions will vary, and those differences should, within reason, be emphasized. The balance of work should focus on interiors, with other work serving to support and clarify your own identity.

In selecting items, it is essential to include a range of project types. Residential, commercial, small and simple, large and complex, concrete and realizable, and highly conceptual projects all have a place in a portfolio. It is also useful to include a range of presentation types.

Some designers come to their job search with a range of educational and/or professional experience, such as double major in graphic design or marketing, or a prior degree in fashion or business. While it is reasonable to include some portfolio elements reflective of this other expertise, those items should be treated as secondary. The primary work should be about interiors, and the other work should indicate a range of skills, talents, and interests. Don't go overboard with the other items unless you have more than one degree or significant professional experience in the other field.

Most students and recent graduates have only a finite number of student projects and a few projects from internships. In such cases, the purpose of the inventory is to seek out quality projects that reflect and clarify strengths and skill sets. The inventory will focus on identifying the best projects, which ones need work (and how much work is required to bring them up to par), which are too terrible to be included, and what projects will present a range of types and aesthetic or conceptual approaches.

As you gain experience in the professional world, student projects are generally culled and replaced by professional work; around three to five years after graduation, student work is often completely replaced by professional work. However, if you conducted significant research (such as a thesis project or graduate work) or if your student work is highly conceptual and leads to a clear understanding of your personal narrative, you may choose to keep it in your portfolio longer.

Portfolios for Other Reasons: Academics and Awards

Portfolios are also used for a variety of reasons that do not relate directly to employment. They are required to move forward in some design programs; to be accepted as a transfer student; to apply for grants, awards, and scholarships; and for acceptance into graduate design programs. In all these cases, it is paramount that applicants pay the utmost attention to the guidelines created by the institution reviewing the portfolio.

While this book will help with the mechanics of making the required portfolio elements look professional, each educational program is very different, and will require that varying items be included. It is best to use the checklist provided by each institution as the ultimate guide to portfolio preparation. Print the guidelines in checklist form—even if this requires creating your own copy of the information. Work from that list, and don't veer off from those requirements. Many graduate programs invite applicants to review successful portfolios and ask questions; attending such a presentation is very beneficial.

In preparing applications for graduate school, awards, and scholarships, those reviewing the portfolios tend to be driven by adherence to guidelines. Put another way, the reviewers are looking for a reason to disqualify applications and narrow the field. Therefore, following instructions and guidelines to a T is key. For example, most guidelines call for admissions portfolios to be prepared in letter or 11 × 17″ size booklet format; those portfolios not presented in that format will typically be tossed!

Some undergraduate programs require that students present foundation-level work as they move into their third year. Other design programs require students to display thesis-level projects. In such cases, work may be presented on pinup boards or in a gallery-type setting, rather than in a portfolio. Basic rules of organization and composition should, nonetheless, be followed. Consider how to best use the space provided. Students are often granted a particular amount of wall space; if this is the case, it is wise to create a scaled thumbnail of how the space will be organized. (Information about graphic design found in chapter 3 may prove helpful for those preparing a personal exhibition of this type. In addition, considering elements of the personal narrative covered in appendix 2 may aid in the preparation and organization.) See Figures 2-5 through 2-8 for illustrations of work displayed on walls rather than in portfolios.

BY NICOLE BANASZEWSKI.

FIGURE 2-5 **Student work on display for a scholarship presentation.** ■

BY NICOLE BANASZEWSKI.

FIGURE 2-6   Detail of the work on display in Figure 2-5. ■

BY LAURA PURCELL. PHOTOGRAPH BY SHELLEY PECHA.

FIGURE 2-7   Student work on display for a thesis presentation. ■

FIGURE 2-8　Student work on display for a thesis presentation. ■

BY MOLLIE DRABIK. PHOTOGRAPH BY SHELLEY PECHA.

If you plan to apply to a design program in the future, keep all your projects and artwork safe, clean, and accessible—you may find you need them someday. Obtaining a specialized storage box—perhaps one that fits under a bed—is highly advisable. Never leave your work accessible to small children or pets.

DESIGN AND PORTFOLIO ORGANIZATION

Once the portfolio inventory and self-assessment are complete, you can begin to design the portfolio and related items. After the inventory is complete, it is helpful to take the projects you plan to use and practice a timed presentation with a friend or acquaintance. This will allow you to gauge how much time it will take you to present the selected projects at an interview. Practice with the raw projects—just as they have been done for class or an employer—prior to conducting any portfolio design.

First interviews rarely last longer than an hour; that includes questions, answers, and your portfolio presentation. It is therefore safe to assume you will have no more than 45 minutes in which to present your portfolio, and some firms only allow about 30 minutes. If the projects that have made your first cut take between 30 and 45 minutes to present, you've probably found a safe number around which to design the portfolio. If the timed presentation is much shorter or longer, however, do more work on the inventory.

After the number of projects has been inventoried and timed, you can begin designing your portfolio. Look over the projects again and utilize the assessment tools in appendices 2 and 3. Then begin to set the design direction for the portfolio. Should it be spare and minimal, with a focus on the projects and plenty of white space in the composition? Or should it be dynamic, with many images per page? These questions can only be answered after you complete a careful self-assessment and inventory.

Keep on hand the collage of images generated in the appendix 2 exercise as you make visual choices. This will help you focus your intentions (it is easy to get lost in the heat of the moment). Each item to be included should be assessed visually. Is it in landscape or portrait format? Is it a large, existing board with multiple drawings on it, or a small, letter-size image? Figure 2-9 shows thumbnails of projects as they were done for various classes and an internship—the raw, unchanged projects. These thumbnails can be used to generate ideas for the final portfolio sheets or images.

The thumbnails can be seen as a visual brainstorming session, done as information from the self-assessment and the personal narrative is integrated. Visual brainstorming is best done quickly and without a lot of editing: generate the ideas first, and edit later. When working with thumbnails, try to come up with at least three completely different approaches, as shown in Figure 2-10. (Information about graphic design that will aid in the preparation of thumbnails can be found in chapter 3.)

After you create several different thumbnails, the best can be selected (either by the designer or in a class or peer-critique session). The best versions should be modified and refined so that a direction for the portfolio can be defined as you move forward.

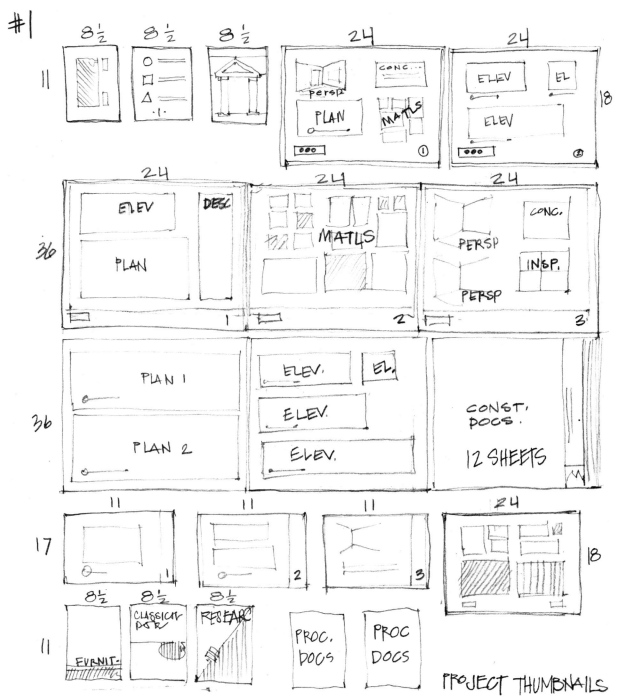

FIGURE 2-9 Thumbnails and visual notes for a number of projects as they were done for classes, prior to revising them for inclusion in a portfolio. ■

As you refine the design, consider the cost and time involved in producing the portfolio: grand schemes mean nothing if there is not enough time to complete them successfully. Consider also what you will send along with the resume and cover letter; as with the larger portfolio, the cost and time involved in producing small mail-away portfolios should be given serious thought.

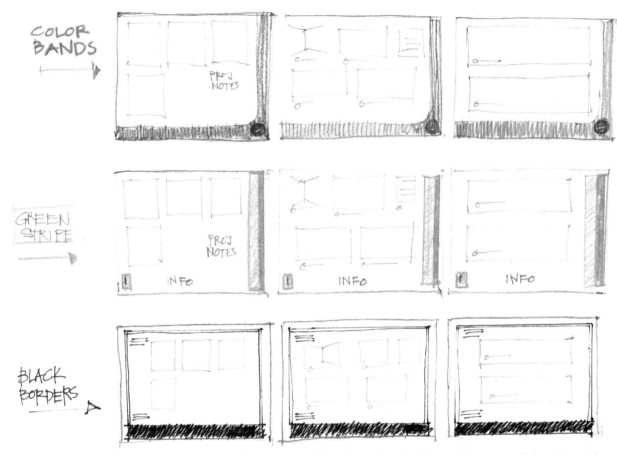

FIGURE 2-10 **Examples of different approaches to a portfolio, these thumbnails consider ways of changing and integrating projects that were done for various classes.** ■

You must also make another basic decision: should boards be redone completely to create a completely consistent visual package, or should just a touch of consistency be maintained across each board or sheet? Once again, there is no correct answer. If your assessment indicates that your story is about perfect cohesion and control, your portfolio should reflect that, and you will probably revise presentations so that they are all consistent. The second section of this book has many examples of highly consistent portfolios, as well as those with some minimal elements added to create a modicum of visual consistency.

In making decisions about visual consistency, another important question arises: will the presentation be completely digitally generated and printed, or will it contain a variety of examples, perhaps both digitally printed sheets as well as physical boards? Making this decision is fundamental to how the portfolio is developed because the physical pieces must relate well visually to the digital elements.

Increasingly, portfolios are completely digitally generated. This does not mean that this is the right solution for everyone's portfolio; there is room for variety within individual portfolios. However, it is important to have an up-to-date portfolio. It is therefore advisable to include a range of presentation types, thereby illustrating your range and depth. Including a range of presentation types requires that significant thought is given to methods of creating graphic cohesion within the portfolio. Another option, should you choose to include a range of presentation types, is to divide the portfolio into sections, or individual booklets based on project type or presentation type.

Some employers wish to see at least one physical material sample board to check for quality craftsmanship. Including as least one physical board is therefore worthwhile (see page 37 for more information about ways to integrate boards into a portfolio). More information about digital portfolios can be found later in this chapter, with additional technical information in later chapters.

Timing and Number of Projects

The purpose of conducting an inventory is to identify which projects will form the portfolio, and which will be excluded. Editing is necessary for two reasons: all portfolio elements must reflect upon you positively, and you will have a limited amount of time at an entry-level interview to present your portfolio. How many items or projects should be included? There is no clear quantitative answer; it is all about the process of presenting the projects in relation to time constraints.

The way to best determine quantity is to rehearse presenting the projects and actually time the presentation—being up against the clock is good practice. Such a rehearsal will be most effective when done in front of another person—not a best friend, with whom there might be the temptation to joke around, but with an acquaintance you do not know all that well. Such practice will help you get used to questions and pacing. Rehearsing your presentation often throughout the development of your portfolio is highly recommended.

Deciding the order of projects within the portfolio is an ongoing question. Should the best or most advanced projects appear first? Or should the earlier (and often weakest) work be followed by the more advanced? The answer lies partly in your self-assessment. Perhaps your great improvement is a key part of the presentation. If so, it is reasonable to include weaker projects near the beginning. In general, however, it is best to lead with some strong projects and not spend too much time building toward your best work. Otherwise, the interviewer might be called away and leave without ever seeing what you are proudest of.

Grouping projects by scope and function also has merit, because it allows you to target certain areas for certain interviews. For example, if all hospitality projects are clustered together, you can focus on them in an interview with a hospitality-oriented firm. When clustering projects functionally, it is common to lead with the strongest projects and work backward.

Design Process Documentation, Construction Documents, and Sample Boards

Most professionals agree on the need to include in-process work with your projects. Many students document their design process with booklets or binders that are separate from the final refined projects. Figure 2-11, for example, shows a series of images used in the design process; however, you cannot include such a booklet for each project (two is probably the maximum). Another option is to include some in-process work, such as drawings, diagrams, and sketches within the final presentation (as shown in Figure 2-12) and have the full binder or book ready for backup.

Interior designers make material sample boards as a means of conveying the use of finishes and materials on projects. Students typically use these boards as the record for material decisions (whereas those with more professional experience may use photographs of the final built environment in their portfolios). By the time a student graduates, he or she may have ten to twenty of these large, heavy boards.

As more and more digital content is included in portfolios, the question arises: should these physical boards be included in the portfolio, or merely photographed and included in that form. Furthermore, on some projects, materials are often scanned and incorporated into digital presentations, without the use of a physical sample board at all.

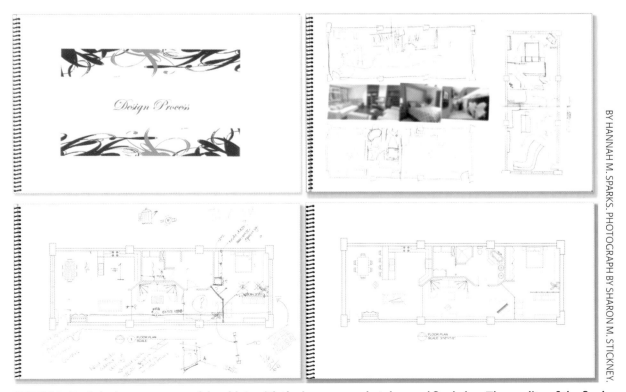

BY HANNAH M. SPARKS. PHOTOGRAPH BY SHARON M. STICKNEY.

FIGURE 2-11 A design process work booklet, with the in-process sketches and final plan. The quality of the final plan overcomes the early messy sketches, and the packages serve as a good record of the process. ■

BY JENNIFER IREY.

FIGURE 2-12   The incorporation of in-process sketches into the final digital presentation. ■

Many of those who hire entry-level designers still want to see the actual physical sample boards for at least a few projects: they want to know that the people they are hiring can make these boards with good craftsmanship and attention to detail, and they want to see and feel the physical qualities of the materials.

One option for resolving the issue is to include one to three physical boards in the portfolio, along with digital images of the other sheets and/or boards for those projects. An entire project, including the finishes, can thereby be handled by taking photographs of the sheets and/or boards, printing them, and showing them alongside the physical sample board, as shown in Figure 2-13.

In cases where the entire portfolio has been created digitally and then printed, the sample board for a few projects can be brought into the interview and kept available in case the employer asks to see it. Clearly, in cases where the portfolio is contained on a CD or on the Web, sample boards should be photographed. (Additional information on photography can be found in chapter 4.)

But it is always worth saving sample boards for projects that are included in the portfolio, even if they do not become part of the final portfolio itself (digital or otherwise). Should an employer ask to see them, they can then be retrieved and brought in for a second interview. (It is always a good idea to have additional work to show at a second interview.)

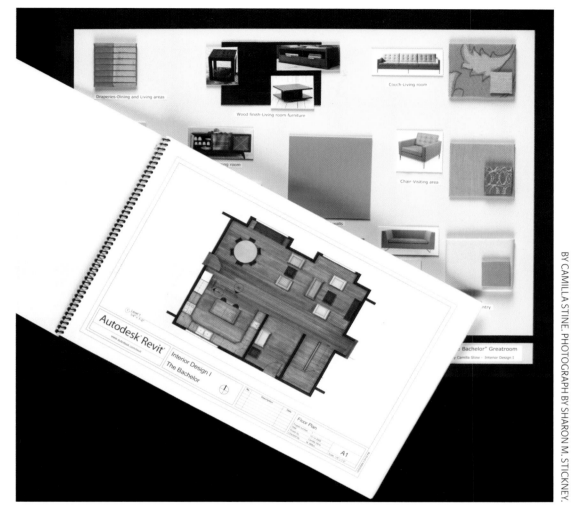

BY CAMILLA STINE. PHOTOGRAPH BY SHARON M. STICKNEY.

FIGURE 2-13 **A freestanding sample board used in conjunction with a bound portfolio.** ■

Depending on the nature of the job, employers may want to review technical drawings, such as construction documents and design details, along with other elements of the portfolio. Options for including these are to reduce the drawings to a size such as 11 × 17″ and incorporate them into a separate booklet (these can be bound at a copy shop).

If such a reduction in scale makes the drawings difficult to read, the set of drawings can be rolled up and presented much like a standard set of working drawings. These can either be placed within the portfolio or carried separately in a drawing tube. It is worth practicing arriving at the interview with a portfolio case and rolled drawings. Remember, you will need to shake someone's hand at the same time you are setting down your portfolio, drawings, and perhaps a coat or bag.

Including technical drawings directly in the digital portfolio is also an option. This involves including the final presentation drawings and technical drawings in "sheets" that are created digitally and printed. Several examples can be found in section 2 of this book (see Figures 8-1e, 8-7, 8-15b, 8-17, 8-26, 8-31, and 8-32).

THE CONTAINER

As they begin to create thumbnails, students often ask, "How can I design the portfolio without knowing what the case for it looks like?" It can indeed be difficult to get a feel for the portfolio without knowing how it will be housed. Therefore, thinking about the container can be seen as part of the brainstorming process.

What type of portfolio container to use (or make) is dependent on what was learned in the self-assessment. If you do everything differently than the norm or like to push the envelope, then making your own portfolio or using a nontraditional container can make sense.

If the portfolio is going to be completely digital (meaning composed with software using digital imagery and then printed on photographic paper), then it will tend to have a slicker look. The slickness of the digital portfolio can be emphasized by simply binding the edge and using a clear plastic cover page over a cover image. (This can be done at most copy stores and on college campuses.) This type of portfolio is a common requirement for graduate school application (see Figure 2-14).

When this type of simply bound, printed portfolio is used, it can be supplemented by including sample boards from specific projects. (As a project is presented, the sample board can be presented at the same time.) While this can involve a bit of a balancing act, it can be worthwhile. Doing so requires the use of an additional portfolio case—one that houses both the bound portfolio and the loose boards.

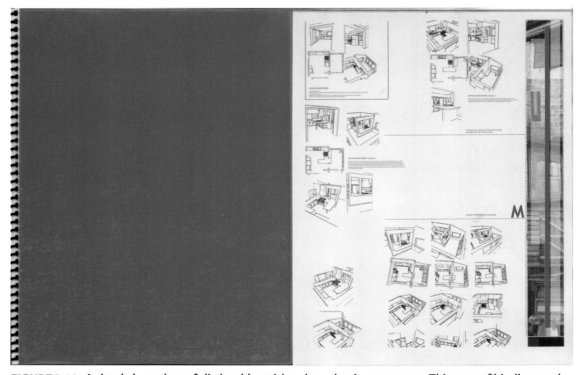

FIGURE 2-14 A simply bound portfolio booklet with a clear plastic cover page. This type of binding can be done at most copy stores. ■

A portfolio case or presentation case consisting of a cover, a binder mechanism, and polypropylene, polyester, or acetate sheet protector sleeves is shown in Figures 2-15 and 2-16. This is the most common type of portfolio. It is easy to carry, open, and review, and is often reasonably priced. Refill pages are available for most models.

This type of portfolio often includes interior and/or exterior pockets and a zipper. The inclusion of a zipper allows for boards and other loose elements not contained within the sleeve to remain safe and intact. These are available in a range of materials, from vinyl to leather, and range in cost from under $50 to over $200.

PHOTOGRAPH COURTESY OF ALVIN & COMPANY INC.

FIGURE 2-15 **Alvin vinyl presentation case with binder, sheets, and a zipper.** ■

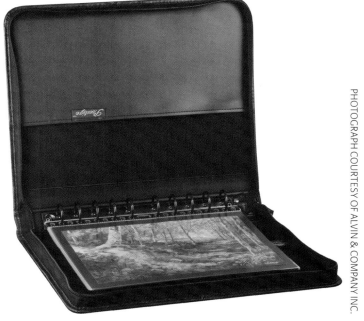

PHOTOGRAPH COURTESY OF ALVIN & COMPANY INC.

FIGURE 2-16 **Alvin leather presentation case with binder, sheets, and a zipper.** ■

Some people dislike this type of portfolio, thinking that it is too ordinary and that the sleeves create glare and are, on occasion, difficult to turn. This type of case is also available without sleeves, so that printed sheets can either be put in the binder portion or mounted on softer paper. The paper is then bound, creating a softer, more natural look.

Another type of portfolio looks similar from the exterior but has no interior binder mechanism, allowing for boards or sheets to be contained for carrying but not tied to any type of binder within the portfolio (see Figure 2-17). These are sometimes referred to as art portfolio cases.

PHOTOGRAPH COURTESY OF ALVIN & COMPANY INC.

FIGURE 2-17 **A presentation case with no interior binder, which allows for loose sheet and board storage. These are sometimes referred to as studio portfolios.** ▪

Another option is a portfolio book, which typically consists of a cover and interior binding mechanism. Some booklet-style portfolios have unusual cover materials such as bamboo, aluminum, or acrylic, as shown in Figures 2-18 through 2-20. These are available in a range of standard paper sizes, including letter, legal, and 11 × 17″ (and in some cases larger sizes as well).

You can purchase special adhesive hinges with prepunched holes for inclusion in a binder or portfolio. The adhesive has a peel-off label and can be attached directly to sheets you have printed, eliminating the need for the plastic sleeves. (These strips also allow for special art papers to be included in the portfolio without the use of sleeves.)

In the past, portfolios consisted of many boards, drawings, sketches, and materials, all of which were mounted on mat or fiberboard. This created a rather thick, cumbersome portfolio. For some, the solution was to build a custom box or case to contain the boards and other items. Such a solution continues to have merit, especially when sample boards and other bulky items are included in the portfolio.

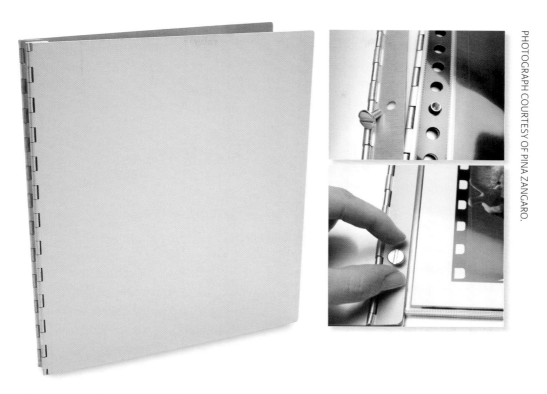

FIGURE 2-18 Aluminum portfolio cover with screw-post binding. ■

FIGURE 2-19 Bamboo portfolio cover with screw-post binding. ■

PHOTOGRAPH COURTESY OF PINA ZANGARO.

FIGURE 2-20 **Acrylic portfolio cover with screw-post binding.** ■

Creating a custom box or container is an especially good choice for someone with woodworking or furniture-making skills; it is a great way to make a statement. Those without such skills may want to consider purchasing a special storage box, as shown in Figures 2-21 through 2-23. These are available through art supply stores and online sources. You can also purchase special jackets to protect such a box, as shown in Figure 2-24. Some presentation cases combine box-like qualities with a binder mechanism, as shown in Figure 2-25.

PHOTOGRAPH COURTESY OF PINA ZANGARO.

FIGURE 2-21 **Aluminum storage boxes may be used to house a portfolio.** ■

FIGURE 2-22 Another type of storage box that can be used to house a portfolio. ■

FIGURE 2-23 Some box-type portfolios come equipped with handles, like this one from Pina Zangaro. ■

PHOTOGRAPH COURTESY OF PINA ZANGARO.

FIGURE 2-24 A jacket or portfolio shell used in conjunction with a portfolio box. ■

PHOTOGRAPH COURTESY OF ALVIN & COMPANY INC.

FIGURE 2-25 This presentation case is a bit of a hybrid. It is boxlike yet contains an interior binder mechanism. ■

For those unhappy with the look or cost of manufactured portfolios and binders, relatively simple methods of binding can be used to create handmade portfolios. The *pamphlet stitch* is a relatively easy binding method that involves binding a batch of pages folded at the center with a series of stitches. Figure 2-26 shows an example of pamphlet stitching; there are also directions for pamphlet stitching in appendix 4.

FIGURE 2-26 **Illustration of a pamphlet stitch.** ■

The pamphlet stitch is quite good for smaller, lighter booklets, but not as useful for the entire portfolio. Another binding method, known as post binding or *screw-post binding*, involves binding loose sheets of paper with a two-piece binding system consisting of screws and screw posts.

To make post-bound booklets, the paper and the cover are prepunched with holes and then the screws and posts are put in place, as indicated in Figure 2-27. A variety of covers can be used for this type of binding, from cloth-covered paperboard to wood. This type of book cannot typically open fully flat, so margins must be planned out in advance, usually by doing a mock-up.

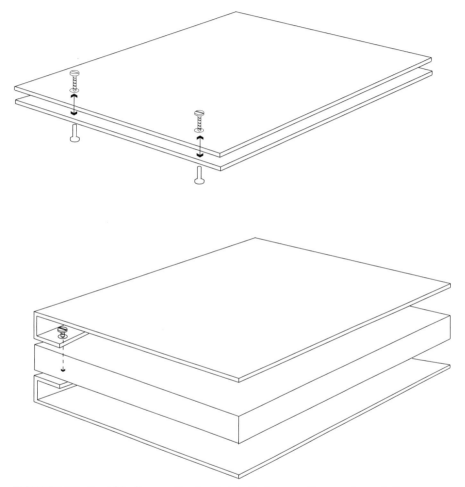

FIGURE 2-27   Post binding methods. (A detail of a manufactured portfolio with post binding is shown in Figure 2-18.) ■

Japanese stab binding (see Figure 2-28) involves using single sheets of paper and a cover material that are bound together using a pattern of stitching visible from the book's exterior. While quite beautiful, this binding has some drawbacks for portfolios: it does not allow the book to lie flat and be opened fully, and the exterior stitching is prone to damage.

Additional research into both screw-post binding and Japanese stab binding (as well as other types) is recommended prior to committing to this type of portfolio. Books and online guides about book binding and book making are available, as are classes about this art form worth further inquiry for those interested. The references section of this chapter contains related resources. Figure 2-29 shows a handmade portfolio.

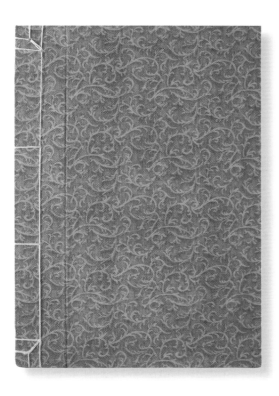 

BY ELIZABETH KRUSE. PHOTOGRAPH BY SHARON M. STICKNEY.

FIGURE 2-28 Japanese stab binding. ■

BY CATHERINE POPP.

FIGURE 2-29 Handmade portfolio cover exterior. (Images from this portfolio can be found in Figures 2-30 and 8-29 through 8-32.) ■

PHOTOGRAPH COURTESY OF ALVIN & COMPANY INC.

FIGURE 2-30 Interior images from the portfolio shown in Figure 2-29. ■

When using a single handmade portfolio, multiple handmade booklets, or some combination of booklets and boards, a larger, soft-sided portfolio can be used to contain the entire array of items. Many design students own these and have been using them for years to carry projects and materials back and forth to classes (see Figure 2-31.) These can be used with success at an interview, as long as the organization of the items inside has been well thought out.

PHOTOGRAPH COURTESY OF ALVIN & COMPANY INC.

FIGURE 2-31 A large, soft-sided portfolio can be used to house several smaller portfolios or booklets and boards. ■

You can even use a simple nylon case (with a carrying strap, as required), as long as the items inside are well designed and the presentation of items is well planned. Organization and overall presentation are key to telling your story. The best portfolio case in the world will not overcome weak work or a lack of organization. On the other hand, if the work is perfect, a clean, attractive case can underscore its excellence.

UNIFYING MANY ELEMENTS

As stated previously, a mini-portfolio or sample of work should be sent along with a resume. Design the portfolio that will be taken to interviews first. After you have set a clear visual direction for the full portfolio, you can then consider the visual qualities for the mini-portfolio. The following is a list of additional items that may be used in a design-related job search.

≫ ITEMS USED IN A JOB SEARCH

Stationery for cover letter

Resume

Mini-portfolio (mailer or CD)

Portfolio

Web site

Thank-you note (use stationery or create a separate piece)

Images from portfolio uploaded to a free portfolio site such as HTTP://WWW.COROFLOT.COM/PUBLIC/PEOPLE_HOME.ASP

It is important to create a cohesive relationship between all of these elements. The elements can be very similarly designed or quite varied, with only a few elements—a logo, band of color, or certain imagery, for example—in common.

Options for mini-portfolios and mailers include simple folded letter-size sheets of paper, as shown in Figures 2-32 and 2-33, as well as small pamphlets and booklets and clever packages that include bound or unbound project images. More and more often, a CD is sent with a cover letter and resume, all in a single, well-designed package. Figures 2-34 through 2-36 are examples of mini-portfolios and mailers.

The most intricate, expensive, and time-consuming mini-portfolios should be sent only as part of a highly targeted job search, for which it may be worth developing a fabulously impressive mailer. As the list of targeted employers expands, seek out mailers that cost less and take less time to produce, such as those shown in Figures 2-32 and 2-33. Once again, a self-assessment will help you decide how many potential employers to target—the key to many aspects of the portfolio, including the mini-portfolio.

FIGURE 2-32 Portfolio images can be sent along with the resume and cover letter in the form of a folded letter-size sheet of paper. ■

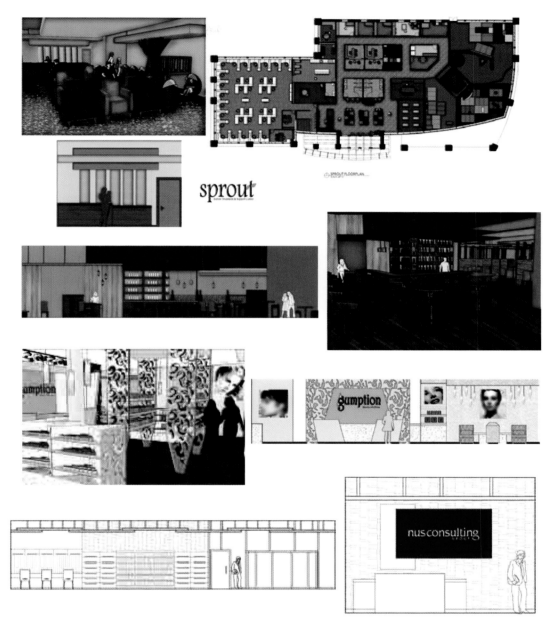

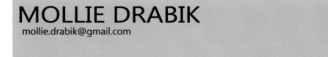

MOLLIE DRABIK
mollie.drabik@gmail.com

BY MOLLIE DRABIK.

FIGURE 2-33   Portfolio images created during the last year of college are combined on a single printed page. Sheets such as this can be included with a cover letter and resume. This sheet works well compositionally because the colors used in the bottom images relate well to the sheet graphics, helping to unify unrelated items. ■

BY JAIME SCHREINER. PHOTOGRAPH COURTESY OF SHARON M. STICKNEY.

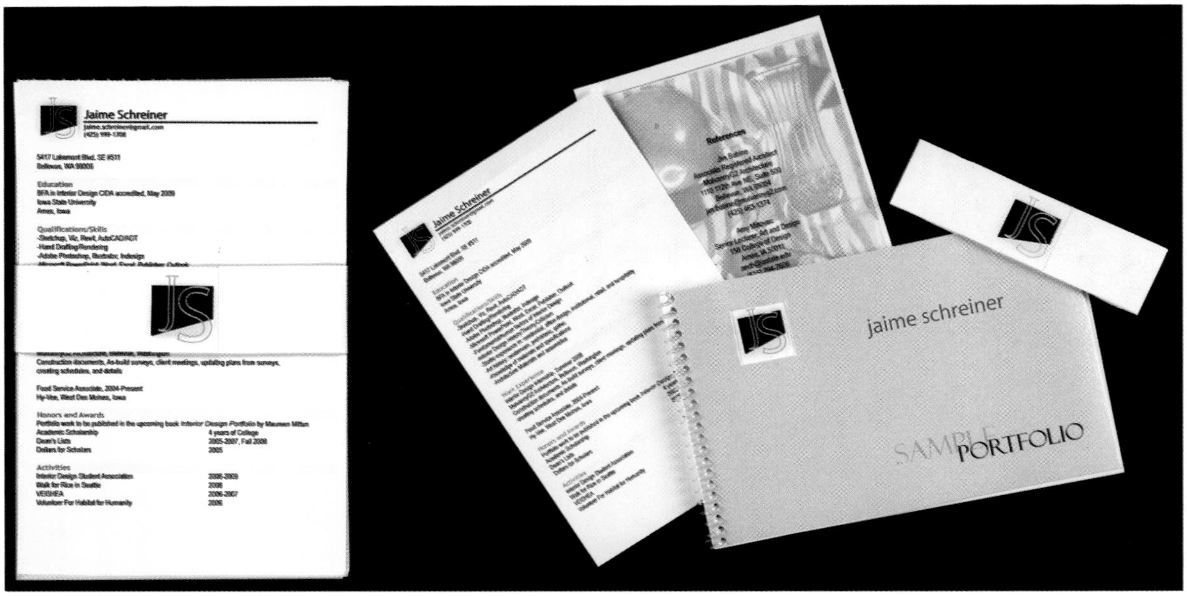

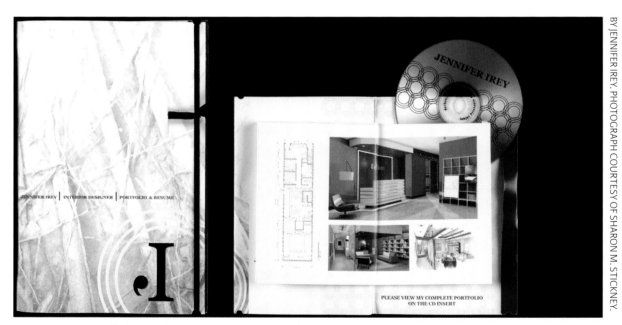

FIGURE 2-34 Bound sample or mini-portfolio. This was sent as a single package with a well-designed wrap to hold all of the elements in place. (More images from this portfolio can be found in Figure 8-33.) ■

BY JENNIFER IREY. PHOTOGRAPH COURTESY OF SHARON M. STICKNEY.

FIGURE 2-35 A well-designed mini-portfolio with CD. (More images from this portfolio can be found in Figures 7-7 and 8-1.) ■

FIGURE 2-36 Portfolio images on a CD with a mini-portfolio in a clever container. (More images from this portfolio can be found in Figures 8-31 and 8-32.) ■

MORE ABOUT DIGITAL PORTFOLIOS

In *Designing a Digital Portfolio* (2004), Cynthia L. Baron writes, "A digital portfolio is a collection of creative assets distributed via computer-based media. This broad definition covers a range of forms: PDF attachments, CD presentations, DVD demo reels, work housed on laptops and websites."

As described previously, interior designers are using various forms of digital portfolios as components of a complete package. While the digital portfolio has not yet replaced the physical or traditional portfolio, it is definitely a viable tool you'll want to have available for certain potential employers.

Some firms hiring designers prefer that only a well-designed cover letter and resume be sent digitally (typically via e-mail), while other firms prefer that the letter, resume, and a digital portfolio be available for review prior to an interview (via a personal Web site or CD). Most prefer that the interview portfolio contain, to some degree, real or physical examples of projects, rather than mere digital representations—although this preference seems to be evolving.

Before going further, a clarification is in order. The term *digital media* refers to anything created using either software or electronic media, like digital photography. But even a portfolio comprised entirely of digital media can still have the feel of a traditional portfolio if it is composed of printed pages within a physical portfolio. On the other hand, a completely digital portfolio is both generated and viewed via computer; it is such a portfolio to which Cynthia Baron refers when she describes the "creative assets" being "distributed" via computer-based media.

 The term *digital portfolio* is used here to describe a portfolio that is meant to be viewed via computer rather than in its printed form. Digital portfolios use RGB (red/green/blue) color as well as graphics files at a lower resolution, usually 72 dots per inch (dpi). If you generate portfolio elements via digital means but ultimately intend to print out the files, use CMYK (cyan/magenta/

yellow/black) color and higher-resolution graphic files (a minimum of 300 dpi), as indicated in Figure 2-37. These important differences require you to make a decision while the portfolio is being developed. Will it be a true digital portfolio, viewed only via digital means? Or will it be designed to be printed, with a secondary version available via electronic delivery?

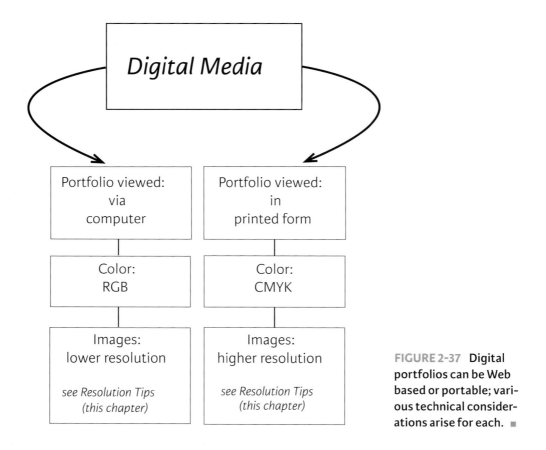

FIGURE 2-37 **Digital portfolios can be Web based or portable; various technical considerations arise for each.** ■

When the digital portfolio will serve as a backup to the physical portfolio, consistency between the two is a worthy goal that can be accomplished with some forethought. Digital images of the physical portfolio's actual pages are very often used to create the "pages" of the digital portfolio. When possible, it's helpful to select background colors or type styles consistent with the elements of the physical portfolio.

Digital portfolios present two distinct choices: the portfolio may either be *Web based* or portable (typically saved to a CD or DVD). Web-based portfolios may require a bit more time to prepare, and they require server space on an ongoing basis, but they have the advantage of being readily available to prospective employers and clients. CDs can be relatively easy to prepare, are viewable without a Web connection, and do not require server space.

Another portable option is the use of a laptop with a preset portfolio presentation readily available for view. (This option is more commonly used by graphic, game, and multimedia designers than by interior designers.)

Portable Digital Portfolios (CDs and DVDs)

As previously mentioned, a digital portfolio can be saved to a disc—CD, DVD, or Blu-ray—and sent to potential employers. CD-Rs are read-only discs that cannot be altered or overwritten. CD-RW (for read/write) discs allow the disc to be both read and rewritten. Portfolios are typically produced on CD-Rs, as these are the least expensive; there is no need to pay extra for the ability to overwrite their contents. DVDs and Blu-ray discs hold more data than CDs, allowing them to handle portfolios with large graphics, video, animation, and/or sound files.

There are two basic options for CD creation. A CD can simply be loaded with portfolio pages saved as single or multiple PDFs, which open on any computer running Adobe Acrobat Reader, a common application that can be downloaded for free. Another option is to set up the CD similarly to a Web site, with a navigation system that allows viewers to move from image to image.

The first is by far the easiest and most straightforward type of digital portfolio to create. The results are not flashy, but they can be opened on most computers and be created quickly, making them ideal for many interior designers—who are not, after all, typically trained in Web authoring. Some designers and students are perfectly content with creating a CD containing such a gallery of images with minimal text. Using PDFs allows images to be selected and enlarged on screen. (Chapter 4 covers common graphic imaging software and describes ways to save files as PDFs.)

If you want the viewer to experience the CD more like a Web-based portfolio or to create a preset visual experience more like a slide show, you must load special files onto the CD. Because CDs are read by browsers using the file system protocol and Web sites are read using the hypertext transfer protocol (http), you cannot simply put HTML pages created by Web authoring software onto a CD—they won't automatically open to the main page.

Creating a self-starting CD on a Windows-based computer involves adding one or two small files to the root directory of the CD during its creation. One file is called autorun.inf, which is required to automatically launch a program with an .exe extension. If the file to be automatically launched is not an application but rather a file such as a Web page, then a second intermediary .exe file should also be added to the root level. One such file is ShelExec.exe, which associates the Web page file with a default browser and launches the page in that program (unless security settings prevent this). ShelExec.exe can be downloaded for free.

You can also use Microsoft PowerPoint for your CD-based portfolio. PowerPoint is presentation software used to generate slide shows. You can create slides with images and descriptions of projects or import portfolio sheets from Photoshop or other imaging software. Organize the PowerPoint slides as you would any presentation, with an eye toward the order and editing of projects. Always make sure that words are spelled correctly and that text, heading sizes, and colors are graphically consistent before burning the file to a CD. Because PowerPoint files tend to be large, saving a PowerPoint file as a PDF prior to burning it to the disc is a good idea. (This can be done using PowerPoint's Print dialog box.)

There are two main problems with using PowerPoint. Some employers find the use of Power-Point less than sophisticated. And even with the files saved as PDFs, PowerPoint must be installed on the viewer's computer in order for the slide show to run. PowerPoint can, however, work well in a pinch. If you use it, avoid using the stock templates that come with the application and design your own layouts, and always make sure that the software will be loaded on the computer used to view the presentation.

CDs can be easily included in an attractive package that also includes a cover letter and resume. The CD label should always be graphically consistent with these elements, as shown in Figure 2-38. CDs can be labeled using labeling software or printers that are able to print directly on the surface of a disc.

BY HANNAH M. SPARKS. PHOTOGRAPH COURTESY OF SHARON M. STICKNEY.

FIGURE 2-38 Create a CD label that is graphically consistent with the other job search tools, such as the resume and portfolio pages. (More images from this portfolio can be found in Figures 8-23 through 8-28.) ■

Portfolio Web Sites

According to Wikipedia, a Web site

...is a collection of related web pages, images, videos or other digital assets that are addressed with a common domain name or IP address in an Internet Protocol-based network. A web site is hosted on at least one web server, accessible via the Internet or a private local area network. Creating a Web site requires the use of some type of Web authoring or editing program; these allow text, links, digital images, and often audio and video to be imported and viewed. Most portfolio sites self-authored by interior designers (that is, not produced by a professional Web designer) are created using either WYSIWYG- or template-based editors.

WYSIWYG is an acronym for *"what you see is what you get."* These editors allow you to view a document while it is being edited so that you can see what the final version will look like. The HTML code is written automatically while you work. WYSIWYG editors such as Adobe Dreamweaver and Microsoft FrontPage (last released in 2003) allow users with limited programming skills to create Web sites, permitting them to focus on aesthetics rather than computer skills. (Professional Web designers usually hand code a site, which requires them to be able to discern from the code how the final page will appear.)

Template-based editors such as Apple's iWeb or Realmac's RapidWeaver offer predesigned templates to which users with no knowledge of HTML code can add information and images. Some find the templates overly limiting, while others enjoy their ease of use.

In addition to considering what type of editing application to use, you must select a file server to host the Web site. Web hosting is a service that allocates space for users on a specific computer—think of it as renting space on the server so the site can exist there twenty-four hours a day. Free Web hosting is available for sites that will receive minimal traffic, such as personal portfolios. One drawback to free hosting services is that they often run advertisements alongside your images, which can be quite distracting.

Most Web-based portfolios start with a *home* or *index page* that provides some sort of introduction as well as *links* to the various pages within the site. Each page should then *link* back to the main page or provide some form of navigation, as shown in Figures 2-39 and 2-40. As a general rule, portfolio Web sites should include links to portfolio pages, a resume, contact information, and additional documents (as required).

There is a need for visual continuity among the various links within the portfolio, so give some thought to the index page's organization and the descriptions for the individual project pages and links. Earlier work with portfolio development will prove useful, providing a foundation for the look and feel of the Web site. (Keep that visual narrative collage handy.) Serious thought should be given to titles and descriptions on the various Web pages.

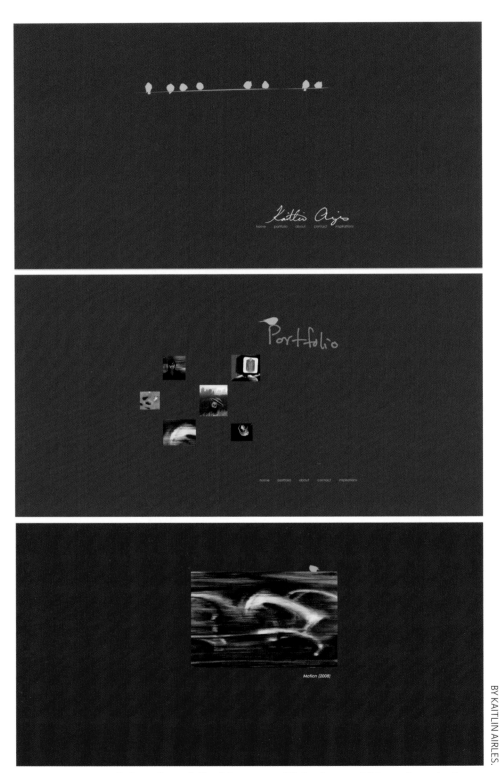

FIGURE 2-39 A Web-based portfolio title page and linked pages. This student site is simple and well-designed. ■

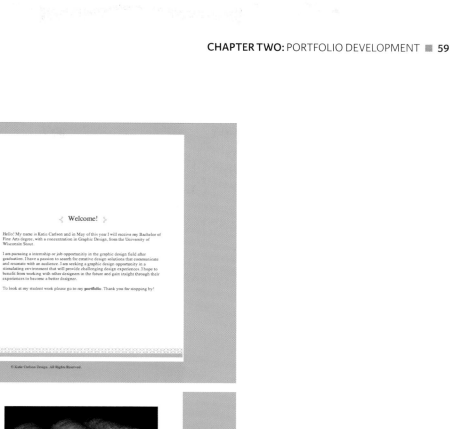

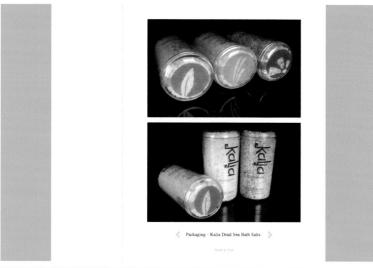

FIGURE 2-40 A Web-based portfolio title page, with related pages. (Additional portfolio-related work by Katie Carlson can be found in Figure 6-5.) ■

In *The Non-Designer's Web Book* (2005), Robin Williams writes, "It's easy to make a web page; to make a well-designed web page, however, is not so easy." As with other portfolio-related items, a strong argument can be made for keeping things as simple as possible when creating Web-based portfolios. Simplicity in the Web site's design allows your own design work to become the focus. Additionally, most interior designers do not have hours invested in the study of Web design; keeping it simple allows you to work within your own skill-set limitations.

If you do have the time and software skills, it may be worthwhile to develop a more complex, original digital portfolio. For those interested in spending the time necessary to move away from standardized templates, read Williams's book, which is easy to understand and covers all aspects of Web-site creation. Additionally, *Web Style Guide: Basic Principles for Creating Web Sites* by Sarah Horton and Peter Lynch (2009) is very useful.

Additional information about working with Adobe Dreamweaver and related software can be found in chapter 4.

As mentioned on page 15, it is possible to upload portfolio images to either free or fee-based Web sites as well. These sites allow a number of project images, or portfolio pages/sheets, to be uploaded and then viewed by anyone with an Internet connection. The drawback to these sites involves limitations related to the number of files, file sizes, and formatting.

PREPARING WORK FOR THE PORTFOLIO

Nondigital items must either be scanned or photographed with a digital camera to prepare them for inclusion in a digital portfolio or for digital output. Three-dimensional items, such as scale models and sculpture, as well as material sample boards, require photography; other items, such as sketches, drawings, and renderings, may require scanning.

Many colleges and universities provide digital photography services and provide high-quality scanners for rent. When these services are unavailable, students photograph their own work using digital cameras or hire professionals to do so.

High-quality cameras must be used to avoid distortion, poor color rendition, and generally poor-quality results. The photography of three-dimensional items such as scale models, furniture, and sculptural elements requires adequate lighting and the selection of an appropriate background.

For those who are not professional photographers, photographing projects with a range of light sources can ensure better results. This involves shooting the items several different times using a different light source each time. Shooting projects both indoors with electric lights and outdoors offers more opportunity for success than does one setup.

For outdoor photography, scale models may be placed against a sky or landscape background. When set indoors, selecting a neutral background on a table or against a vertical element (a wall or some foam board) can work well.

The photography of boards and drawings (such two-dimensional objects are often referred to as *flatwork*) can be quite challenging, lighting and distortion being the typical problems. Many presentation boards and drawings have glossy surfaces that can create glare and reflections. Turning the flash off and lighting with electronic lights set to the sides of the object can reduce glare and reflections. Taking photographs outside on a cloudy day can also reduce glare. The following list provides a summary of tips for photographing your own flatwork.

≫ TIPS FOR PHOTOGRAPHING FLATWORK

Hold the camera steady (use a tripod).

Aim the camera straight at flatwork to avoid perspective problems.

Do not use on-camera flash because this creates glare; keep lights to the sides.

Do not mix different light sources; use one type of light and set your camera accordingly.

Two lights are better than one. Set them up at roughly 45-degree angles to the artwork, but not too close, as that can cause glare.

If the artwork is very light or dark, take several photos at different exposure settings (this is known as bracketing).

Avoid wide-angle lenses, which commonly distort the subject.

Set a zoom lens to midrange or telephoto; using a fixed lens is better than using a zoom.

A copy stand—a flat surface with attachments for cameras and lights—is useful in photographing smaller boards and other flatwork. Distortion in the photography of flatwork can make the edges of boards and drawings look as though they bow out unnaturally. One remedy is to overshoot the edges of the boards by a wide margin and then using image editing software to crop the photographs. Aim the camera directly at the item to avoid odd-looking perspectives.

Distortion and difficulties with focusing on large boards may require that they be photographed in sections and then pieced together using graphic imaging software such as Photoshop. This is preferable to using a wide-angle lens because the wide angle can itself cause significant distortion. Set zoom lenses to midrange or telephoto. In some cases, elements from large presentations may be scanned separately and composed in a new manner using graphic imaging software.

Three-dimensional items such as scale models and sculpture are typically easier to light for photography, and allow for more flexible lighting arrangements. This type of work does not require the camera to be placed level with the work (unless there is some important element worth focusing on in that position). This type of work may benefit from the use of more than one light applied from different directions.

Professional designers are well served by photographing their projects as soon as possible after construction has been completed. Hiring a professional photographer to do so—particularly one with a specialty in architectural photography—is ideal. While this can be expensive, it is generally well worth the price (within reason). Such photos can eventually be used to for publication or as part of a firm's marketing materials.

Depending on the size of the project (and the scanner), scanners can be used for project boards and sheets, freehand drawings, and sketches, as well as for preliminary project doodles. Scanning the original at a high resolution is generally a good idea. High-resolution files can be reduced easily using image editing software for use at a later time. Line drawings are best scanned at an extremely high resolution (above 600 dpi) so that details remain crisp and clear. However, hand-rendered drawing elements, such as wood grain and tile grout lines that look beautiful to the human eye, can look messy when scanned above 300 dpi; the high resolution seems to "explode" pencil and marker lines.

In preparing manually created drawings, renderings, and doodles for scanning, it is imperative that the drawings be very clean. Erase all messy lines and smudges, as these will look much worse when scanned and it is inefficient to try to clean them up digitally. In many cases, it's worth crafting a final version of a beautiful, crisp, clean line drawing so that the scan comes out crisp and clean as well. Cleaning the scanner glass helps to create perfectly clean scans. An overview of image resolution can be found in the following list.

RESOLUTION TIPS (AND FILE TYPES) FOR CREATING WEB AND PRINTED PORTFOLIOS

General Scanning Information

Scan images at a higher resolution than the size suggested for final use; files can then be resampled at a lower resolution later if necessary. If the original resolution is too low, do not rescale up; scan again at the appropriate resolution instead.

Line drawings and sketches should be scanned at a very high resolution so that the linework shows up clearly. Scan these at least double the final resolution required and then scale them down if the lines appear jagged, or to use them for Web-based images. In preparation for scanning, drawings should be cleaned up, with all extraneous marks and lines erased.

Scan Web images so their pixel dimensions are roughly double what they will be on the screen. This means that different sizes of work will be scanned at different pixels per inch (ppi). For example, a small object (like a business card or postcard) might be scanned at 300 ppi, while a larger object, such as an $11 \times 17''$ image, might be scanned at 72 ppi.

Suggested Image Resolution

Web graphic	72 ppi.
Printed (not line art)	300 dpi
Line art	300 to 600 ppi

Digital files are most easily saved in a format native to the application in which they were created, though this may require that they later be copied or saved into a more universal format. The file type you choose depends on the way in which you plan to use the file.

File Type	Recommended Use
EPS	Illustration, conversion of CAD files
TIFF	Photographic images

The following file types are compressed (often for use on the Web) and not recommended for image editing or manipulation, because a loss of image quality will result.

JPEG (.jpg)	Compressed file for photographic and graphic images; 24-bit color depth supported by most Web browsers.
GIF	Compressed file for graphic images; 8-bit color depth (less quality but smaller than JPEGs) supported by most Web browsers. Useful for simple items like logos.
PDF	Used primarily for publications and/or type-intensive documents. Reduces file size for a range of uses. PDFs can be generated from CAD files for later manipulation (such as rendering in Photoshop), but EPS files offer greater options. PDFs can be saved at higher resolutions than the standard 72 dpi, but this requires the installation of the proper software driver.

Presentation elements too large to be scanned as one element can be scanned in sections and knit together using editing software. In some cases a new, better version of the project can result, because elements that were less than successful can be reworked. This is also a way to create a new presentation from elements previously included in a group project. Scanning and changing the composition of projects also allows for inclusion of additional items such as preliminary sketches, diagrams, and in-process work.

This chapter has provided an overview of portfolio development. The next two chapters offer information on graphic design and software commonly used for creating portfolios.

Chapter 3 contains in-depth information about graphic design. Chapter 4 contains information about Adobe Creative Suite 4 software, which can be used in portfolio development, as well as some additional information about Web-based portfolios. Appendix 1 contains statements made by professionals that may prove helpful as you prepare your portfolio.

Before moving on, there is one concept worth reemphasizing. Technology and graphics should never overwhelm the information contained in a digital interior design portfolio. Instead, the technology should be used to support, clarify, and enhance the original work the portfolio contains. A portfolio is about the work, the projects, and the telling of your unique story—not about the bells and whistles of the digital design.

REFERENCES

The references below contain works cited as well as recommended reading. Annotations are included where appropriate.

Amphian Photography. n.d. Bookbinding. HTTP://WWW.AMPHIAN.COM/VIEW/BOOKS.PHP.

A great site, with helpful information on bookbinding and photography.

Baron, Cynthia. 2004. *Designing a Digital Portfolio.* Berkeley, CA: New Riders.

This well-organized book contains helpful technical and design-related information intended primarily for graphic designers.

Bender, Diane M. 2008. *Design Portfolios: Moving from Traditional to Digital.* New York: Fairchild.

DesignM.ag. n.d. Entries Tagged as "Inspiration." HTTP://DESIGNM.AG/CATEGORY/INSPIRATION.

———. n.d. Entries Tagged as "Resources." HTTP://DESIGNM.AG/CATEGORY/RESOURCES.

———. n.d. 101 Awesome Portfolio Sites. HTTP://DESIGNM.AG/INSPIRATION/101-AWESOME-PORTFOLIO-SITES.

Eisenman, Sara. 2008. *Building Design Portfolios: Innovative Concepts for Presenting Your Work.* Gloucester, MA: Rockport.

An exquisite book with beautiful examples of graphic design–related portfolios.

Horton, Sarah, and Peter Lynch. 2009. *Web Style Guide: Basic Design Principles for Creating Web Sites.* 3rd ed. New Haven, CT: Yale University Press.

LaPlantz, Sharon. 1998. *Cover to Cover: Creative Techniques for Making Beautiful Books, Journals & Albums.* New York: Sterling.

Linton, Harold. 2004. *Portfolio Design.* 3rd ed. New York: W. W. Norton.

Marquand, Ed. 1986. *Graphic Design Presentations.* New York: Van Nostrand Reinhold.

Swan, Alan. 1997. *The New Graphic Design School.* New York: John Wiley & Sons.

Weston, Heather. 2008. *Bookcraft.* Beverly, MA: Quarry.

A good bookbinding primer.

White, Alexander. 2002. *The Elements of Graphic Design: Space, Unity, Page Architecture, and Type.* New York: Allworth

Williams, Robin. 2005a. *The Little Mac Book.* Tiger ed. Berkeley, CA: Peachpit.

———. 2005b. *The Non-Designer's Type Book.* 2nd ed. Berkeley, CA: Peachpit.

———. 2005c. *The Non-Designer's Web Book.* 3rd ed. Berkeley, CA: Peachpit.

Highly recommended reading for those interested in learning more about building a Web site. Williams's books are clear and easy to follow.

WonderHowTo. 2009. Make a Book Using the Five-Hole Pamphlet Stitch. HTTP://WWW.WONDERHOWTO.COM/COMMUNITY/MEMBER/WENDILYNN20/PLAYLISTS/CRAFTS/BY-NEWEST/HOW-TO-MAKE-A-BOOK-USING-THE-FIVE-HOLE-PAMPHLET-STITCH-217809.

You Tube. n.d. Bookbinding (Part 1). HTTP://WWW.YOUTUBE.COM/USER/RICEFZ#P/U/58/LVKO6DYOBTG.

WiseGEEK. n.d. What Is Web Hosting? HTTP://WWW.WISEGEEK.COM/WHAT-IS-WEB-HOSTING.

THREE

GRAPHIC DESIGN:
AN OVERVIEW

Ambica Prakash contributed to the content in this chapter;
figures in this chapter were created by Ms. Prakash and her students.

To design means to plan. The process of design is used to bring order from chaos and random-ness. Order is good for readers, who can more easily make sense of an ordered message. ■
—ALEXANDER WHITE, *THE ELEMENTS OF GRAPHIC DESIGN: SPACE, UNITY, PAGE ARCHITECTURE, AND TYPE* (2002)

White's succinct description is a great starting point for understanding graphic design. While interior designers are educated to understand that to design means to plan, methods of creating order out of chaos for a *reader* fall outside of most interior designers' training and experience. This chapter is meant as an introduction to understanding how "to bring order from chaos" for those without training in graphic design, thereby creating what White calls an "ordered message."

AN INTRODUCTION TO TYPOGRAPHY

Many of us who do not have formal graphic design training use terms in reference to type and the printed page the meaning of which we are not quite sure. For example, the term *typeface* is often confused with the term *font*. A typeface is a set of alphanumeric characters, punctuation marks, and symbols all designed to work together within a type family. Within a typeface, such as Times New Roman, there are many fonts in various styles to choose from, such as bold and italic.

In practice, we choose typefaces from a font menu by specifying the typeface, point size, style, and so on in an application such as Adobe InDesign or Illustrator. While the distinction between font and typeface is not an issue to the average at-home desktop publisher, it becomes very important when working with printers and print services.

There are two main categories of type: *serif* and *sans serif*. *Serif typefaces* have short finishing strokes called serifs at the top and bottom of the letterforms, numerals, and symbols. Sans serif typefaces are without (*sans* in French) such serifs. Figure 3-1 illustrates serif and san serif typefaces.

serif
sans serif

FIGURE 3-1 **Serif and sans serif typefaces.** ■

Additional terminology related to type includes *point size,* which is the standard unit of measurement (see Figure 3-2). Historically, it stood for the height of the metal block of type used to create the letterform. The term leading *refers to* interline spacing; the term comes from a time when thin strips of lead were placed between lines of metal type to increase the spatial interval between them.

8-point type
9-point type
10-point type
11-point type
12-point type
14-point type
18-point type
21-point type
24-point type

FIGURE 3-2 **An illustration of various point sizes.** ■

The *baseline* is an imaginary line on which the base of all the letters sit, while the *mean line* is an imaginary line that touches the tops of nonascending lowercase letters such as, a, c, e, and x. The *cap line* is an imaginary line that touches the top of uppercase letters. The term *x-height* refers to the distance between the baseline and the mean line—most easily measured on the letter x. This height is different in different typefaces. (See Figure 3-3.)

FIGURE 3-3 An illustration of baseline, leading, mean line, cap line, and x-height. ■

The term *letterspacing* refers to the space between the letters, whereas *word spacing* describes the space between the words. *Kerning* refers to the adjustment of the space between two letters. Awkward letterspacing can occur around some uppercase letters with angled or curved strokes (such as W, Y, V, and O) and those that have open spaces (such as T and L). (See Figure 3-4.)

To kern or not to kern? Auto Letterspacing
To kern or not to kern? Optical Letterspacing

LOVE INTERIORS
LOVE INTERIORS

Love Interiors
Love Interiors

Kerning: Compare the space between each O, V, R, and T and the letters adjacent to them.

FIGURE 3-4 This example shows some awkward combinations to illustrate the importance of kerning. ■

It is also important to adjust the space between large letters, as excessive spacing can result from the size of the letterforms. *Tracking* is used to increase or decrease the spacing across an entire word, line, or column of text, as indicated in Figure 3-5. It is common practice to letter-space uppercase letters and small capitals to make the letters stand apart.

We're just scratching the surface of typography.

We're just scratching the surface of typography.

We're just scratching the surface of typography.

Negative, normal, and loose tracking in lowercase letters.

WE'RE JUST SCRATCHING THE SURFACE OF TYPOGRAPHY.

WE'RE JUST SCRATCHING THE SURFACE OF TYPOGRAPHY.

WE'RE JUST SCRATCHING THE SURFACE OF TYPOGRAPHY.

Negative, normal, and loose tracking in uppercase letters.

WE'RE JUST SCRATCHING THE SURFACE OF TYPOGRAPHY.

WE'RE JUST SCRATCHING THE SURFACE OF TYPOGRAPHY.

WE'RE JUST SCRATCHING THE SURFACE OF TYPOGRAPHY.

Negative, normal, and loose tracking in small capital letters.

FIGURE 3-5 Comparing tracking with lowercase, uppercase, and small capital letters. ■

Uppercase or capital letters are a set of large letters used in English for the first letter of a sentence and the first letter of a proper noun, as well as for initials. Capital or uppercase letters are also known as majuscule letters. *Lowercase letters* are the set of smaller letters used for most other purposes; they are also called miniscule *letters*. (Interestingly the term *case* refers to the type cases that used to hold movable type for letterpress printing.)

Small caps are a complete set of capital letters the same height as, or slightly taller than, the x-height of a typeface's lowercase letters. These are used often for abbreviations, cross reference, and emphasis. Uppercase numerals, *or* lining numerals, are numbers that are the same height as capital letters and sit directly on the baseline. Lowercase numerals, also called old-style numerals *and* nonaligning numerals, are a set of numerals that are more compatible with lowercase letters. These are often used with paragraphs of text. Figure 3-6 illustrates these concepts.

As described previously, a type family is a group of alphanumeric characters designed to work together. A typical type family consists of four styles: *regular, bold, italic,* and *bold italic,* as shown in Figure 3-7. Roman, also known as *plain, regular,* or *book,* is considered the parent of the type family and is the standard upright version of a typeface. Italic is not just a slanted version of the roman, but is rather redesigned to match specific characteristics and is therefore structurally different. (*Oblique* is the slanted version of sans serif typefaces, and is similar to italic type.)

abcdefghijklmnopqrstuvwxyz

ABCDEFGHIJKLMNOPQRSTUVWXYZ

ABCDEFGHIJKLMNOPQRSTUVWXYZ

Lowercase, uppercase, and small capitals in Garamond Premier Pro.

0123456789   0123456789

Aligning and nonaligning numerals.

FIGURE 3-6   Lowercase letters, uppercase (or capital) letters, small caps, aligning numerals, and nonaligning numerals. ■

abcdefghijklmnopqrstuvwxyz	Regular
abcdefghijklmnopqrstuvwxyz	Italic
abcdefghijklmnopqrstuvwxyz	Bold
abcdefghijklmnopqrstuvwxyz	Bold Italic

Set in Baskerville.

abcdefghijklmnopqrstuvwxyz	Thin
abcdefghijklmnopqrstuvwxyz	Light
abcdefghijklmnopqrstuvwxyz	Roman
abcdefghijklmnopqrstuvwxyz	Medium
abcdefghijklmnopqrstuvwxyz	Bold
abcdefghijklmnopqrstuvwxyz	Heavy
abcdefghijklmnopqrstuvwxyz	Condensed
abcdefghijklmnopqrstuvwxyz	Extended

Set in Helvetica Neue.

FIGURE 3-7   A variety of styles can exist within one type family. ■

Script is italic letters with connecting strokes. *Medium, semibold,* and *bold* have stroke weights of increasing thickness. *Light, ultralight,* and *thin* are faces with strokes of varying weights lighter than the regular or roman style. *Condensed* and *compressed* letterforms' widths are thinner than that of the roman. *Extended* and *expanded* letterforms are wider than the roman version, and are usually used for display purposes, such as headlines; they are not usually used for body copy, such as passages of text.

Working with Type

The previous discussion provides a framework for understanding the basic components and terms related to working with type. It should enable you to begin to work with typefaces and make informed design decisions; one of the first decisions involves choosing between a serif or sans serif typeface. Some serif and sans serif recommendations follow later in this chapter.

As expressed in the words of Robert Bringhurst, "Typography exists to honor content." You should consider both the style and the purpose of the content in relation to the audience. This consideration should then lead to the selection of a typeface that embodies the look and feel of that style. Is the text wry? Humorous? Dark? Poetic? The typeface should support that style.

In making a selection it is wise to use well-designed typefaces—and to avoid using some of the millions of free typefaces available on the Web. A limited knowledge of typography can become problematic when combined with this world of free fonts, which can make it confusing and difficult to choose correctly. Readability and legibility are of the utmost importance when working on professional presentations. Figure 3-8 illustrates some free fonts available on the Web that could do more harm than good.

>> SOURCES FOR QUALITY TYPEFACES

Adobe: WWW.ADOBE.COM/TYPE

Bitstream: WWW.BITSTREAM.COM/FONTS/INDEX.HTM

Fonts.com: WWW.FONTS.COM

Linotype: WWW.LINOTYPE.COM

Typefaces are designed differently for screen and print, and it is important to know the intention behind the design of a particular typeface: a typeface that looks good on screen may not necessarily look good in print. Use a typeface designed for print for your resume. And always print proofs before printing a final version, not only for editing, but also to check point size, white space, and other graphic elements.

A Charming Font
A Yummy Apology
ACME SECRET AGENT
A770 Deco
A780 Deco
Aardvark Cafe
ACTION IS
Advert
Aerovias Brasil
AGENT ORANGE
Agnes
Airmole Stripe

FIGURE 3-8 **Free fonts available on the Web are often worth avoiding.** ■

When working with type, novices should keep things simple—this is surely a case where less is more. The following are some additional rules of thumb for novices.

» QUICK GUIDE TO WORKING WITH TYPE

Less is more; stick to one or two typefaces within an extended type family.

Body type should be between 8 and 12 points.

Contrast is an important design element.

Always spell-check your work.

It is easy to say that things should be kept simple, but often that requires selection of appropriate typefaces. The following is a list of recommended typefaces that work well in a variety of situations.

» SIXTEEN TRIED AND TESTED TYPEFACES

Serif	Sans Serif
Baskerville	Franklin Gothic
Bodoni	Frutiger
Caslon	Gill San
Centaur	Helvetica
Century Expanded	Meta
Clarendon	News Gothic
Didot	Trade Gothic
Garamond	Univers

Visual examples of these tried-and-true typefaces are shown in Figure 3-9.

Baskerville	Franklin Gothic
Bodoni	Frutiger
Caslon	Gill Sans
Centaur	Helvetica
Century Expanded	Meta
Clarendon	News Gothic
Didot	Trade Gothic
Garamond	Univers
Serif Typefaces	Sans Serif Typefaces

FIGURE 3-9 Examples of some tried-and-true typefaces. ■

HIERARCHY

The term *hierarchy* refers to the arrangement of elements in order of importance within a composition. Hierarchy is created through the use of a variety of elements, including scale, weight, placement, and spacing. The words commonly used to describe hierarchical order are *primary,* *secondary,* and *tertiary.*

In terms of directing the viewer's eye, *primary* is the most important information. *Secondary* information follows primary information in importance; *tertiary* is the third most important information within the composition. Creating contrast between the various elements in a composition is essential in creating hierarchy; it provides emphasis and lends vitality to the design, as illustrated in Figure 3-10.

FIGURE 3-10 An example of a composition with a well-defined hierarchy. Headings stand out well, and body copy is clearly defined. ■

In developing hierarchy, it is important to consider content and relationships as described in the following checklist.

>> CHECKLIST FOR DEVELOPING HIERARCHY

☑ What is the breakdown of the information?

Identify the information, from the most important to the least important; the most important becomes the primary information, followed by secondary and tertiary information.

☑ Which content is to be the main focus of the reader's attention?

Think about how this information should be highlighted to give structure to the piece being designed. The use of a slightly larger point size, color, or bold type can serve you well, but remember: less is more.

☑ What are the relationships between the different parts of the information?

Cohesive design elements with hierarchy create distinct points of interest while unifying the overall design. If one element stands out too much from the rest, it may abuse the principle of hierarchy and become a distraction.

Creating Hierarchy

With the various hierarchical elements identified, a number of methods and elements can be employed to create hierarchy. These include *scale, weight, color, typographical color, space, uppercase and lowercase letters, type families,* and *placement.*

Scale is the relationship of small, medium, and large elements in a design. Larger elements appear to move closer to the reader because they are perceived as darker, due to their scale. Smaller elements recede from the reader, as they appear lighter.

Weight refers to fonts of varying styles (such as semibold or thin) within a type family. Varying weights can be used to highlight important information. Used properly, weight can provide contrast and clarity to design elements. Typographic hierarchy can be achieved by varying point size and weight. Larger, bolder elements will become the focus of the reader's attention, as shown in Figure 3-11.

Color and *typographic color* are two additional methods of creating hierarchy. Typographic color should not be confused with using color in typography. Typographic color is the blackness or darkness of the text, determined by the relative thickness of the strokes of the letters combined with the their point size, leading, and letterspacing. The hue, value, and saturation of the type color and the background color are also important considerations in generating contrast.

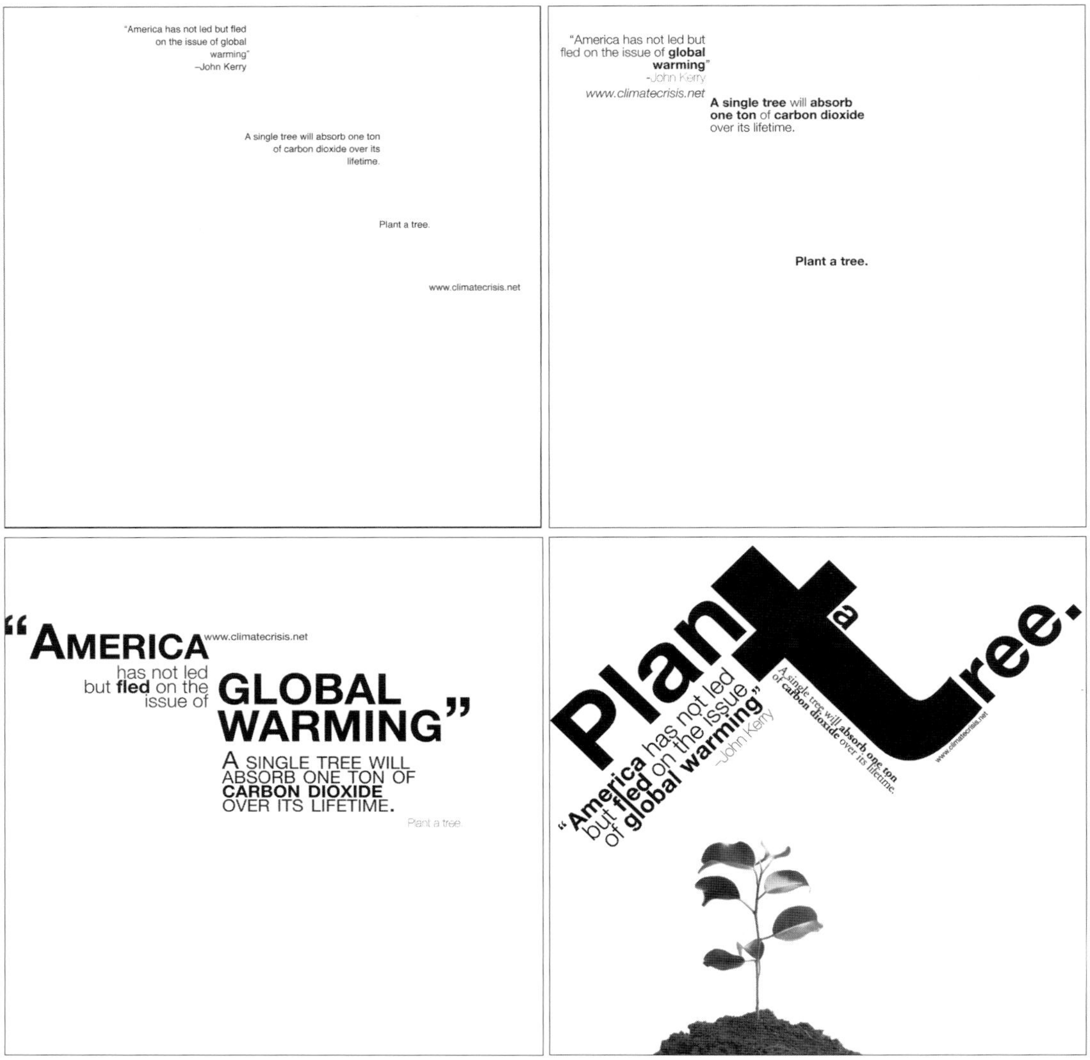

FIGURE 3-11 Varying point size and weight within a type family can provide contrast and clarity. ■

BY IVAN TRUSHIN.

In terms of hierarchy, the term *space* refers to the interrelationship between the negative or white space on a page and the positive space—namely, the elements (text and images) that are placed on the page. Grouping related items together helps develop clear spatial organization and establish a sense of order. Leading, paragraph spacing, and indents are tools helpful for achieving spatial relationships, as shown in Figure 3-12.

Uppercase letters draw more attention than lowercase letters, as they tend to look bigger, even when used at the same point size. Because they occupy more space, they should be used sparingly; otherwise, you may compromise the text's legibility. *Lowercase letters* are easier to read in large passages of text and should be seen as the standard or default approach.

Type families can provide both variation and consistency. Using the variants within one type family will successfully create contrast while maintaining consistency within the hierarchy. In other cases, mixing typefaces can add visual interest. The key is to use contrasting typefaces that make a visual statement. Using two different typefaces in one design project typically suffices—more than two can be overwhelming. It is worth exploring the variety within type families to establish successful hierarchy, as shown in Figure 3-13.

Placement on the page is another important consideration when developing hierarchy. In English, the reader reads from top to bottom and left to right. Remembering this can be helpful when deciding where to place the most (and least) important design elements. (See Figure 3-14.)

BY JESSICA LEAFBALD.

BY HANNA ROESLER.

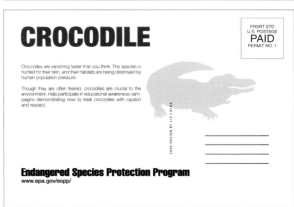

BY LIZ CALKA.

BY IVAN TRUSHIN.

FIGURE 3-12 **Space can be used to create hierarchy.** ■

In some cases it is worth challenging this convention by using some of the other methods discussed earlier in this chapter, such as scale, weight, and color. Such an approach can direct the viewer's eye in a more controlled and unexpected manner while creating visual interest—by placing a title in bold on the right side of the page, even though we read from left to right, for example.

Various approaches to text alignment, including the use of grids, provide multiple avenues for working with the placement of page elements. Grids will be discussed in depth later in this chapter.

A

B

FIGURE 3-13A BY KATIE CARLSON. FIGURE 3-13B BY ELIZABETH CALKA.

FIGURE 3-13 A,B The use of uppercase letters and limited type families can provide contrast and create visual interest. ■

FIGURE 3-14A BY HANNAH ROESLER. FIGURE 3-14B BY NATHAN PIEPER.

FIGURE 3-14 A,B Placement can be used to develop hierarchy. ■

The notion that *less is more* should take precedence over all the tools for creating hierarchy discussed in this chapter. Seek out consistency by making use of just one or two of the methods described in creating your composition; doing so will ensure visual order and create a successful design. Too many shifts and variables will become distracting and create confusion for the reader. The "keep it simple" approach is highly recommended for novice graphic designers (see Figure 3-15).

BY AMY STEMPER.

FIGURE 3-15 Keeping it simple. In these examples, one typeface is used consistently; its size is varied to create hierarchy. The controlled color palette and repeated use of center alignment provides consistency. ■

THE GRID

The use of the grid implies:

the will to systematize, to clarify

the will to penetrate to the essentials, to concentrate...

the will to integrate elements of colour, form and material

the will to achieve architectural dominion over surface and space ■

—JOSEF MÜLLER-BROCKMANN

A *grid* is an underlying framework of invisible horizontal and vertical guides that give structure to the page. It helps to create hierarchy as well as a cohesive message. It can be restrictive and mechanical or liberating and organic.

The construction of a grid starts by identifying the text and images in the design. Think about the audience. Who will be reading or reviewing this item? How can the content be designed to achieve optimum readability? The larger purpose of the piece must also be considered.

Specific compositional elements must be inventoried as the grid is developed. Consider the longest and shortest lines of text, as well as the largest and smallest images. It is similar to a jigsaw puzzle whose pieces must all fit together to create the overall composition, but with the addition of negative space, which helps to focus the viewer's eye on the content. (A lack of negative space can often create visual chaos.)

Grids are created with horizontal and vertical guidelines. Use fewer guidelines to create a tighter, more controlled grid, or use more guidelines to allow greater flexibility, as shown in Figure 3-16. While using more guidelines offers a greater number of options for aligning page elements, it can create confusion, especially for those new to the technique. When creating a grid be aware that most printers have print margins of about ¼ inch, beyond which no information can be printed.

The compositional space of a grid is inactive until a piece of information is placed into it. As information is added, you must decide whether to break up the space into *symmetrical* or asymmetrical units; these form a foundation for various choices related to the alignment of the information. Symmetrical proportions and use of type can create balanced but static layouts. Asymmetry, either in the division of space or between the different parts of the content, can enliven the page and engage the viewer.

FIGURE 3-16 **Using guidelines to create grids. More guidelines create more choices; fewer guidelines create tighter grids.** ▪

Alignment

Alignment is the relationship of lines of text to the margins. A grid's functionality is based on how various elements are aligned in relation to one another. There are four types of alignment; they are illustrated in Figure 3-17.

Flush left alignment occurs when the left edge of the text is straight, with the soft edge—or rag—on the right. (A *rag* is the pattern formed by the words at the edge of lines in a paragraph of unjustified text.) Here the emphasis is on the beginning of the text, as the viewer's eyes always go back to the same straight left edge. Strive for an even rag; an uneven rag, with drastic contrast between the short and long lines, can be distracting to the reader.

Flush right alignment is the reverse of flush left alignment, with the straight edge on the right and the rag on the left. Western languages are read left to right, making this alignment difficult to read when large amounts of text are involved. The emphasis here is at the end of the line, since our eye knows the resting point is at the right edge.

Centered alignment refers to when text is centered within the text box. This alignment creates symmetry, as it uses the central axis. The lines can jump dramatically from the start and end of one line to the next, creating uneven rags.

Justified alignment has a straight edge on both the left and right. This is a uniform block of text. It is important to achieve a uniform rag before justifying a paragraph of text. This helps to avoid large white gaps in the text that can be distracting to the reader.

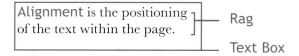

Flush left alignment occurs when the left edge of the text is hard with the soft edge or rag on the right.

Flush right alignment is the reverse of flush left alignment with the hard edge on the right and the rag on the left.

Centered alignment refers to when the text is centered within the text box.

Justified alignment has a hard edge on both the left and right. This is a uniform block of text.

FIGURE 3-17 Examples of flush left, centered, flush right, and justified alignment. ■

Types of Grids

Grids can be simple or complex. There are four main types of grids, and these can be combined to create more complex grid systems. Figure 3-18 illustrates the basic types.

The *manuscript grid* developed from traditional written manuscripts. The grid structure is a simple rectangular area made of one column that uses most of the page area. When using this grid, it is important to consider the margins and the size and placement of the text column.

The *column grid* is based on multiple vertical columns. This grid structure provides flexibility. You can either create a continuous relationship between columns of flowing text, or some columns can be combined to create a larger area for more prominent text.

A *modular grid* is made of vertical and horizontal divisions called modules. Each module provides an informational space. Some modules can be combined to create spatial zones. A modular grid provides both greater control and flexibility, but can also be confusing and restrictive if the intention behind the creation of the grid is not clear.

A *hierarchical grid*, unlike the previous three grids, is more organic and intuitive. It is based on the designer's visualization of the space in relation to the elements' hierarchy. This type of grid has little or no repetition of intervals or grid lines, but can still provide structure to the page by aligning various parts of the content. This type of grid is often used for Web sites.

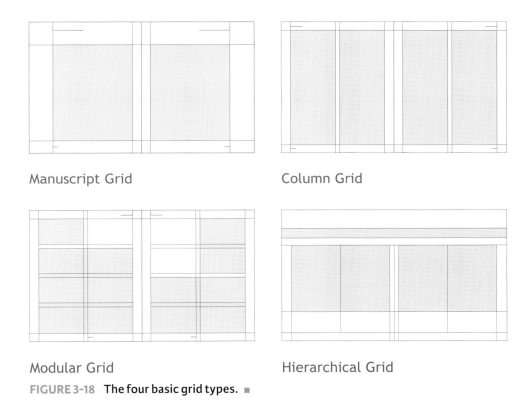

Manuscript Grid

Column Grid

Modular Grid

Hierarchical Grid

FIGURE 3-18 **The four basic grid types.** ■

While not specifically one of the four types of grids, the *golden section*, also called the *golden ratio* and the *golden rectangle,* are all synonymous, with a ratio of 1.618, or 3:5 or 5:3. This proportion exists all around us—in nature, mathematics, physics, art, and design. Using this proportion as a guide to page structure (see Figure 3-19) can improve the communication of your design because it is thought to draw on the inherent natural language embedded in the human brain.

Another compositional guideline is known as the *rule of thirds,* which is considered the *golden grid rule.* The rule of thirds is applied by dividing a space into thirds both vertically and horizontally, creating a grid of nine rectangles. Elements can be aligned to these lines, or at points where the lines intersect, to create a layout more dynamic than one in which the elements are placed in the center of the page.

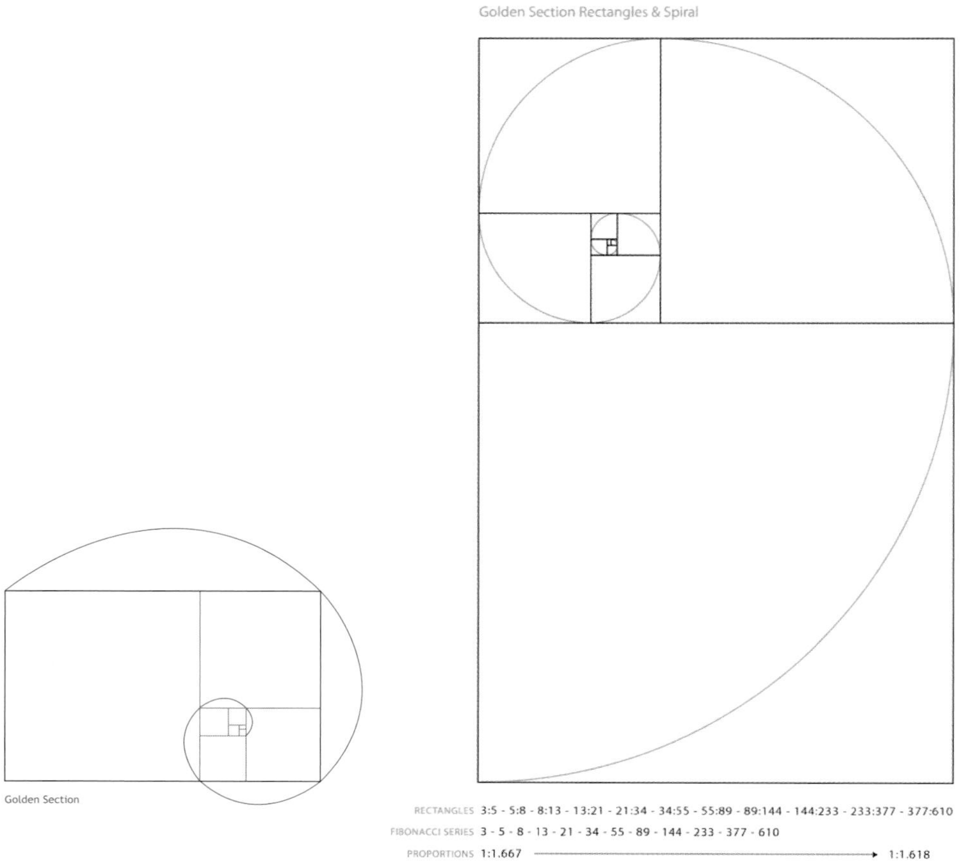

Golden Section Rectangles & Spiral

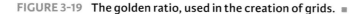

RECTANGLES 3:5 - 5:8 - 8:13 - 13:21 - 21:34 - 34:55 - 55:89 - 89:144 - 144:233 - 233:377 - 377:610

FIBONACCI SERIES 3 - 5 - 8 - 13 - 21 - 34 - 55 - 89 - 144 - 233 - 377 - 610

PROPORTIONS 1:1.667 ⟶ 1:1.618

Golden Section

FIGURE 3-19 **The golden ratio, used in the creation of grids.** ■

REFERENCES

Heller, Steven, and Meggs, Phillip. 2001. *Texts on Type: Critical Writings on Typography.* New York: Allworth.

The Müller-Brockmann quote was taken from this publication, which contains texts by designers and critics.

Jute, André. 1996. *Grids.* New York: Watson-Guptill.

Lidwell, William, Kritina Holden, and Jill Butler. 2009. *Universal Principles of Design.* Beverly, MA: Rockport.

Lupton, Ellen. 2004. *Thinking with Type.* New York: Princeton Architectural Press.

Swan, Alan. 1997. *The New Graphic Design School.* New York: John Wiley & Sons.

Tondreau, Beth. 2009. *Layout Essentials: 100 Design Principles for Using Grids.* Beverly, MA: Rockport.

White, Alexander. 2002. *The Elements of Graphic Design: Space, Unity, Page Architecture, and Type.* New York: Allworth.

Williams, Robin. 2005. *The Non-Designer's Type Book.* 2nd ed. Berkeley, CA: Peachpit.

FOUR

ADOBE CREATIVE
SUITE SOFTWARE AND PORTFOLIO DEVELOPMENT

*Robert Atwell contributed to the content in this chapter;
figures in this chapter were produced by him unless otherwise indicated.*

You will likely need to use digital design software for the layout, refinement, editing, and image manipulation of any of the elements you include in your portfolio. This chapter provides a brief overview of the Adobe software products most commonly used for these tasks. This information is a mere introduction and should be supplemented with additional publications and tutorials. The goal of this chapter is to clearly explain the software, what it is used for, and some of the most commonly used tools in each—but only in relation to portfolio and resume development. The reference section contains resources for further study.

Adobe Creative Suite (known as CS) is a collection of diverse software for image manipulation, graphic design, video editing, and Web development. Adobe Illustrator is useful for typesetting and tracing, as well as creating linework; Adobe Photoshop is geared toward retouching digital photography and also used for compositing. Adobe InDesign is used to lay out publications, periodicals, documents (such as resumes), and other print media. Adobe Acrobat is used to view, and create files. Adobe Dreamweaver is a Web development application, and Adobe Flash is a used for adding animation and interactivity to Web pages.

For general information about file types and resolution, see page 62. Please note that upcoming versions of Creative Suite may require modifications to instructions found in this chapter.

ADOBE ILLUSTRATOR

Adobe Illustrator is a *vector*-based program. Such applications create items that remain smooth when enlarged, rather than becoming pixilated (see Figure 4-1). This makes Illustrator ideal for lines, type, and tracing. (The software's name can help you remember its purpose: it is used for *illustration* and illustration-like single-page artwork.)

Illustrator should be used for anything that is line and tracing oriented and must retain its sharpness and crispness, such as type, logos, illustrations, signage, maps, packaging, and labels. Such sharp, enlargeable lines contrast with the functionality of *raster*-based applications like Adobe Photoshop, which work by manipulating pixels.

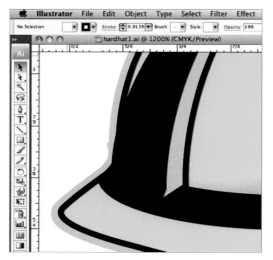

FIGURE 4-1A A vector-based image. Notice the smooth contours and lack of pixilation. Adobe Illustrator is vector based. ■

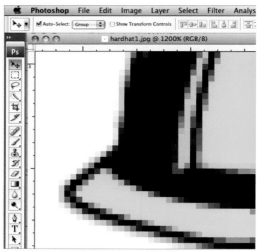

FIGURE 4-1B A raster-based image. Notice the pixilation and lack of clarity. Adobe Photoshop is raster based. ■

Illustrator Tools

Pen Tool

The *Pen tool* shown in Figure 4-2 is used to make the paths that create images; these *paths* can then be stacked and grouped. The Pen tool is used for tracing and drawing freeform objects. It can also be used to manipulate type for typographic design.

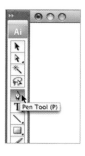

FIGURE 4-2 The Pen tool is used for tracing and drawing. ■

Using the Pen tool takes a bit of getting used to because it is not like typical drawing tools in other drawing programs. It doesn't work by clicking and dragging the mouse; rather, it is a point-to-point drawing tool that you use to "connect the dots." To get smooth curves, click and drag to manipulate the curve using a tangential line. Rather counterintuitive, this takes some practice, especially for those with experience with CAD and other drawing programs. Figure 4-3 illustrates the use of the Pen tool.

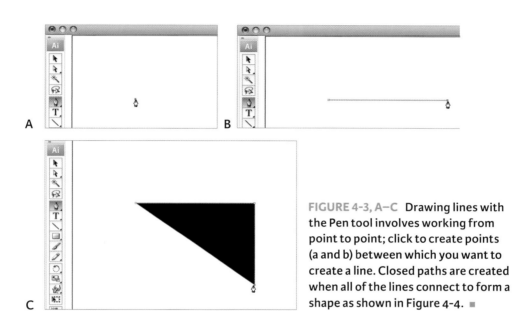

FIGURE 4-3, A–C Drawing lines with the Pen tool involves working from point to point; click to create points (a and b) between which you want to create a line. Closed paths are created when all of the lines connect to form a shape as shown in Figure 4-4. ▪

An object in the process of being traced or drawn is an *open path* (c) as shown in Figure 4-4. It is prudent to close the path as the object is completed, because many of the tools used to manipulate objects will only work with closed paths. It is also good to get in the habit of completing items (with closed paths) before finishing a file. If you are giving it to a client or another designer, closing the paths makes the files more useful.

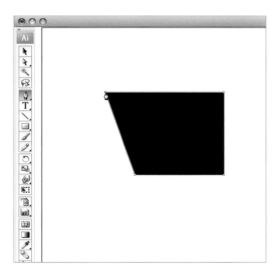

FIGURE 4-4 With the paths closed, the object or shape can be manipulated. Here the object is filled by clicking the Fill Color tool, which sits in front of the Stroke tool. (Activate each tool by selecting or clicking on it.) ▪

Objects can have a fill color (Figure 4-5a), a fill and stroke color (Figure 4-5b), or a stroke color with no fill (Figure 4-5c). (Objects can have only one fill color and one stroke color each.) When tracing artwork using the Pen tool, it is often best to keep the fill color turned off, so that as you trace the object, you see only the line you are drawing, rather than the entire shape of what is being traced.

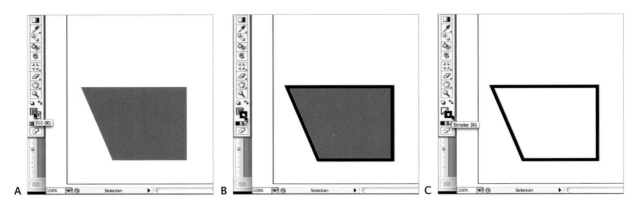

FIGURE 4-5, A–C Objects can have just a fill color with no stroke (a), different fill and stroke colors (b), or just an outline, with no fill color (c). ▪

Selection and Direct Selection Tools

The Selection tool allows you to select any object and move, scale, and rotate it, as shown in Figure 4-6. To move the object, click on it and drag it. When you select an object, it creates a *transformation box* around the object. To scale an object, clicking on one of the transformation box's handles and move it to achieve the desired size. To maintain the object's proportions as you resize it, hold down the Shift key while scaling it. Objects can be rotated in a similar fashion.

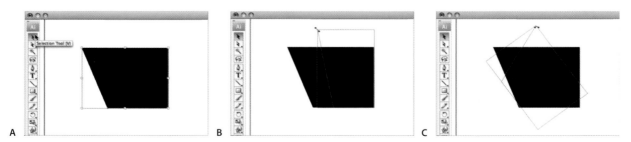

FIGURE 4-6, A–C Using the Selection tool. Selecting an object creates a transformation box that allows you to move, scale, and rotate the object. To maintain an object's proportions, hold down the Shift key while selecting and moving its handles. ▪

CHAPTER FOUR: ADOBE CREATIVE SUITE SOFTWARE AND PORTFOLIO DEVELOPMENT ■ 87

The Direct Selection tool allows you to select individual points or nodes along the path that defines your object. This, in turn, allows you to delete individual points or make minor adjustments as needed (see Figure 4-7).

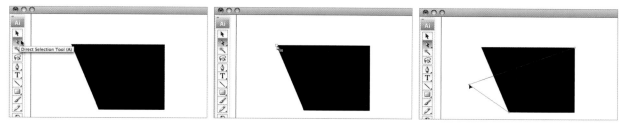

FIGURE 4-7, A–C **The Direct Selection tool allows you to select individual points along the path defining the object. These points can then be adjusted or deleted.** ■

Type Tool

The Type tool is used widely in graphic design; it allows you to break type into paths so that it can be manipulated. Examples of the use of the Type tool can be found in Figure 4-8.

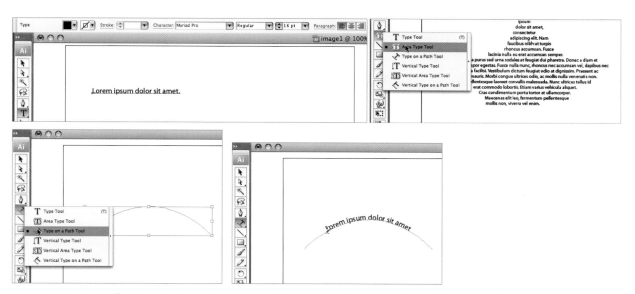

FIGURE 4-8, A–D **The Type tool can place type within a rectangle, on a path, and in other orientations.** ■

Additional examples related to the use of Illustrator can be found in Figures 4-9 through 4-11.

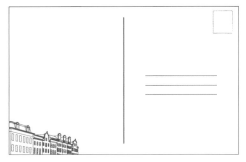

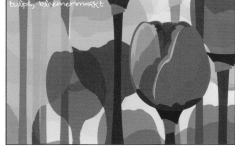

BY HOLLY SIVULA.

FIGURES 4-9, 4-10, 4-11 Examples of images created using Illustrator. All of these images were done primarily using the Pen tool and were created for postcards. ■

ADOBE PHOTOSHOP

Adobe Photoshop is a graphics editing and manipulation program that works with *bitmapped* images, also known as raster-based images. *Bitmaps* rely on small units called *pixels* to deliver visual information. The number of pixels along a bitmap's height and width create that image's pixel dimensions; these are measured in pixels per inch (ppi). The more pixels per inch, the more detail in an image. This is important: unlike Illustrator's vector-based graphics, bitmapped images cannot be scaled up without losing detail and becoming pixilated (see Figure 4-1b).

The name *Photoshop* suggests the best use for the software: the manipulation of photographs and images, including digital compositing (putting images together). This software allows you to manipulate color and, to some extent, scale. You can also use it to render, blend, fill, and crop images, as well as apply filters to them. Photoshop's bitmapped images have a soft, painterly quality—for hard, clean lines, use Illustrator.

Photoshop Tools

Marquee Tool

The *Marquee tool* is used to select an area of an image so that you can alter it in some way (see Figure 4-12). The tool comes in rectangular and elliptical versions.

FIGURE 4-12 **The Marquee tool is used to select a rectangular, or elliptical area for manipulation.** ■

Lasso, Polygonal Lasso, and Magnetic Lasso Tools

The *Lasso tool* is a modified marquee tool that allows you to draw a freeform shape around an area, thereby selecting that shape (see Figure 4-13). Within the Lasso tool is a pull-down menu for the Polygonal Lasso tool and Magnetic Lasso tool. The Polygon tool allows you to draw freeform geometric shapes, as shown in Figure 4-14. The Magnetic Lasso tool detects differences between pixel colors and uses that difference to create an outline, as shown in Figure 4-15. It is typically used to identify the pixel edge of the object being traced. If used slowly, it works quite well; moving the tool too quickly tends to create imperfections in the outline.

FIGURE 4-13 **The Lasso tool is used to draw a freeform shape around an area, thereby selecting it.** ■

FIGURE 4-14 **The Polygonal Lasso tool is used to draw a freeform geometric shape around an area, thereby selecting it.** ■

FIGURE 4-15 **The Magnetic Lasso tool detects color variations among pixels and selects areas based upon that difference. Move the cursor slowly when using this tool.** ■

Move Tool

Once an image or area is selected with a Marquee tool, it can be moved—either within the original document or to a new file—with the Move tool.

Crop Tool

The Crop tool resizes the canvas to the selected area, eliminating unselected part of the image (see Figure 4-17). After selecting the Crop tool, go to Image > Crop to execute the command, or press Enter.

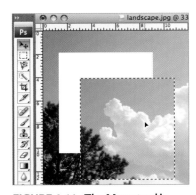

FIGURE 4-16 **The Move tool is used to move a selection within the document or to another file.** ■

FIGURE 4-17, A,B **The Crop tool resizes the canvas to the selected area. First select the Crop tool, then go to Image > Crop, or press Enter.** ■

Color Chips and the Color Picker

Clicking on the color chip (also known as the color square) located toward the bottom of the toolbar for either the foreground or background color will display the Color Picker dialog box, as shown in Figure 4-18. This dialog box includes the color field (the large square box) and a color ramp (the narrow, rectangular box), and indicates whether it applies to the foreground or background color. You can change the color by clicking anywhere on the field or by moving the slider on the ramp. By default, the color palette shown is HSB (hue/saturation/brightness), but it can be set to RGB, CMYK, Web, or Lab color.

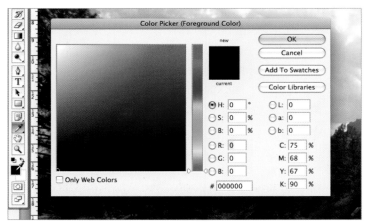

FIGURE 4-18 **The Color Picker can be displayed by clicking on the foreground or background Color Chip, located in the toolbar.** ■

Photoshop Palettes/Panels

Layers Palette/Panel

Layers, a key aspect of working in Photoshop, help in composing and manipulating images. The term *layers* means something very different in Photoshop than it does in Autodesk AutoCAD and other CAD programs. Think of Photoshop layers like the different pictures cut out to a create a collage. The way each layer is manipulated, as well as its location, level of transparency, and use of masks, will contribute to the final Photoshop image.

Pixel information on its own layer can be manipulated (by moving it, changing its color, or applying various filters and modes) without changing the information on other layers, thereby preserving those parts of the original image. By using a separate layer, you can also try out new ideas without affecting the underlying image. This is sometimes referred to as working "non-destructively."

Photoshop allows for an infinite number of layers; however, as the number of layers increases, the file size increases. For this reason, after portions of the image are completed, layers can be merged together to keep files sizes smaller (Layer > Merge Layers). After the entire composition is complete, you can use the same command to "flatten" all of the layers into one, reducing the file size considerably. This prevents changes to flattened layers later.

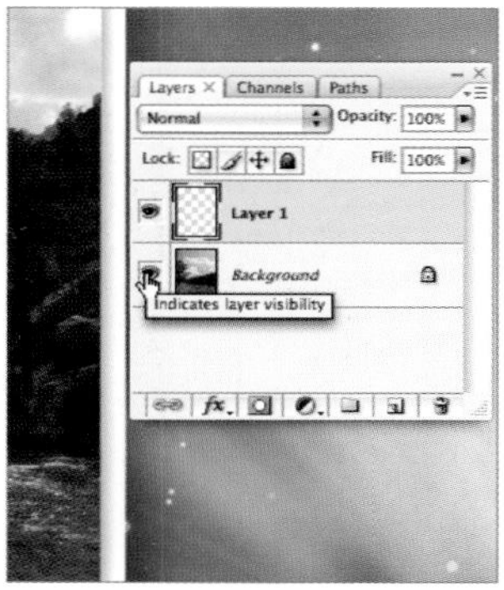

FIGURE 4-19 **Individual layers can be turned on and off by selecting the "eye" icon on the left side of the Layers palette.** ▪

Individual layers can be turned on and off (displayed and hidden) by selecting the "eye" icon on the left side of the Layers palette, as shown in Figure 4-19. This enables you to try out various ideas and then revert back to the original without affecting the original image.

To begin working with layers, create a new document by choosing File > New. In the New dialog box, select a size from the Size drop-down menu. You can also set a white, colored, or transparent background and establish the color mode (bitmap, grayscale, RGB, CMYK, etc.), as shown in Figure 4-20.

In many cases, working with a transparent background (which looks like a checkerboard) is advantageous; in other cases, you will desire a white background and can start the file with that selection. When an existing document such as a photograph is opened, that image will become the background. This can be changed later on through the use of new background layers as well as duplicate layers.

To make sure you are working on the correct layer, use the Layers palette to select the layer that contains the object you want to manipulate (see Figure 4-21).

The order in which Photoshop layers are stacked is important. The stacking order dictates what image (or what portion of an image) sits on top of another and, therefore, which is visible—much like layers of film lying on top of one another. The stacking order can be changed by selecting a layer in the Layers palette and moving it to the desired location.

FIGURE 4-20   When creating a new file, its size, background contents, and color mode can be set in the New dialog box (File > New). ■

FIGURE 4-21   Changes can only be made to the selected (or active) layer. Click on the appropriate layer in the Layers palette and execute your changes for that layer. If your changes don't "take," make sure the correct layer is selected. ■

Figure 4-22 shows the Layers palette's Blending Options command, as well as the look created by certain options. You can select various blending modes and effects from the Layer Style dialog box. By cycling through the various blending options, you can review what looks good—and what doesn't.

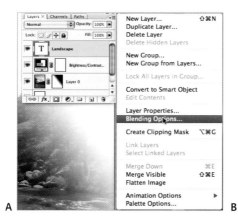

FIGURE 4-22, A–C   Blending options listed under the Styles section in the Layer Style dialog box (a) include Drop Shadow (b) and Outer Glow (c). ■

History Palette/Panel

While the Edit menu's Undo and Redo commands move you stepwise through recent changes, the History palette allows you to revert the file directly to previous states many steps removed from the current one. When you open any image in Photoshop, the History palette snaps a picture of it that becomes visible on the palette. Click on this icon to revert the file to that state. Make new "snapshots" by choosing New Snapshot from the History palette menu or by clicking the New Snapshot icon.

The History palette also lists each change made to the file. You can undo any of these changes by clicking on the change to which you want to revert, or by dragging the slider that appears next to each change. Figure 4-23 illustrates the History palette, snapshots, and the descriptions of various changes made to this file.

FIGURE 4-23 Click on a line in the History palette, or a snapshot icon, to revert a file to a previous state. ◼

Color and Swatches Palettes/Panels

In addition to the Color Picker, you can make color selections by using the Color and Swatches palettes. The Color palette includes a ramp for quick color selection. You can also adjust the palette's sliders or enter numeric values, as shown in Figure 4-24. The current background and foreground colors are displayed in the palette. As a default, selections change the foreground color, and RGB color is its default color scheme; however, these settings can be changed to HSB, CMYK, or Web color (and made to affect the background color).

FIGURE 4-24 Use the Color palette's ramp, sliders, or value fields to change color. ◼

The Swatches palette is set up with a default set of colors. Custom swatches can be added to this palette.

Working with Photographic Images

According to A Few Scanning Tips, a Web site by Wayne Fulton, the three most common image file formats—and the three most important for printing, scanning, and Internet use—are .tiff, .jpg, and .gif. (However, .tiff files cannot be used in Internet browsers.) Photoshop works with these three file types, as well as with .pdf, .png, .ai, and .psd files. The .psd file type is Photoshop's native file format: each time a new Photoshop file is created, it will be saved, by default, as a .psd file. To save Photoshop files as a different file type, go to File > Save As, select the file type you want to use, then click Save.

Files that are saved in formats supported by Photoshop can be opened directly in Photoshop by going to File > Open and browsing for the desired file. This will display the image in a new image window; it will be sized according to its original image size. To find information about image size, go to Image > Image Size to display the Image Size dialog box, shown in Figure 4-25. It gives information about pixel dimensions, document size, and resolution. These dimensions can all be altered by entering new numbers in the value fields.

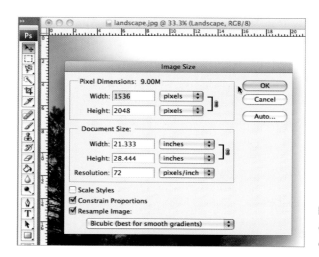

FIGURE 4-25 The Image Size dialog box displays information about image size, document size, and resolution. ■

You will find the Canvas Size and Image Size commands under the Image menu. *Canvas size* refers to the size of the complete working space. When the canvas size is increased, blank space will be added around the image. When the canvas size is decreased, part of the image may be cropped (a warning will appear if this is about to happen). To add height or width to the Canvas Size, go to Image > Canvas Size and make the necessary changes in the dialog box that appears. The background of the larger canvas will default to whatever color is selected in the background color chip. (That color can then be changed.)

Image size refers to the size of the actual image. When the image size is increased, the image will appear bigger and may become blurry. In fact, increasing image size in Photoshop will always result in a decrease in image quality. That decrease may not be perceptible if the image is viewed at 50 percent, so be sure to view images at 100 percent or greater to determine if enlarging it has been detrimental to its quality.

It is common to work on multiple images simultaneously in Photoshop; this allows you to copy and paste portions of one image into another. To do so, select the appropriate layer (or image), go to Edit > Copy, select the open file for the image you want to paste into, and go to Edit > Paste (see Figure 4-26). Each time the Paste command is used, a new Layer is automatically created. Alternatively, you can use the Move tool to drag an image from one to another; this also creates a new Layer.

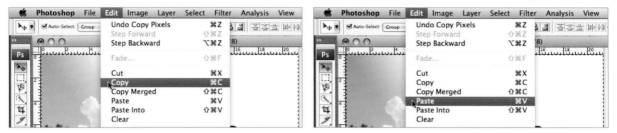

FIGURE 4-26, A,B To copy and paste images from one document to another, select the appropriate layer (or image), go to Edit > Copy, select or open the file for the image you want to paste into, and go to Edit > Paste. ■

Filters are used to apply special effects to images, portions of images, and/or layers. Filters can be used to clean up photographs and apply effects that give images the appearance of sketches and paintings, as well as other stylized appearances. Filters are found in Photoshop's Filter menu. While filters are useful and powerful tools, they can be overused, creating images that are overly distorted, unnatural, and too "Photoshopped" in appearance. Experiment with restraint. Figure 4-27 shows an image with two different filters applied.

FIGURE 4-27, A,B An original image with two different filters applied. Gaussian Blur (a) allows for controlled blurring. The artistic filters, like Palette Knife (b), allow for various visual treatments. ■

Transformation is another useful Photoshop operation. Free Transform mode (Edit > Free Transform) allows you to stretch and reshape selected areas of layers and images by clicking and dragging. Transform mode allows you to scale (resize), flip, rotate, skew, and make other changes to selected portions of images. Both types of transformation are particularly useful in rendering with Photoshop because they allow for layers of color and texture to be tweaked to relate to organic shapes and perspective lines. Figure 4-28 shows a type of transformation.

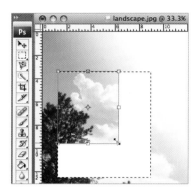

FIGURE 4-28 **A portion of an image with Edit > Transform > Scale applied. Notice that the selected portion of the tree has been scaled down (made smaller) in relationship to the original tree size (retained at left). ■**

ADOBE INDESIGN

Adobe InDesign is used for creating and laying out publications, posters, and other print media. While it makes document publishing relatively straightforward, it can be used in the design of the most sophisticated print media. Because both raster- and vector-based images can be used with InDesign documents, it works well with Photoshop and Illustrator.

Defining a New Document

Opening and creating new documents is similar in InDesign to other CS software. By going to File > New > Document, you can define the document's size, format, and number of pages. Additional page spread details, such as margins, gutters, and columns, can also be established at this time (Figure 4-29).

Once you've created a document, you can use the tools described below to locate type and images on the page. InDesign is a highly flexible application; many of the tools create page elements that can easily be moved and resized.

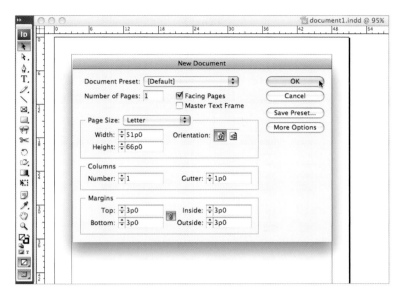

FIGURE 4-29 Create a new document by selecting File > New > Document. Page size, page format, number of columns, and number of pages can all be defined in the New Document dialog box. ▪

The InDesign Toolbox

Some tools in the InDesign toolbox (Figure 4-30) are for selecting and editing, while others are for choosing type shapes, drawing lines, and creating gradients

Type and Type On Path Tools

The Type tool defines where type is placed within a document. Clicking and dragging the Type tool icon creates a text box (Figure 4-31). Type can then be put inside the box. Think of the box as a text container; it can be resized, rotated, or moved. A variation of the Type tool, the Type On Path tool, can be used to define a path, allowing type to follow a curve (or another form defined by the path), as in Figure 4-32.

FIGURE 4-30 The InDesign toolbox. ▪

Frame Tool

This tool is used to create areas for content on a page. Click and drag the tool to define the frame's location. The frame can then be resized, rotated, or moved. Type, color, and/or images can be added to the frame (Figures 4-33 and 4-34).

FIGURE 4-31   The Type tool defines where type is placed. ■

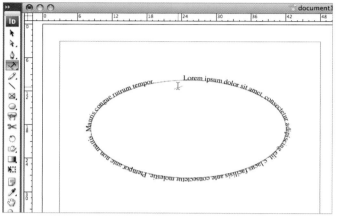

FIGURE 4-32   The Type On Path tool allows you to flow type around a curve (or on some other path). ■

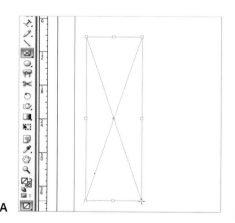

A

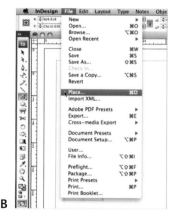

B

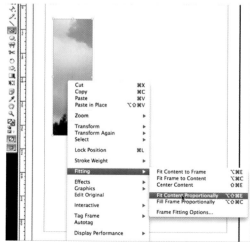

C

FIGURE 4-33, A–C   The Frame tool creates content areas. Clicking and dragging creates and defines the frame location (a). Using the File > Place command allows images to be placed inside the frame (b). Content can be made to fit in a number of proportional options by using the Object Fitting menu (or CMD>Click) as shown in (c). ■

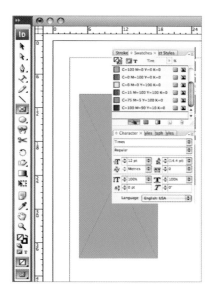

FIGURE 4-34   Color can be added to a frame by clicking on a color in the Swatches panel, the Color panel, or the Color Picker. ▨

Additional Tools

Many InDesign tools are similar to those in Photoshop and Illustrator. The Rectangle, Pen, and Rotate tools are used in the same way as they are in Illustrator and Photoshop. This allows you to work directly in the InDesign document with these tools rather than juggling the various programs (Figure 4-35).

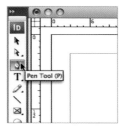

FIGURE 4-35   The Rectangle, Pen, and Rotate tools are all used just as they are in Illustrator and Photoshop. Using them within an InDesign document saves you from having to switch back and forth between applications. ▨

InDesign Palettes/Panels

The Page palette (Figure 4-36) is used to create new pages and define master pages. When an object is added to a master page, it appears on all of a document's pages. So, for example, if the same heading is required on all the pages of a document, you can save time by placing it once on the master page.

The Character palette (Figure 4-37) allows the user to review the font you are working with, as well as its size and style, all at a quick glance. Kerning, leading, and tracking can also be adjusted here.

Many of the resumes featured in Chapter 6 were created using InDesign; they are all examples of this software being put to good use.

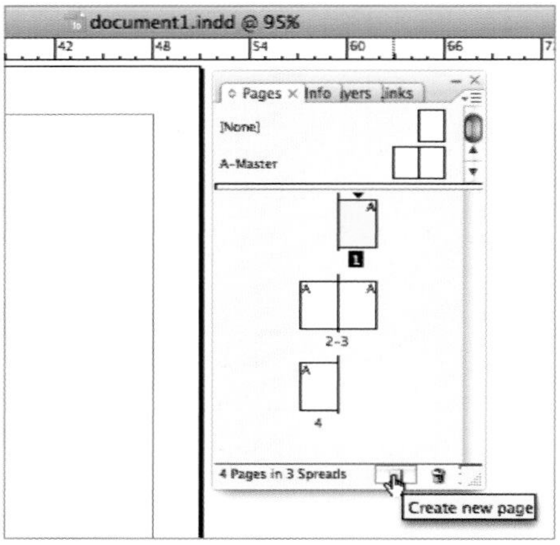

FIGURE 4-36 The Page palette is used to create new pages and define master pages. ■

FIGURE 4-37 The Character palette displays font-related information. ■

Exporting

Once an InDesign document is complete, it can be exported to .pdf format by going to File > Export and then selecting .pdf as the format from the drop down menu. More information about PDFs can be found on page 103. Additional export options include EPS and JPEG, among others (see Figure 4-38).

FIGURE 4-38 InDesign's Export dialog box. ■

ADOBE DREAMWEAVER

Adobe Dreamweaver is WYSIWYG (what you see is what you get) Web development software, although it can also operate in HTML (hand-coding mode). Dreamweaver enables users with limited programming skills to create Web sites, which in turn allows them to focus on aesthetics rather than technical skills.

Dreamweaver is a complex application, and using it requires instruction beyond the scope of this book. A brief overview of the software follows, but it is a mere introduction. Additional coursework, workshops, or books can provide the technical expertise for developing a personal Web site using Dreamweaver.

Because it is a Web site authoring application, upon opening, Dreamweaver requires that a site be defined. This helps keep files and information organized. Usually, the first thing you will see after you launch the application is its welcome screen (Figure 4-39), which gives you the option to open an existing item, create a new one, or create one based on a template. If the welcome screen has been disabled, Dreamweaver will open to a blank Web page with three floating panels: *the Insert, Properties,* and *Answer* panels. These can all be moved, opened, and closed using the Window menu.

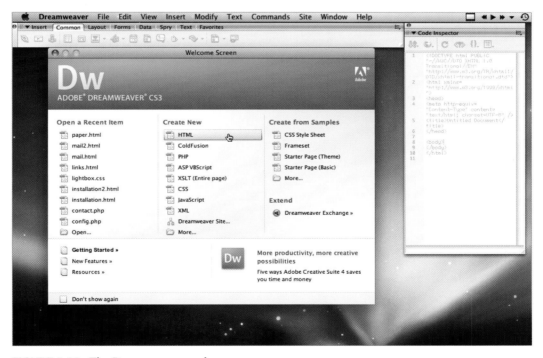

FIGURE 4-39 The Dreamweaver welcome screen. ■

Insert tables into an HTML document to divide the page and create containers for information, such as images or text boxes. To insert a table, use the Common Menu tab, and click on the Table Icon (Figure 4-40a). This will display the Table dialog box. In it, the number of rows and columns, as well as the overall size, can be defined (Figure 4-40b).

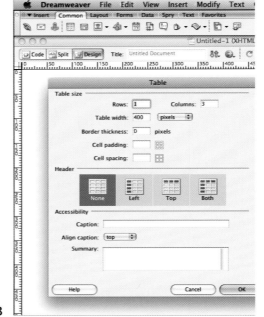

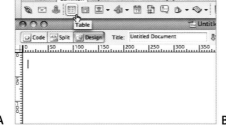

A   B

FIGURE 4-40, A,B Clicking the Table button (a) displays the Table dialog box (b), which allows you to define information regarding the size and quantity of tables. ■

You can insert hyperlinks by selecting the text or table you want to use as a button and then typing the desired link into the Properties menu, as indicated in Figure 4-41.

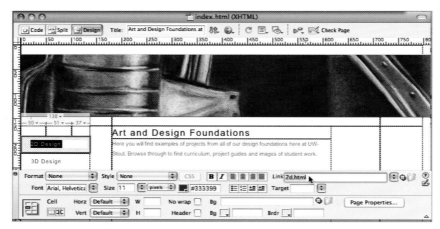

FIGURE 4-41 Select the text or table you want to use as a button to create the hyperlink. Enter the URL to which the hyperlink should be connected. ■

Dreamweaver works with *cascading style sheets* (CSS), another computer language used to describe the look and formatting of documents written in HTML and other markup languages. This allows you to create sophisticated sites with less work than previous applications required. CSS allows a style to be applied to numerous pages within a site, so each page does not need to be individually styled. This can save a lot of time when updating or changing the site content. CSS also allows one style to be applied to all of a site's pages, obviating the need to design each one individually. CSS has its own markup language. Dreamweaver has a CSS menu that can guide you in integrating CSS into Web sites, but you should augment your knowledge with additional research and study of cascading style sheets.

FIGURE 4-42   CSS has its own markup language. Dreamweaver has a CSS menu that can serve as a guide in integrating cascading style sheets into Web sites. ▪

Regardless of the type of Web authoring software you use, the current standard for Web sites usability is 800 × 600 pixels at 72 dpi, and in RGB mode.

ADOBE ACROBAT

Adobe Acrobat is a family of software used to view, create, and manipulate files in Adobe's portable document format (PDF). Acrobat Reader is available as a free download; it allows you to view and print PDF files. For this reason, and because they look the same when viewed on any operating system, PDF files are used widely. Saving your resume, cover letter, and portfolio as PDFs is an excellent idea, especially when these items will be sent via e-mail. (Sending these documents via e-mail in other file formats can become awkward because the applications in which those files were created will be required to view them, and the recipient may not have that software available.)

Whereas Acrobat Reader can be used only to view PDF files, Acrobat Pro can create, edit, and publish PDF documents, and is therefore quite useful in daily design practice. With Acrobat Pro, a series of files, including text, graphics, and Web images, can be combined into a PDF file by selecting File > Create PDF > Merge Files into a Single PDF or, from the other options, the Create PDF menu. To edit PDF files, go to File > Document Properties to display the Document Properties dialog box; editable items can be changed there.

This chapter is intended as a primer on the Adobe Creative Suite family of software. Each application is sufficiently complex to merit many books of instruction: the Lynda.com online tutorials are an excellent source of additional information, as are each application's *Help* menu and the tutorials that come with the software.

REFERENCES

Adobe Creative Team. 2008. *Adobe Illustrator CS4 Classroom in a Book.* Berkeley, CA: Adobe Press.

Alspach, Ted. 2008. *CS4 For Dummies.* Hoboken, NJ: John Wiley & Sons.

Blatner, David, and Bruce Fraser. r.d. Adobe Press. Essential Photoshop 6 Tips: The History Palette. HTTP://WWW.ADOBEPRESS.COM/ARTICLES/ARTICLE.ASP?P=22789&SEQNUM=6.

This is part of a very good series of articles about working with Photoshop.

Chastain, Sue. 2006. About.com: Graphics Software. The Photoshop History Palette. HTTP://GRAPHICSSOFT.ABOUT.COM/OD/PHOTOSHOP/SS/HISTORYPALETTE.HTM.

Cohen, Sandee. 2007. *InDesign CS3 for Macintosh and Windows (Visual QuickStart Guide).* Berkeley, CA: Peachpit.

The *Visual QuickStart Guides* are generally helpful.

Fulton, Wayne. 2008. A Few Scanning Tips. Image File Formats. HTTP://WWW.SCANTIPS.COM/BASICS09.HTML.

Lynda.com. 2010. HTTP://WWW.LYNDA.COM.

This subscription-based Web site has online tutorials for many different software packages useful to the interior designer.

Smith, Jennifer. 2008. *Aquent Creative Team Photoshop CS4 Digital Classroom.* Hoboken, NJ: John Wiley & Sons.

VanWest, Jeff. 2007. *Adobe Illustrator CS Hands-On Training.* Berkeley, CA: Peachpit.

Weinmann, Elaine, and Peter Lourekas. 2009. *Photoshop CS4, Volume 2: Visual QuickStart Guide.* Berkeley CA: Peachpit.

RESUMES AND
RELATED CORRESPONDENCE

Anytime a resume is sent by mail it must be accompanied by a cover letter. The resume is an impersonal description of your qualifications, much like a product brochure. The cover letter is your opportunity to personalize your resume and target your skills to that specific employer. ▪

—Minnesota Department of Employment and Economic Development, *Creative Job Search (CJS) Online Guide* (2009)

In many ways, your resume and cover letter are the "paper interview," and only by winning the paper interview do you have a chance at an in-person one. ▪

—Scott Bennett, *The Elements of Resume Style* (2005)

The resume is one of three important types of correspondence used in the search for employment. As stated above, the resume must be accompanied by a cover letter. In addition, a thank-you letter or note should be sent after every interview. A business card can also be designed and produced. Business cards can be handed out in situations such as social gatherings, when a resume would be inappropriate.

Because of the nature of their work, designers must have resumes and related items that are top notch in both content and design. Creating them therefore requires careful consideration—of the appropriate content, of the clear communication of that content, and of the most effective and appropriate design. Put another way, designers are on the hook for doing two things very well in their resumes and related correspondence: they must look good and read well!

This chapter covers the basics of resumes and related correspondence in terms of development, content, and format and presents some guidelines for the design of these documents as well.

THE RESUME

In *Your First Resume* (1992), Ron Fry defines a resume as

...a written document that attempts to communicate what you can do for an employer—by informing him what you have already done—and motivate him to meet you. However, content alone cannot do that job; presentation is almost equally important. ■

The importance of the presentation of a resume is echoed by John Marcus in *The Resume Makeover* (2003): "The problem is that most resumes don't get read. They get glanced at." He continues, "When it's your resume's turn, it will be given just a brief moment—perhaps 10 seconds—to see if it merits an in-depth evaluation or should be filed away."

Resume Design

In order to get a resume read, it must clearly illustrate your attributes in an eye-catching manner. It must be brief and legible but at the same time elevate you above other applicants. Many of those hiring design professionals look for creative (yet concise and legible) resumes. Burdette Bostwick states in *Resume Writing* (1990) that "creative resumes do not follow a formal pattern or standard format." Bostwick goes on to describe the necessity of including only relevant, condensed information in creative resumes. In designing and writing a creative resume, you must meet all of the requirements of a traditional resume, yet do so in a creative manner.

Professional designers often disagree about resume (and portfolio) styles and formats, and students hoping for a single clear approach to resume formats and wording tend to find this troubling. The inconsistency is engendered by the designers' different focuses and specializations. For example, many professionals involved in facilities management, office planning, and furniture dealerships are looking for more traditional, restrained resume designs, while those engaged in retail, hospitality, or exhibition design seem more comfortable with extremely creative and nontraditional resume designs.

The disparity underscores a key to resume writing: you must analyze your own personality, strengths, weaknesses, and employment objectives prior to writing and designing your resume. You must figure out who you are, what you are comfortable with, and what your objectives are before you can create a successful resume. In other words, your personal narrative should be reflected in your resume: it must illustrate who you are. If you are comfortable with a simple, straightforward resume, that is what you must use. If, on the other hand, you prefer a dynamic or nontraditional resume, you must undertake creating one. Differing resume styles will appeal to different employers and will set you on your way to making the appropriate employment connections. Revisiting the information uncovered in your self-assessment (see chapter 1) will be very helpful in this endeavor; keep the collage and assessment lists handy.

One caveat about the creative resume: do not make "creativity" an excuse for an unrefined design or an unstructured, ill-conceived resume. Resumes must be professional looking, legible, and work within standard business practices.

There are some basic guidelines for the design of creative resumes. Always make use of the components of good graphic design. Pay particular attention to layout and typography—the use of a grid is highly recommended, as is restraint in type selection (no more than two different typefaces). It is also important to moderate your use of kerning and tracking and to retain white space on the page. Consider that languages are read from left to right in Western countries when developing headings and clusters of text. (See chapter 3 for an overview of these graphic design elements and principles.)

Employers find it easiest to deal with resumes on standard, letter-size paper because most business correspondence is formatted this way. Resumes printed with a horizontal (landscape) orientation can become lost in files; using nonstandard paper sizes can present problems because odd-size sheets of paper also tend to get lost.

Paper selection should be based on legibility. Very dark or highly decorative papers may present problems; they can be distracting and thwart photocopying. It is also best to avoid folds and staples, both of which can make filing problematic for potential employers. Additional guidelines for resumes include careful consideration of the location of your name. There are a number of appropriate locations, but never make your name hard to locate. For filing purposes, some employers prefer the name to be placed close to the top margin.

Generally speaking, your name, address, and phone number should be presented in a straightforward manner. Do not confuse creativity with unduly clever complications that can frustrate potential employers. Remember, the goals are to attract attention, sell yourself, and allow employers to find you. The following is a checklist of items to consider when designing a resume.

⟫ RESUME DESIGN CHECKLIST

- ☑ Is the document on standard letter-size paper, with the information laid out in a standard portrait, or vertical, orientation?

- ☑ Does the paper selected allow the viewer to read the information easily, or is the paper too dark or distracting?

- ☑ Is the information easy to read from left to right?

- ☑ Do headings and clusters of text make sense in terms of visual hierarchy (i.e., is the most important information easy to find, and does related information coordinate well visually)?

- ☑ Is your name and contact information easy to locate, read, and file?

☑ Does the resume's layout, use of type, and additional graphic elements clearly rein-force the image you are trying to convey to employers (e.g., traditional, dynamic, cutting-edge, etc.)

☑ Does the resume relate well to the personal identity/logo and cover letter (stationery)?

☑ Do the visual qualities of the resume relate well to the elements of your portfolio through the use of some consistent graphic device(s)?

☑ Does anything look out of place or poorly thought out?

☑ Are there any errors or typos?

☑ Will the paper you have selected work well? It should be thick and luxurious, but not so thick that it cracks when folded.

Resume Organization

The previous discussion concerns how a resume is organized visually. The actual organization of content is equally important and requires serious forethought. There are three basic types of organizational formats: chronological, functional, and a combination of the two. In addition, there is a special type of resume, known as a curriculum vitae, used by teachers and academics.

Chronological Resume

In a chronological format, work experience is described in reverse chronological order, with the current or most recent employment listed first. This type of resume often includes employers' names, your position titles, and the dates you held those positions. Short statements relating to activities, duties, and accomplishments are clustered together with each position. Chronological organization makes it easy for an employer to quickly determine your work history and education. Chronological resumes are most commonly used by those with several years of experience in design and by those remaining in a given field or area of specialization.

According to the Minnesota Department of Employment and Economic Development's *Creative Job Search (CJS) Online Guide* (2009),

The chronological resume is for those with a consistent employment history, no gaps in employment, and whose past employment experiences are directly related to their current employment goals. A steady work record with increasing responsibilities can be effectively showcased using this format. ■

The following is a checklist of components that should be included in a resume with a chrono-logical format.

≫ CHRONOLOGICAL RESUME FORMAT AND CHECKLIST OF ITEMS TO INCLUDE

☑ **Personal and contact information**

    ☑ Name

    ☑ Address (considered optional by some)

    ☑ Phone number

    ☑ Fax number (if applicable)

    ☑ E-mail address

This information should appear at the top of the document.

☑ **Objective**

There is no agreement as to whether an objective must be included; however, it should only be included when it meets one of the following criteria:

    ☑ The statement is true and focused.

    ☑ You are pursuing a very specific job goal and/or you are targeting the resume to a specific position.

☑ **Employment history**

List the company name and location, your title (e.g., interior designer, project manager, etc.), and the dates you were employed (at least by year, if not by month and year). For each position, write a very brief descriptive statement about your duties, responsibilities, and successes. The descriptive statement should convey the most information in the least amount of space; this requires editing and more editing, as well as the use of short action words. (See page 116 for a list of words to use.)

☑ **Education**

In reverse chronological order, list the name of the institution(s) you attended, the type of degrees you received, and the dates they were awarded. If you are a recent graduate and/or have limited work experience, the section on education can be moved above the employment history section.

☑ **Awards, memberships, affiliations, and certifications/licensures**

List memberships in professional organizations and scholarly associations, as well as qualifications such as the National Council for Interior Design Qualification (NCIDQ), the Leadership in Energy and Environmental Design Accredited Professional (LEED AP), and any state certifications or licensures.

☑ **Additional activities**

List items such as travel or study abroad, volunteer work, and extracurricular activities. References are not typically listed directly on a resume. A line at the bottom of the resume can indicate that they are available upon request.

Those with gaps in their employment history, those who are changing careers, and those with limited directly related job experience may not be well served by the chronological format. Another limitation of this format is that by focusing on recent experience, it can place important experiences at the end of the resume, where they may get overlooked.

Functional Resume

The functional format groups work experience by function and job duties. Functional resumes highlight related work experience and focus attention on the types of job you've held, rather than the order in which you held them. The organization of a functional resume allows you to emphasize particular experiences by organizing them into skill-group paragraphs. This type of resume organization is useful for designers who may have held non-design-related jobs but wish to focus the reader's attention on their design experience.

According to the Minnesota Department of Employment and Economic Development's *Creative Job Search (CJS) Online Guide* (2009), this type of format

...works very well for people changing careers, including military personnel moving into civilian employment. It's also effective for first-time job seekers, those reentering the workforce after a gap in employment and people who want to emphasize experience that may be viewed as outdated. ■

The functional format may work well for recent design graduates who have recently held a non-design-related job but wish to focus attention on a successful, previously held internship. The functional resume also provides an opportunity to describe skills that may transfer to a design position from another profession, such as project management. However, some employers frown on purely functional resumes due to concerns that the applicant may be trying to disguise a spotty job history, limited experience, or a lack of progress.

The following is a checklist of components that should be included in a resume with a functional format.

⟫ FUNCTIONAL RESUME FORMAT AND CHECKLIST OF ITEMS TO INCLUDE

- ☑ **Personal and contact information**
    - ☑ Name
    - ☑ Address (considered optional by some)
    - ☑ Phone number
    - ☑ Fax number (if applicable)
    - ☑ E-mail address

This information should appear at the top of the document.

☑ **Objective**

There is no agreement as to whether an objective must be included; however, it should only be included when it meets one of the following criteria:

☑ The statement is true and focused.

☑ You are pursuing a very specific job goal and/or you are targeting the resume to a specific position.

☑ **Highlights of qualifications statement**

Provide a brief overview of your skills and experience—a summary of the experience and qualifications that relate directly to the job for which you're applying.

☑ **List of work/employment experience**

List skills, accomplishments, and responsibilities within specific functional categories. This area will include work experience in nonchronological order. To do this well, you will need to select appropriate categories and make concise, active statements about your experiences. Any specialized design expertise and experiences should be included. Those with limited experience can list volunteer and internship experiences, as long as they are clearly identified as such.

☑ **Education**

In reverse chronological order, list the name of the institution(s) you attended, the type of degrees you received, and the dates they were awarded. If you are a recent graduate and/or have limited work experience, the section on education can be moved above the employment history section.

☑ **Awards, memberships, affiliations, and certifications/licensures**

List memberships in professional organizations and scholarly associations, as well as qualifications such as NCIDQ, LEED AP, and any state certifications or licensures.

☑ **Additional activities**

List items such as travel or study abroad, volunteer work, and extracurricular activities.

References are not typically listed directly on a resume. A line at the bottom of the resume can indicate that they are available upon request.

Combination Resume

The combination format features a functional section that describes skills, accomplishments, and experience; also included is a section with a chronological listing of employment, education, and related experiences. When done well, this brings together the best of both formats. In most cases, a chronological format will be strengthened with a section highlighting skills (thereby benefiting from aspects of the functional format). Similarly, a primarily functional format can be enhanced with a chronological listing of experiences. The following is a checklist of components that should be included in a resume with a combined format.

≫ COMBINATION RESUME FORMAT AND CHECKLIST OF ITEMS TO INCLUDE

☑ **Personal and contact information**

    ☑ Name

    ☑ Address (considered optional by some)

    ☑ Phone number

    ☑ Fax number (if applicable)

    ☑ E-mail address

This information should appear at the top of the document.

☑ **Objective**

There is no agreement as to whether an objective must be included; however, it should only be included when it meets one of the following criteria:

    ☑ The statement is true and focused.

    ☑ You are pursuing a very specific job goal and/or you are targeting the resume to a specific position.

☑ **Summary statement**

A summary provides a brief overview of your skills, qualifications, and experience most pertinent to the job for which you're applying. This section is optional and may be included in cover letter instead.

☑ **Key skills and/or experience**

List your skills and experience, using brief, active statements. Group them into various skill sets, if possible.

☑ **Employment history**

List your most recent employment first. A general rule of thumb is to list your last three jobs or your last ten years of experience, but this history should focus on jobs most relevant to your goals. Unpaid positions and internships can also be included here.

☑ **Education**

In reverse chronological order, list the name of the institution(s) you attended, the type of degrees you received, and the dates they were awarded. If you are a recent graduate and/or have limited work experience, the section on education can be moved above the employment history section.

☑ **Awards, memberships, affiliations, and certifications/licensures**

List memberships in professional organizations and scholarly associations, as well as qualifications such as NCIDQ, LEED AP, and any state certifications or licensures.

☑ **Additional activities**

List items such as travel or study abroad, volunteer work, and extracurricular activities.

References are not typically listed directly on a resume. A line at the bottom of the resume can indicate that they are available upon request.

Keyword and Targeted Resumes

The *keyword resume* contains a list of skills at the beginning, regardless of the rest of the resume's format. The *Creative Job Search (CJS) Online Guide* (2009) states, "Critical occupational skills placed at the beginning add impact to the resume and help capture the reader's attention. This variation is effective for all career fields and skill levels. It's a very effective strategy for creating scannable resumes."

In interior design (and related professions), skills related to industry-specific software, project management, and specific project types can be included in the keyword section.

Unlike most resumes, which focus on needs related to a specific occupation, a *targeted resume* is aimed at one specific employer. Targeted resumes require in-depth research into the employer and its needs, which allows you to describe your skills and experiences in the most relevant manner possible. This type of resume strategy can be useful for top-level jobs or those that are highly specialized.

Research for the creation of targeted resumes can be done through employer profiles, industry publications, association meetings, personal relationships, and networking. A targeted resume can be created using a template containing the basic information, with the functional skills, accomplishments, and qualifications tweaked to reflect the needs of that particular employer.

Curriculum Vitae

In the United States, the term *curriculum vitae* (also called a CV or vita) is used to describe a specific format used for academic and research positions (whereas the term *resume* is used to describe the specific format used for business and industry). A curriculum vitae typically includes information about education, research, professional publications, presentations, committee work, grants received, and other career-related details.

Due to the nature of the information included, curriculum vitae tend to run to several pages. Although it is acceptable for an experienced academic to have one that is five pages long, they should nonetheless be written very concisely and in an easy-to-follow manner The following is a checklist of components that should be included in a curriculum vitae. Chapter 6 contains examples of curriculum vitae.

≫ CURRICULUM VITAE FORMAT AND CHECKLIST OF ITEMS TO INCLUDE

☑ **Personal and contact information**

  ☑ Name

  ☑ Address (considered optional by some)

  ☑ Phone number

  ☑ Fax number (if applicable)

  ☑ E-mail address

This information should appear at the top of the document.

☑ **Education**

In reverse chronological order, list your undergraduate and graduate degrees, along with the names of the institutions you attended and the dates the degrees were awarded.

☑ **Honors and awards**

List any grants, fellowships, and/or awards you received (see next item).

☑ **Teaching and/or research experience**

Depending on your strengths, you may want to lead with a list of where you have taught and/or done research. This may be moved directly below the education or contact information section, depending on the depth of you experience.

☑ **Publications, papers, and presentations**

The placement of this section depends on the strength of your record—it may fall toward the top of the document or be listed separately, toward the end of the document. Use standard bibliographic forms for publications and list dates, locations, and titles for presentations.

☑ **Related Professional Experience**

List experience related to teaching, research, and administration (e.g., organizing, committee work, tutoring, etc.).

☑ **Languages**

Assess your level of proficiency with each language (e.g., fluent, native speaker, etc.).

☑ **Memberships, affiliations, and certification/licensures**

List memberships in professional organizations and scholarly associations, as well as qualifications such as NCIDQ, LEED AP, and any state certifications or licensures.

☑ **Additional activities**

List items such as travel or study abroad, volunteer work, and extracurricular activities.

☑ **References**

References are often required on curriculum vitae. Include the each person's full name, title, institutional affiliation, address, telephone number, and e-mail address.

☑ **Project list**

Designers often include a list of completed projects; for each one, include: the name and/or type of project, your role on the project, its square footage, and a description of any special issues or constraints.

Word Choice

There is some debate about ideal resume length; some people insist that they must limited to one page, while others say that resumes of two pages are acceptable. One school of thought holds that in the first five years after graduation, resumes should be kept to one page. In *The Elements of Resume Style* (2005), Scott Bennett writes:

...There is a bias among hiring managers in favor of a brief, clear, and compelling document. But this can take many forms. Many people with twenty years' work experience have a successful one-page-resume. Some people with ten years' work experience require 1¼ pages to pitch their skills most effectively. ▪

Bennett goes on to describe the importance of selecting words that are short and clear so that the resume is as brief as possible, yet highly effective in describing your skills and attributes. (As mentioned previously, the curriculum vitae is, by its nature, a longer document not limited to one or two pages.)

There are some additional concerns related to resume length for designers. The pages of multiple-page resumes run the risk of becoming separated, yet designers have a space-intensive need to list and describe projects they have worked on. One way to solve this problem is to create a single-page resume that is then enriched by a separate project list. Think of the project list as a bridge between the resume and the portfolio: it should inform the reader about the type and quality of work you have done. Include the role you played on the design team (or as an individual or consultant), the project or client name, the location, and appropriate dates.

It is important to use the best words—and take up the least amount of space possible—when describing your skills, experience, and what you are capable of accomplishing. The following are action words that apply particularly well to design-related employment.

Action Words and Sentence Starters

achieved	consolidated	equipped	initiated	named
administered	contracted	established	inspired	narrated
advised	controlled	estimated	installed	negotiated
affected	converted	evaluated	instituted	notified
analyzed	convinced	examined	integrated	nurtured
applied	coordinated	excelled	interviewed	observed
appraised	correlated	executed	introduced	obtained
approved	counseled	expanded	invented	offset
arranged	crafted	experimented	inventoried	operated
assembled	created	fabricated	investigated	optimized
assessed	critiqued	facilitated	joined	ordered
attained	customized	fielded	justified	organized
authored	decided	figured	launched	oriented
awarded	defined	filed	led	originated
budgeted	delegated	formed	lectured	overhauled
built	delineated	formulated	licensed	oversaw
calculated	delivered	founded	limited	outpaced
catalogued	designed	fulfilled	located	packaged
centralized	detailed	functioned	localized	painted
chaired	developed	furnished	made	participated
challenged	devised	gained	maintained	partnered
changed	diagnosed	gathered	managed	passed
clarified	directed	generated	mastered	patterned
coached	distributed	governed	mapped	performed
collaborated	documented	grouped	marketed	persuaded
collected	doubled	guided	maximized	phased
combined	drafted	handled	measured	photographed
commissioned	drew	harmonized	mentored	pinpointed
communicated	earned	harnessed	merged	placed
compared	edited	helped	minimized	planned
compiled	effected	highlighted	mobilized	planted
completed	eliminated	identified	modeled	played
composed	enabled	illuminated	moderated	portrayed
computed	encouraged	illustrated	modernized	positioned
conceived	enforced	implemented	modified	prepared
conducted	engaged	improved	monitored	presented
constructed	engineered	increased	motivated	preserved
consulted	enlarged	influenced	multiplied	presided

prevented	redesigned	routed	stated	turned
printed	reduced	safeguarded	steered	tutored
prioritized	reengineered	salvaged	stimulated	uncovered
probed	referred	saved	stocked	undertook
procured	referenced	scanned	stopped	underwrote
produced	refined	scheduled	streamlined	unified
profiled	refocused	screened	strengthened	united
programmed	refreshed	searched	structured	unraveled
projected	registered	secured	studied	unveiled
promoted	regulated	selected	submitted	updated
prompted	rehabilitated	sent	succeeded	upgraded
propelled	reinvigorated	sequenced	summarized	upheld
proposed	rejected	served	summoned	upholstered
protected	relocated	serviced	superseded	used
proved	remodeled	sewed	supervised	vacated
provided	removed	shaped	supplied	validated
publicized	rendered	shared	supported	varied
published	renegotiated	sheltered	surpassed	verified
purchased	renewed	shifted	surveyed	vied
pursued	renovated	shipped	synchronized	viewed
quadrupled	reorganized	showcased	synthesized	vindicated
qualified	repaired	showed	systematized	visited
quantified	replaced	signed	tabulated	vitalized
quoted	reported	sketched	tailored	voiced
raised	repositioned	slashed	targeted	volunteered
rated	represented	simplified	taught	watched
reached	reproduced	sold	tightened	weathered
reacted	reshaped	solved	trained	weighed
reassembled	resolved	sorted	transcended	welcomed
rebuilt	restored	sourced	transcribed	welded
received	researched	specialized	transferred	won
reclaimed	restructured	specified	transformed	wired
recommended	revamped	sponsored	transitioned	withstood
reconfigured	revealed	spurred	translated	witnessed
recorded	reviewed	stabilized	transmitted	won
recognized	revised	staffed	transported	worked
recovered	revitalized	staged	traveled	wrote
recruited	rewrote	standardized	trimmed	yielded
rectified	rotated	started	tripled	

In addition to careful word choice, noting special experiences—those that may set you apart from others, such as foreign study or travel, fluency in foreign languages, specialized training, software skills, volunteer work, and/or extracurricular activities—can also enhance a resume. Including such items is particularly helpful for recent graduates or those just returning to the workforce. (Those who have served in the military should translate military jargon into more easily understood keywords for clarity.)

Recent graduates should assess the strength of their educational programs and highlight these in their resumes. Any coursework in construction and construction documents, business, specialized computer software, human factors engineering, universal design, or sustainability—and any related fine arts activities—should be noted. Student membership in design organizations and service projects should be included as well. This does not mean that you should list every course you took; focus instead on what made your education extraordinary. Remember, your resume must set you apart from the competition.

A grade point average should only be included if it is an A– or above—and only in the first few years after graduation. (After that, academic honors can still be included in a resume, even when the grade point average is omitted.)

Scannability

Corporations (including large design firms) and employment agencies often use electronic resume scanning systems set up to search for specific skills, making a careful listing of those skills very important. In scanning for design-related jobs, the systems may be programmed to look for specific software skills, such as Adobe Photoshop or Autodesk Revit, or for specific project experience, so these should be listed clearly on your resume.

Many of the same features that make resumes easy for humans to read allow for scanners to read them as well. Simple graphics, good type selection, good use of white space and high contrast (dark type on a white page) are important for resumes to be scanned. The following is a checklist of items to consider in the design of scannable resumes.

⏩ RESUME SCANNABILITY CHECKLIST

☑ Is there enough contrast between dark type and light paper? The paper must not be too dark, and there should be no shaded areas of type.

☑ Is the information easy to read from left to right?

☑ Is your name and contact information easy to locate and read? Can the resume therefore be easily filed by your name?

☑ Are all keywords and skills mentioned clearly and concisely? Are they industry specific, when appropriate?

☑ Is the text spaced so that it is not overly condensed?

☑ Are the typefaces and text easy to read, with no underlined, script, highly decorative, or hard-to-read italic type?

☑ Are the margins generous at the top, bottom, and sides?

☑ Are there any errors or typos?

☑ Have you avoided using staples or fasteners?

Sending the Resume Electronically

Potential employers may request that a resume be sent via e-mail or posted to a Web site. This can be advantageous, because the resume will land in the correct hands—often immediately. To preserve the resume's graphic integrity, send it as an attachment rather than as text within the body of the e-mail message. Prior to e-mailing your resume, it is prudent to send a test message to yourself or a friend to make sure that the attachment can be opened.

Saving the resume as a PDF file allows it to be opened and viewed easily by most computers. Always title the PDF—or any other files you send—with a straightforward file name that includes your own name.

COVER LETTERS AND THANK-YOU NOTES

Cover Letters

Cover letters should follow the standard conventions for business letters. Always include the date; a heading consisting of your name and contact information; a salutation (that, when possible, addresses a specific person); paragraphs comprising the body of the letter; a valediction (like the word *sincerely*); and a signature with your name printed below it.

While there is room for some variation, the first paragraph of a cover letter should state the reason for writing, naming the type of work or specific position (including information about how you learned of the opening can be helpful).

The second paragraph generally covers the ways in which you would be an excellent fit for the position (or firm) and/or why you are interested in the job. This paragraph may therefore contain information about the unique skills and attributes you have that relate to the employer or position.

The third paragraph typically states that the resume or other materials are enclosed and discusses your availability for an interview or meeting. It's also wise to thank the reader, either in the concluding paragraph or in some other appropriate portion of the letter.

Cover letters should be brief and to the point; keeping them to one page is best. The language used should not be overly familiar or too informal. It's best to state things about a current position or experience in a positive manner, focus on what you have to offer and your career-related goals, and not to overstate qualifications or be too vague.

Something in the body of the letter should relate to your purpose in sending your resume. If you are responding to a publicized job listing, you'll want to note the advertisement or listing in the letter; if you have learned about an open position through networking, contact with employees, or informational interviews, mention that. Figure 5-1 is an example of a cover letter sent in response to a specific job opening.

FIGURE 5-1 A cover letter sent for a specific, known position or job opening. ■

In some cases the letter is sent unsolicited, or sent "cold." In these cases, research the nature of the work done by that particular employer in order to personalize the letter and allow you to match your skills to that employer's needs. Letters sent with unsolicited resumes fit into two broad categories. One type , which targets specific firms, should provide evidence that the applicant has done research into the firm—perhaps by mentioning a successful project, for example. The other type is sent out to a number of firms or companies (known as broadcasting) and casts a very wide net, but without some firm-specific information included the letters may come across as generic. Therefore, as stated in chapter 1, a broadcast resume is made stronger with a cover letter that mentions at least some firm-specific information. Figure 5-2 is an example of a cover letter for an unsolicited resume.

Your logo (or personal identity mark) could be in the header and should be consistent in design and location with your resume. The logo or address heading may appear centered or to the right. If the logo contains the address information, be sure to add the current date in the header. Be sure to include an email address.

This letter could be adapted for an internship postition (in place of entry-level designer). For internships state time to graduation or year in program. Discuss coursework, rather than the completed degree.

Your name
Address and/or email address
Phone number

Date

Ms. Jane Doe
Design Studio XYZ
111 Fifth Street
San Carlos, CA 91111

It is best to address the letter to an actual person rather than "To Whom It May Concern." Often a search of the the firm's Website can reveal the name, as can a phone call.

Dear Ms. Doe,

I am very interested in an entry-level interior design position (or whatever the position is) with your firm. The work your firm has done on recent projects such as Fancy Restaurant and Great Retail Space is very impressive (you could list reasons here). (*Substitute for previous sentence*: Soon I will be relocating to Denver and I would like to work with a design firm such as yours. *This is used a general statement to explain the situation when you are broadcasing many resumes.*) I believe my skills and qualifications could be of benefit to your firm.

Try to keep sentences starting with I to a minimum: using a few is reasonable.

Listing something about the work the firm or company does is ideal. However, if you are broadcasting many resumes in a geographical region, a more general statement may work.

My qualifications include the successful completion of a degree (could list BA, BS, BFA) from a CIDA-accredited interior design program and internship experience with Big Dogs Design Firm. As my enclosed resume indicates, my education and internship have given me hands-on experience with software programs including AutoCAD, Revit and Photoshop as well as top-notch sketching and rendering skills. Through my internships I gained experience in the creation of construction documents, project presentation boards, and drawings, as well as familiarity with product specifications.

The middle paragraph should describe why you are perfect for this type of position. Specifics are helpful, but this should not be a repetition of what is on the resume.

Enclosed are my resume and examples of my work for your review and consideration. I believe I have much to offer and look forward to meeting with you to present my portfolio and discuss my qualifications in greater detail. I plan to call you to determine when an interview might be possible. Thank you.

You may want to include a statement that requires a response, such as an indication of possible meeting dates and times. Be sure to close with a thank-you.

Sincerely,

(Signature)
Typed Name

Enclosure

Sign your name in blue or black ink and indicate that there is an enclosure (resume and in some cases a mini-portfolio), with the word "Enclosure."

FIGURE 5-2   A cover letter sent to accompany an unsolicited resume. ▨

Resumes sent to an employer electronically still require a cover letter: a cover letter serves as an introduction and clarifies your skills as they relate to a specific position. This role remains vital whether the resume is sent electronically, by mail—or even if it is hand delivered.

The cover letter may be sent as a separate e-mail attachment so that it appears much like a traditional letter on your stationery, or it may be included in the body of the e-mail message. Sent as a separate attachment, it may be missed by a person reviewing the application in a hurry; however, including the text in the body of the e-mail message can make the e-mail overly long. Therefore, the contents of the letter should be shortened when included in an e-mail. Following up the electronic submission with a hard copy is also a good idea.

Thank-You Notes

Sending a thank-you letter or note to employers, employment contacts, and those who have offered assistance in your job search is an essential part of the search process.

Some form of thank-you correspondence should be sent after all interviews. The style of correspondence—from a more formal letter to a hand-written note—depends upon the situation, the interview's level of formality, and your own personal style. If you were interviewed by a group of people, writing either separate letters to each person or a single letter thanking each person by name but directed to one individual for distribution are both acceptable.

The basic parts of a thank-you correspondence are the greeting (to a person, by name); a statement of appreciation for the interview; a restatement of interest in the job and your qualifications; and in some cases, a time and date to follow up the interview. You will often learn more about the job during the interview, and this knowledge can be expressed in the thank-you letter as a reason for your continued or enhanced interest in the job. Figure 5-3 is an example of content found in a thank-you note.

All written documents included in the job search—the resume, the cover letter, and the thank-you note—should be related graphically. In most cases all three documents will contain elements that unite them visually, such as a logo (or personal identity system), page layout, graphic composition, and/or use of type and color. This means that when you create a resume, you must consider the design of each of these associated documents in order to create a unified visual when all of them are viewed together. Put another way, the three forms of correspondence are each a part of a whole that should be designed to create unity and visual consistency. Chapter 6 contains many examples of visually consistent cover letters, thank-you notes, and resumes.

And remember, all components of a job application or inquiry should be perfect—they should never be sent out with any grammatical, typographical, or other kinds of errors. Have a number of different readers proofread these documents so you get a number of different points of view. Small errors give reviewers and human resources professionals an easy excuse for moving your documents from the "maybe" pile to the "no" pile—and then all of your hard work will be for naught.

Your logo (or personal identity mark) could be in the header if this is written on stationery rather than a note card. When possible, aim for consistency in design.

Dear Ms. Doe,

If you find it appropriate you may write the person's name here, as in, Dear Jane.

It was very enjoyable to speak with you about the open interior design position at Cool Firm. The position, as you presented it, seems to be a very good match for my skills and interests. The team approach to design management that you described seems to be a very productive approach (subsitute something that seemed positive about the firm/company). My up-to-date Revit skills would be an asset as your firm moves into using this software on upcoming projects.

It was a pleasure to meet Jim Samples and Carole Jones; I enjoyed my conversation with them. As I toured the firm, I was very impressed with the design of the workspaces and the way teamwork is enhanced by the design of the space. I appreciate the time you took to interview me. I am very interested in working for you and look forward to hearing from you about this position.

It is not necessary to list all of these. if you met with other people mention that; if you toured the firm mention that.

The idea is to thank them for some part of the experience and to thank any other participants. Make sure to thank the person for their time!

Sincerely,

Your Signature

If you have not been given any clear direction on follow-up, you can let them know when you will be contacting them.

Sign your name in blue or black ink.

FIGURE 5-3 **A sample of the content found in a thank-you letter sent after an interview.** ■

REFERENCES

Bennett, Scott. 2005. *The Elements of Resume Style: Essential Rules and Eye-Opening Advice for Writing Resumes and Cover Letters that Work.* New York: AMACOM/ American Management Association.

The opening citation is from the introduction, page xv.

Berryman, Gregg. 1990. *Designing Creative Resumes.* Menlo Park, CA: Crisp.

Bostwick, Burdette E. 1990. *Resume Writing: A Comprehensive How-To-Do-It Guide.* New York: John Wiley & Sons, 1990.

Coxford, Lola. 1995. *Resume Writing Made Easy.* Scottsdale, AZ: Gorsuch Scarisbrick.

Farr, Michael. 2007. *Same-Day Resume.* Indianapolis, IN: JIST.

Marcus, John. 2003. *The Resume Makeover: 50 Common Problems with Resumes and Cover Letters—and How to Fix Them.* New York: McGraw-Hill.

Minnesota Department of Employment and Economic Development. 2009. *Creative Job Search (CJS) Online Guide.* HTTP://WWW.DEED.STATE.MN.US/CJS.

Piotrowski, Katy. 2008. *Career Coward's Guide to Resumes.* Indianapolis, IN: JIST.

Whitcomb, Susan. 2007. *Resume Magic.* 3rd ed. Indianapolis, IN: JIST.

PART II

EXAMPLES

SIX

RESUMES
AND RELATED CORRESPONDENCE

Clarity, consistency, and visual unity are the keys to tying together the many elements involved in correspondence related to a job search, including a cover letter, resume, and thank-you note. These items must also share some elements of visual consistency with the larger portfolio, Web site, and sample or mini-portfolio. Figures 6-1 to 6-16 are high-quality examples of stationery, business cards, envelopes, and resumes designed by graphic design graduates. Figures 6-17 to 6-19 are well-refined resumes for designers with academic experience. Figures 6-20 to 6-26 are examples of well-designed resumes for interior design graduates.

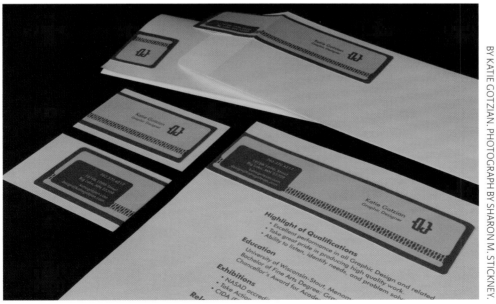

BY KATIE GOTZIAN. PHOTOGRAPH BY SHARON M. STICKNEY.

FIGURE 6-1   Visual consistency in stationery, business card, envelope, and resume design. (Figure 6-11 is an enlarged image of the resume.) ■

FIGURE 6-2 Visual consistency in stationery, business card, envelope, and resume design. (Figure 6-12 is an enlarged image of the resume.) ■

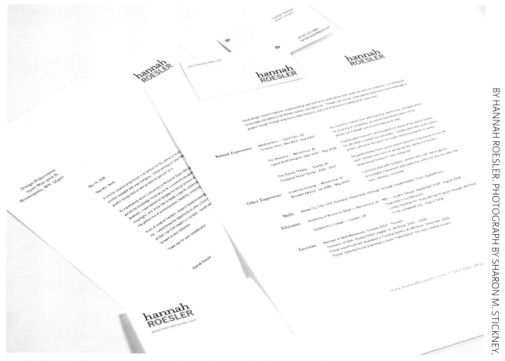

FIGURE 6-3 Visual consistency in stationery, business card, envelope, and resume design. (Figure 6-13 is an enlarged image of the resume.) ■

BY KATIE HANSON. PHOTOGRAPH BY SHARON M. STICKNEY.

FIGURE 6-4 Visual consistency in stationery, business card, envelope, and resume design. (Figure 6-14 is an enlarged image of the resume.) ▪

BY KATIE CARLSON. PHOTOGRAPH BY SHARON M. STICKNEY.

FIGURE 6-5 Visual consistency in stationery, business card, thank-you note, and resume design. (Figure 6-15 is an enlarged image of the resume.) ▪

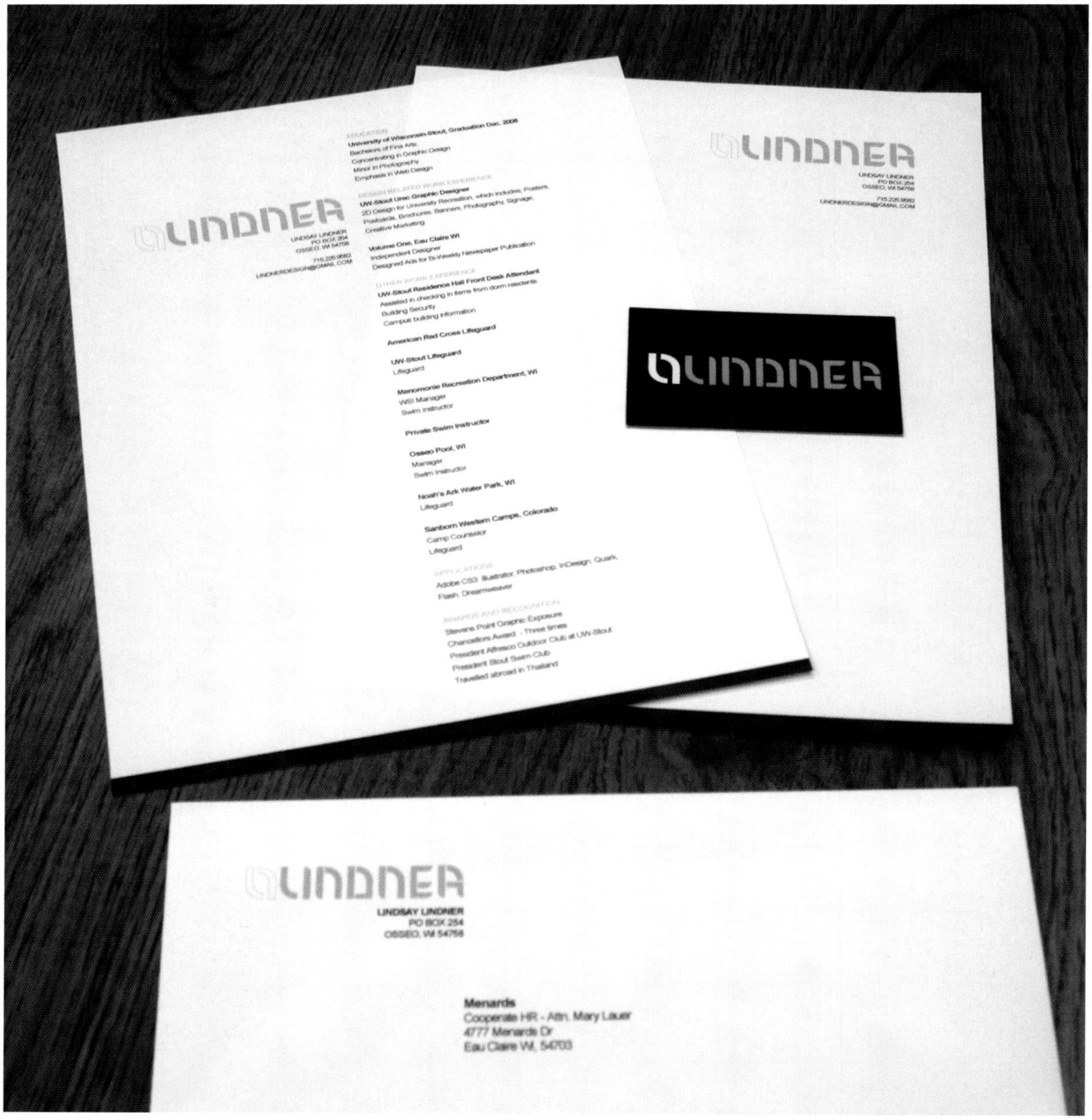

BY LINDSAY LINDNER. PHOTOGRAPH BY SHARON M. STICKNEY.

FIGURE 6-6 Visual consistency in stationary, business card, envelope, and resume design. ■

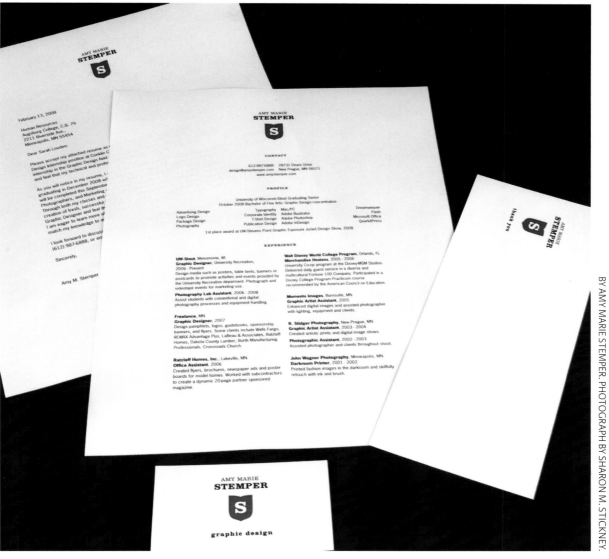

FIGURE 6-7　Visual consistency in stationery, business card, envelope, and resume design.　■

FIGURE 6-8 Visually consistency in stationery, business card, envelope, and resume design. ■

FIGURE 6-9A Visual consistency in the design of stationery, business cards, and portfolio elements. ■

JULIA
STEPHAN

OBJECTIVE

Energetic, dependable graduate from the acclaimed BFA graphic design program at University of Wisconsin-Stout. Presently seeking an experience to assist myself in growing in my career.

EDUCATION

University Wisconsin Stout | Menomonie, WI
- BFA Graphic Design
- GPA of 3.5
- Graduated May 2008

WORK EXPERIENCE

IBM Design Source | RTP, NC
- 2007-present
- Hired as co-op Graphic Designer
- Responsible for improving visibility, design quality and competitive image of IBM offerings through the application of contemporary design practice and within corporate guidelines.
- Worked closely with clients and team members to develop icons, print, multimedia, packaging, and other graphical support.
- Developed strong verbal and written communication, negotiation and problem solving skills.
- Software included the CS2 Adobe Suit, Dreamweaver, Flash, Coral Draw, and Microsoft Office Suit.

Knaacks Advertising | Menomonie, WI
- 2006, hired as Graphic Designer
- Responsible for designing t-shirts, logos and other memorabilia for various companies and individuals.
- Responsible for customer communication and gaining customer approval while working within there budget and their requirements.
- Software included Adobe Illustrator, Adobe Photoshop, and CorelDraw.

Xcel Energy | Eau Claire, WI
- 2005, hired as Customer Care Representative
- Responsible for providing customers with answers to their questions and inspiring a confident and positive opinion of Xcel Energy.
- Gained valuable communication skills and techniques.
- Trusted with time sensitive and high security information.

Julia Stephan
4836 Ritsch Court
Eau Claire, WI 54703
715-864-9431
julia@**juliastephan.com**

BY JULIA STEPHAN.

FIGURE 6-9B An enlargement of the resume shown in Figure 6-9A. ■

Lisa Schwennsen
Graphic Designer & Photographer

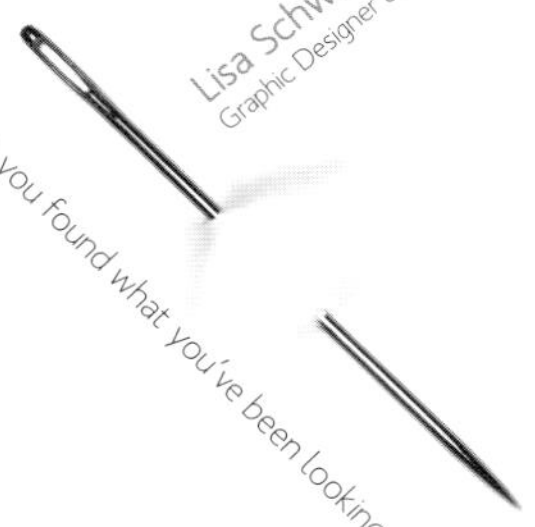

Have you found what you've been looking for?

Education
University of Wisconsin-Stout, Menomonie
B.F.A, Graphic Design May 2008
Minor, Digital Photography July 2008
Study Abroad Program, Scotland May—June 2008
(Digital Photography Portfolio Class)

North High School, Eau Claire
Study Abroad Program, Mexico June 2002
(Intermediate Spanish Class)

Awards & Honors
North High School Certificate of training/completion
for Printing Apprentice Program Aug 2002—June 2004

Work-Related Experience
UW-Stout Photography Department, Lab Assistant Aug 2007—May 2008
Equipment management
Assist students/mentor
Clean/maintenance equipment
Mix chemistry

Software Experience (Pc or Mac)
Microsoft Office Suite
Adobe Illustrator CS3
Adobe Photoshop CS3
Adobe InDesign CS3
Adobe Dreamweaver CS3
Adobe Flash CS3
Adobe Bridge CS3
Adobe Acrobat
QuarkXPress
Final Cut Pro
iMovie

Johnson Litho Graphics, Production Assistant June 2002—Dec 2004
Contact customers
Process production orders
Edit printed and digital proofs
File management

Professional Experience
Kohl's, Ad Set Associate Dec 2005—July 2007
Update price/signage
Merchandise products

Design Specialization Courses
Publication Design
Package Design
Photography
Videography
Web Design

Pepsi Bottling Group, Merchandiser July 2007—Current
Promote sales
Work Independently
Manage Inventory
Build displays & apply signage

Online Portfolio
www.lisaschwennsen.com

2915 Starr Ave
Eau Claire, WI 54703
schwennsenl@uwstout.edu
(715) 864-6083

FIGURE 6-10   The resume of a recent college graduate. ■

763.370.4217

19198 109th Street
Big Lake, MN 55309

katiegotzian.com
design@katiegotzian.com

Katie Gotzian
Graphic Designer

Highlight of Qualifications
- Ability to listen, identify needs, and problem solve to meet client needs.
- Take great pride in producing high quality work.
- Excellent organization and communication skills.

Education
University of Wisconsin-Stout, Menomonie, Wisconsin
Bachelor of Fine Arts Degree: concentration in Graphic Design
Chancellor's Award for Academic Excellence received for eight semesters.
Graduated with Cum Laude honors.

Related Work
UW-Stout University Housing, Graphic Designer, Menomonie WI, June 2007-April 2008
- Arrange and prepare for client meetings.
- Self directed projects to meet the client's needs and deadlines.
- Prepare files for a variety of output.

Activities
Portfolio One-on-One, April 2008

Seek Design Conference, November 2007

AIGA Design Camp, October 2007

AIGA Member, 2007-Present

Graphic Design Association, 2006-2008

Exhibitions
- NASAD accreditation gallery exhibition at University of Wisconsin-Stout, 2007.
- Take Action, poster exhibition at Furlong Gallery, University of Wisconsin-Stout, 2006.
- CIDA (FIDER) accreditation gallery exhibition at University of Wisconsin-Stout, 2005.

Technical Skills
Proficient skills using Illustrator, InDesign, Photoshop, and Microsoft Word working on a Mac platform.

Experience with digital and film cameras, black and white 35mm film development, serigraphy, and metal forming.

References and Portfolio available upon request.

FIGURE 6-11 The resume of a recent college graduate. ■

objective
To achieve a position in the graphic design field to bring new ideas and designs with the education I received from the University of Wisconsin-Stout.

jessica
leafblad
Graphic Design & Illustration

514 21st. Ave. E. #23 Menomonie, WI 54751   (612) 250 9797   schloegelj@uwstout.edu

education

BFA Graphic Design
2004 - 2008   University Of Wisconsin-Stout
2003 - 2004   University Of Minnesota, Duluth

design related skills

Strong background in Illustrator, Photoshop and InDesign. Some work in Dreamweaver, ImageReady and Quark Express. Extensive background in fine arts, specializing in illustration. Experience in both Macintosh Apple computers and PC computers.

Advanced Design Classes
Advanced Computer Imagery, Publication Design, Screenprinting (Monotypes) Product & Packaging Design, and Senior Project.

design experience

2007 - May 2008   The Stoutonia Newspaper
Advertising Designer & Illustrator
Responsibilities include updating, fixing and designing ads; obtaining article story topics and illustrating for that particular story or any other illustration needed for the paper.

Oct - Dec 2007   The Niche Boutique
Graphic Design Internship
Responsibilities included logo design, department identities, poster design for each department and printing and preparing signage.

1999 - 2007   Other Experience
Throughout these years, from my first job to the recent I have obtained skills such as using different machinery, tools, computers, working with people, serving people and other important life skills that were obtained through these jobs.

references

Available on request.

FIGURE 6-12   The resume of a recent college graduate. ■

hannah ROESLER

Good design requires passion, understanding, and a drive to create great work under all sorts of conditions. A fulfilling life encourages the ability to be flexible, humor, and optimism. Though I am young, I have gained experience and knowledge of graphic design through long hours, hard research, and a lot of practice in doing what I love most.

Related Experience

BKGElements — Sioux Falls, SD
Creative Intern, May 2007 - Aug 2007

Assisted the creative team with branding, advertising, and publications for a variety of companies, as well as learned the basics of the production manager and account executive roles.

The Stoutonia — Menomonie, WI
Layout & Ad Designer, Sept 2007 – May 2008

Created advertisements and designed the layout of the sports section for UW-Stout's student-led newspaper. Collaborated with sports editor, writers, and other designers to create interesting layouts bi-weekly.

The Stanley Theater — Stanley, WI
Freelance Poster Design, 2006 - 2007

Designed holiday movie poster advertisements to be placed around the town; worked with client on designing new identity for theater; experienced freelance client interaction.

Other Experience

University Housing — Menomonie, WI
Resident Advisor, Jan 2006 – May 2007

Communicated with residents, worked with staff, led programs, encouraged involvement and leadership, enforced policies within the halls, referred, counseled.

Skills

Adobe CS, CS2, CS3; Illustrator, Photoshop, InDesign, Acrobat, Dreamweaver, Flash, QuarkXPress.

Education

University of Wisconsin-Stout — Menomonie, WI

BFA — Graphic Design, September 2004 - August 2008
Chancellor's List Recipient

Goldsmith's College — London, UK

London Summer Art Study Abroad Program through UW-Stout
To be completed July - August 2008

Activities

Member of AIGA-Minnesota, October 2007 – Present.
Treasurer of GDA, student AIGA chapter of UW-Stout, 2007 – 2008.
Poster advertisement displayed in Furlong Gallery at UW-Stout, December 2006.
Poster selected to be published in book "Take Action" for class related project.

www.hannahroesler.com » 507.525.3892 » hannahroesler@gmail.com

BY HANNAH ROESELER.

FIGURE 6-13 The resume of a recent college graduate. A related Web site can be found in Figure 7-14. ■

KATIE HANSON graphic designer

5575 Park Place Drive, Shoreview, MN 55126 • 651.442.1456 • hansonka@uwstout.edu

OBJECTIVE

To obtain a graphic design or related position where there is a need to use numerous design tools creatively and with a focus on customer satisfaction.

ACADEMICS

University of Wisconsin–Stout – Menomonie, WI
Bachelor of Fine Arts, Graphic Design
Projected Graduation: May 2008
GPA 3.71

HONORS/ACTIVITIES

AIGA Student Member 2006–08
Delta Zeta National Sorority 2005–08, Web Designer, Academics Chair
UW-Stout Dance Team Member 2004–07, Captain 2005–06
Chancellor's Award for Academic Excellence: 6 semesters

TECHNICAL SKILLS

Skilled in Adobe CS3 Photoshop, Illustrator and InDesign. Experience in Dreamweaver, Flash and Acrobat. Knowledge of Microsoft Word, Excel, and PowerPoint. Proficient in Mac and PC platforms.

DESIGN EXPERIENCE

GRAPHIC DESIGNER

Shop Your Colors, LLC – Eau Claire, WI (Dec. 2007–Present)
- Logo design for apparel and advertisements for print and web.
- Demonstrated creative problem-solving and excellent time-management.

MARKETING INTERN

Core Products International, Inc. – Osceola, WI (Jan. 2007–Jan. 2008)
- Redesigned product packaging, displays and posters, and catalog design.
- Showed knowledge of creative problem-solving and use of technical skills.

WORK EXPERIENCE

OFFICE ASSISTANT

University Dining Services – Menomonie, WI (Aug. 2006–Dec. 2006)
- Office tasks, poster and postcard design, updated and maintained website.
- Demonstrated initiative, resourcefulness, and ability to solve problems.

SERVER

Stout Ale House – Menomonie, WI (Jan. 2006–Aug. 2006)
- Reputation for being energetic, enthusiastic, and helpful to other coworkers.
- Understand the importance of customer service to repeat and referral of business.

HOSTESS/SERVER

Byerly's Minnesota Grill – Roseville, MN (Mar. 2004–Nov.2005)
- Extremely reliable, covered extra shifts, and worked extra hours.
- Conducted all interactions with customers and staff with courtesy and efficiency.

BY KATIE HANSON.

FIGURE 6-14 The resume of a recent college graduate. ■

Katie Carlson
carlsonkat@uwstout.com

N5650 W. Channel Dr.
Shawano, WI 54166
715-851-4414

Education

The University of Wisconsin-Stout
Menomonie, Wisconsin
Bachelor of Fine Arts, concentration Graphic Design
Business Administration Minor
GPA 3.880

Qualifications: Adobe Photoshop, Illustrator, InDesign, Flash 8, Dreamweaver 8, and Quark X-press. Experience with Microsoft Office. Proficient in both MAC and PC platforms.

Relevant Experience

Outreach Services, UW-Stout
Menomonie, WI
Graphic Designer (June 2006-Present)
Design promotional materials for credit courses, conferences, and workshops of Outreach Services

Learning Technology Services, UW-Stout
Menomonie, WI
Photography Assistant (April 2007- May 2008)
Help maintain the UW-Stout photo database, assist Senior Photographer in and out of the studio, scan negatives, and digital photo editing

Exhibitions, Awards, Activities
CIDA (FIDER) accreditation, Furlong Gallery exhibit
University of Wisconsin-Stout (2006)

Take Action, poster exhibit at Furlong Gallery
University of Wisconsin-Stout (2006)

Larsen Design Scholarship Recipient
(2006–2007)

London Summer Art Program Participant
Studied advanced drawing and painting (Summer 2007)

Graphic Design Association
(2005-2008)

Portfolio and references available upon request

BY KATIE CARLSON.

FIGURE 6-15 The resume of a recent college graduate. ▪

SPARKS
CREATIVE LABOR

DUSTIN SPARKS
740 Northern Meadows Pkwy #204
Menomonie, Wisconsin 54751

715.556.0240
dustinsparks@gmail.com
www.creativelabor.com

- -

EDUCATION

2005-2008
Bachelor of Fine Arts, Graphic Design
University of Wisconsin, Stout

2000-2003
Associate in Applied Arts Degree, Commercial Art
Madison Area Technical College

1999-2001
Certificate, Web Page Design
Madison Area Technical College

- -

EXPERIENCE

2004-2005
The Hiebing Group, Madison, Wisconsin; graphic designer
Assisted in and completed projects in branding, print collateral,
packaging, and web site design

2003-2004
Aesention Interactive, Madison, Wisconsin; graphic designer
Responsible for projects from concept to completion including
promotional collateral, corporate identity, and websites

2003
Olille Design, Madison, Wisconsin; freelancer

2003
Maddox Design Works, Madison, Wisconsin; intern

- -

ACHIEVEMENTS

2007
Letterhead & Logo Design 10, Rockport Publishers
Published entry

2003
Print Magazine: Regional Design Annual

2003
How Magazine: Self Promotion Annual

2002
Step By Step Magazine: Illustration Annual

2002-2005
Addy Awards: 1 Gold and 6 Silver

- -

SERVICE

Design Madison; Education Chair Designer
Worked with the Design Madison Education Chairman
in developing posters for upcoming events

FIGURE 6-16 The resume of a recent college graduate. ■

Ambica Prakash

520 N Street SW, Apt S232, Washington DC 20024
ambicaprakash.com • design@ambicaprakash.com • 812.320.4401

WORK EXPERIENCE

Projects | 2004–present
Indego Africa, Washington, DC
Gutenberg Communications, New York, NY
Swechha – We for Change Foundation, New Delhi, India
Hagar International, Eau Claire, WI
TunaHAKI Foundation, Santa Monica, CA
Phoebe A. Hearst Museum of Anthropology, Berkeley, CA
Center for Sustainable Living, Bloomington, IN
Bloomington Parks and Recreation, Bloomington, IN

Applied strategic thinking & research to logo redesigns; Designed & produced print & online marketing collateral; Developed layouts for a book chapter; Redesigned newsletters to increase readership; Designed bold illustrations for promotional materials from concept to final production; Created web design, wrote site map and worked with developers; Implemented cohesive branding; Used social media & networking tools.

Assistant Professor | 2008–2009
Department of Art, American University

Courses taught: Beginner Typography, Intermediate Typography & Advanced Narrative Design.

Assistant Professor | 2005–2008
Department of Art & Design, University of Wisconsin-Stout

Courses taught: Graphic Design One, Branding, Publication Design, Senior Capstone, and Art & Design Perspectives in Northern India (study abroad course).

Other duties: Liaison with local & international organizations via service-learning while working with the press; Area Representative; Faculty Advisor for AIGA student chapter; Mentor for junior faculty.

Graphic Designer | 2005–2008
Furlong Gallery, University of Wisconsin-Stout

Designed print marketing collateral – postcards, brochures, invitations, mailers, posters – following university brand identity standards.

EDUCATION

MFA Graphic Design | 2005
Indiana University, Bloomington, IN

BFA (Visual Communication) with honors | 2002
Herron School of Art, IUPUI, Indianapolis, IN

BFA (Applied Art) | 1998
College of Art (Delhi University), New Delhi, India

French Diploma | 1998
Alliance Française de Delhi, India

SKILLS

Adobe Creative Suite; Microsoft Office; Conceptual & Technical Expertise; Production; Art Direction; Problem Solving; Strategic Thinking; Project Management; Illustration; Scanning & Photo Editing; Typography; Identity & Branding; Publication Design; Social Media.

AFFILIATIONS

Marketing, PR & Sales Committee Chair, Indego Africa | 2009
American Institute of Graphic Arts | 2001–present

REFERENCES available upon request.

AWARDS & GRANTS

Guest Juror | 2008
Louisiana Tech, Ruston, LA

Badger Award for "Take Action" Book | 2007
Printing Industry of Wisconsin

Faculty Research Initiative Grant | 2007
University of Wisconsin-Stout, Menomonie, WI

AIGA Minnesota Design Show Award | 2006
Minneapolis, MN

Academic Student Appointee | 2002–05
Indiana University, Bloomington, IN

Service-Learning Grant | 2004
Indiana Campus Compact, Indianapolis, IN

Grants-in-Aid of Research Awards | 2003
University Graduate School, IU, Bloomington, IN

World Studio Foundation Scholarship | 2002

French Government Scholarship | 1999
L'Ecole des Beaux-Arts, St. Etienne, France

BY AMBICA PRAKASH.

FIGURE 6-17 The resume of a graphic designer with design and teaching experience. A related Web site can be found in Figure 7-12. ■

LECTURES

Workshop On Civic Engagement | 2008
Swechha, New Delhi, India

An IDEA For Change Workshop | 2008
National Service-Learning Conference, Minneapolis, MN

Design & Social Responsibility | 2008
Louisiana Tech University, Ruston, LA

Cultural Perspectives In Design | 2007
CCPVC, University of Wisconsin-Eau Claire, WI

Service-Learning: Helping The Community | 2006
Design Frontier (AIGA), Lakewood, CO

I Profess: The Graphic Design Manifesto | 2006
Furlong Gallery, Menomonie, WI

PUBLICATIONS

Aksharam © **Ambica Prakash** | 2009
Cover Art for book, "Passage to Manhattan:
Critical Essays on Meena Alexander"

Introduction to Graphic Design | 2009
Authored chapter in forthcoming book for Interior
Designers to be published by Wiley Higher Education

So Far, So Good | 2009
Authored & designed book on India study
abroad course to be published in 2009

An IDEA For Change | 2009
Authored & designed workbook on civic
engagement to be published on Lulu.com in 2009

Graphic Design For Social Change | 2005–08
Authored chapter in forthcoming book *Integrating Service-
Learning into the University Classroom* to be published

Elements Of Nature: Earth, Wind, Fire & Water | 2006
Posters published in *Reflections Artists Journal*

**Learning Service Or Service Learning:
Enabling The Civic** | 2006
Co-authored paper, *International Journal of
Teaching and Learning in Higher Education*

Transient Connections | 2006
Outside In: An International Poster Exhibit Catalog

BIBLIOGRAPHY

**Environment: Design For Social Change – A
Wisconsin-India Connection** | March 4, 2008
Jyoti Gupta, SAJA Forum

Designs From India | December 27, 2007, 16
Ryan Toppin, Volume One

Designing Ways To Change The World | Fall 2007
Kay K. Stanton, Chippewa Valley Business Report

Students Take Action With Art | 2007
Stout Quest: The Journal of Research at University of WI-Stout

Measuring Up | February 11, 2007, A7
Tom McDonald, Dunn County News, Menomonie, WI

**University of Wisconsin-Stout Students' Designs Grace
United Way Posters** | February 11, 2007, 1C
Pamela Powers, Leader-Telegram, Eau Claire, WI

An IDEA For Change | Winter 2005
Jennifer Piurek, IU School of Fine Arts Newsletter, Bloomington, IN

EXHIBITIONS

To Death With A Smile | 2007
Juried show, Mexican Museum of Design, Mexico City; Poster
titled, *Reincarnation* was selected with 140 other posters from
1,300 international entries

PDN PhotoPlus Expo | 2007
Group exhibition New York, NY

Urban Forest Project | 2006
Times Square, New York, NY

Multicultural, Syncretism | 2006
Juried show, Appleton Art Center, Appleton, WI

An IDEA For Change | 2005
MFA thesis work, SoFA Gallery IU, Bloomington, IN

I Profess: The Graphic Design Manifesto | 2005–07
Juried traveling show, East Lansing, MI; Portland, OR; Troy,
NY; Toledo, OH; Memphis, TN; Menomonie, WI, Mississippi, MS

OUTSIDE IN An International Poster Exhibit | 2004
Juried traveling show, Boston, MA; Detroit, MI; Beverly, MA;
Portland, ME and Muncie, IN

अम्पिच
Ambica Prakash   ambicaprakash.com • design@ambicaprakash.com • 812.320.4401

BY AMBICA PRAKASH.

FIGURE 6-17 (Continued) ■

Robert Atwell

Education
2002   M.F.A. Iowa State University, Ames, IA
1995   B.F.A. Iowa State University, Ames, IA

Solo Exhibitions
2009   *Robert Atwell,* Simon Gallery, Morristown, NJ
2008   *Robert Atwell,* Walker Art Gallery, University of Nebraska-Kearney, Kearney, NE
2007   *New Paintings,* Gilman Contemporary, Ketchum, ID
         Today and Tomorrow, James Watrous Gallery, Madison, WI
2005   *Saturday Morning Swim,* Schwalbach Gallery, Baraboo, WI
2004   *A Day in the Life*, Pioneer Gallery, Ames, IA
2002   *Master of Fine Arts Thesis Exhibit,* Iowa State University, Gallery 181, Ames, IA

Selected Group Exhibitions
2008   *Fusion,* Gilman Contemporary, Ketchum, ID
         UW-Stout Faculty Show, Furlong Gallery, Menomonie, WI ('04, '05, '06, '07)
         Focus Grant Reunion Exhibit, The Gallery, Iowa State University, Ames, IA
         Red Dot Art Fair-NYC, and London, UK, Kathryn Markel Fine Arts, New York, NY
         Big Impressions, Gilman Contemporary, Ketchum, ID
2007   *Red Dot Art Fair-Miami,* Kathryn Markel Fine Arts, New York, NY
         Summer Group Show, Kathryn Markel Fine Arts, New York, NY
         Affordable Art Fair NYC, Kathryn Markel Fine Arts, New York, NY
2006   *Waterfall,* Mahan Gallery, Columbus, OH
         Liquid/Solid: New Abstractions by Contemporary Painters, Rice Gallery, Westminster, MD
         Visiting Abstractions, LE Philips Gallery, Eau Claire, WI
         Northern / Southern Exposure, HIte Art Institute, University of Louisville, Louisville, KY
2005   *The Joy of Jell-O,* Ephemeral Space, Saint Paul, MN
         AAF-NYC, Margaret Thatcher Projects, New York, NY
         3Views, Gallery 106, Menomonie, WI
         Waterfall, Vermont Studio Center, Johnson, VT
2004   *HeyYEAH!,* University of Iowa, Iowa City, IA
         Group Exhibition, Sioux City Art Center, Sioux City, IA
         Faculty Show, Iowa State University, Ames, IA
2003   *AAF-NYC,* Margaret Thatcher Projects, New York, NY
         Scene/Unseen, Runnells Gallery, Portales, NM
         Soundtoys.net, London, UK
         Greater Midwest International XVIII, CMS Art Center Gallery, Warrensburg, MO
2002   *Combined Talents, the Florida National,* FSU Museum of Fine Arts, Tallahassee, FL
         58th Juried Exhibition, Sioux City Art Center, Sioux City, IA
1999   *Iowa College Salon XXI,* Brunnier Art Museum, Ames, IA
1998   *Wall Paper, Brilliant New Abstract Prints*, Gallery 181, Ames, IA
         Iowa College Salon XX, Brunnier Art Museum, Ames, IA

Grants, Fellowships, Awards, and Honors
2006   Bush Fellowship Finalist, Bush Foundation, St. Paul, MN
2005   Vermont Studio Center Fellowship, Johnson, VT
2003   2nd Place, *Scene / Unseen,* Runnells Gallery, Portales, NM
2002   2nd Place, ISU Animation and Film Festival, Ames, IA
1995   Focus Grant Recipient, Iowa State University, Ames, IA

BY ROBERT ATWELL.

FIGURE 6-18   The resume of a fine artist with studio and teaching experience. A related Web site can be found n Figure 7-13. ■

Bibliography

Brown, Rick, "Reduced to Abstraction ' a lot of sketching' helps artist Atwell create abstract works", Kearney Hub, Sept. 17, 2008.

Smith, Jennifer A, "A world of their own, Two artists have their way with reality", *Isthmus*, August 10, 2007.

Stockinger, Jacob, "Side-by-Side reveals This-n-That", *Wisconsin State Journal,* July 17, 2007.

Stahl, Kathy, "Interview with Robert Atwell" *Spectrum West, Wisconsin Public Radio WHWC 88.3(wpr.org)*July 12, 2007.

Mayr, Bill, "Personal Galleries: Young adults start private collections by prowling central Ohio exhibits."*The Columbus Dispatch,* January 28, 2007.

Zappardino, Pam, "Still Liquid / Still Solid", *Carroll County Times,* Friday, June 2, 2006.

Pamela Powers, "Creative Space, New art gallery caters to contemporary works." *Leader Telegram,* Nov.7, 2005

Kyle Kingston, "Gallery 106 opens its doors with "3views"", *The Stoutonia.* v96.08. October 27, 2005

Cameron Campbell, *Iowa Architect*; v04.247, 2004

Jay Kim, "Atwell draws from multiple media: Artist experiments with motion media." *Iowa State Daily,* July 8, 2004

Joe Spragon, "Sketch off gets dirty: Professors draw each other for charity. "*The Stoutonia,* v95.12. Nov. 18, 2004

Steve Tanza, "Interview with Robert Atwell." *Soundtoys.net,* June 2003

Sunghyun Ryoo Kang, *Journal of Asian Design,* 2003.

Kathy Svec, "Cream of the College Crop" *Tractor; Iowa Arts and Culture* v6.2 1998

Shuva Rahim, "Bob and a Mural." *Ethos;* v41.3 December 1994

Works in Public Collections

Comcast Corporation
Houston Four Seasons

Employment

Assistant Professor, Foundations Coordinator, 2005 - present
Department of Art and Design, University of Wisconsin-Stout, Menomonie, WI

BY ROBERT ATWELL.

FIGURE 6-18 (Continued) ■

timothy d. [tim] dolan

908 shady lane
johnson city, tennessee 37601
423 . 676 . 3092
dolantd@appstate.edu

education

Master of Science, Technology: Engineering Technology, East Tennessee State University, August 2003.
Master's Thesis: Designers' Perceptions of Interdisciplinary Design Education

Bachelor of Science, Human Ecology: Interior Design, Magna Cum Laude, The University of Tennessee at Chattanooga, May 1993.

research focus

The correlative association of foundational studies among multidisciplinary design education disciplines, service-learning, and design & culture

employment history

Assistant Professor, Appalachian State University, College of Fine and Applied Arts, Department of Technology, August 2004 to present. Responsibilities: Course development, instruction, and assessment of interior design courses at all levels: lecture and studio, student advisement, and creative scholarship. Emphasis in this program is centered on hands-on instruction and experimentation through the Technology Department's multidisciplinary offerings; Construction [...]
Design: Furniture, and related production industries: ce[...]
Students are integrally trained as designers and prob[...]
sets. Additionally, students are exposed to related dis[...]
knowledge necessary for professional development in [...]

Courses Taught Include:

* INT 1300 Introduction to Interior Desi[...]
* INT 2110 Studio III; Fall 2006, Sprin[...]
* INT 2200 Interior Design Systems I; F[...]
* INT 3001 Internship Workshop; Sprin[...]
* INT 3100 Studio IV; Fall 2007, Fall 2[...]
* INT 3311 Commercial Interior Design[...]
* INT 3331 Interior Building Materials [...]
  2005, Spring 2006
* INT 3400 Interior Design Junior Field[...]
* INT 3531 Impact of Interior Design: [...]
* INT 4100 Studio VI; Spring 2007
* INT 4320 Professional Practices in De[...]
  2007, Spring 2008, Spring 2009
* INT 4323 Professional Practices in Int[...]
  2005, Fall 2005, Spring 2006
* HON 4010 General Honors Thesis

timothy d. dolan

908 shady lane
johnson city, tennessee 37601
423 . 676 . 3092
dolantd@appstate.edu

biography:

With an eye for detail and a love of the unique, Tim brings over fifteen years of design experience to projects, clients and students. NCIDQ certified [National Council for Interior Design Qualification] and a Registered Interior Designer in the State of Tennessee, his background ranges from stage and set design, to textile printing, graphic design, and commercial development. Currently, he is an Assistant Professor at Appalachian State University in Boone, North Carolina, and maintains a private practice specializing in health care design.

Academically, he received a B.S. degree Magna Cum Laude from The University of Tennessee at Chattanooga and an M.S. degree from East Tennessee State University, where his research focused primarily on the correlative association of foundational studies among multidisciplinary design education disciplines. For over nine years he has had the opportunity to serve as an instructor in university interior design programs. His teaching has covered senior design studios to architectural study tours including visits to the International Home Furnishings Market in High Point, NC, and NeoCon World's Trade Fair in Chicago, IL. A student favorite, Tim structures his classes with hands-on learning, industry experience, high expectations, and healthy doses of fun.

Professionally, he most recently has been involved in the new construction, addition and renovation of over forty long-term care, assisted living and retirement facilities, with an average value of two million dollars; functioning primarily as project coordinator for a management and development company. Geographically, his projects have covered the east coast and central states. Prior experience includes hospitality design, educational facilities, corporate offices, churches, as well as corporate identity and branding. He is an active professional member of the International Interior Design Association [IIDA] and the American Society of Interior Designers [ASID]. Additional memberships include the Interior Design Educator's Council [IDEC] and the International Code Council [ICC].

Personally, Tim enjoys traveling, jazz music and theatre. In his free time, he is in frequent demand as a designer, clinician, and adjudicator for marching band programs. He currently splits his time between homes in Northeast Tennessee and Western North Carolina, with his wife Nikki and yellow Labrador Pearl.

FIGURE 6-19 A biography and curriculum vitae for an interior designer with design and teaching experience. ■

Rosa C Brandt

612.226.9454 | rosacbrandt@yahoo.com | 10124 Wentworth Ave. S Bloomington, MN 55420

objective

To obtain a sales position with a strong, forward thinking, progressive company where I can fully utilize my knowledge and experience as a designer.

professional experience

Opus A & E	Smart Associates	Shea Inc.
Minnetonka, MN	Minneapolis, MN	Minneapolis, MN
Interior Designer	Interior Designer &	Interior Design Intern
Aug 2007 - Jan 2009	Studio Manager	June 2003 - Aug 2003
	Jan 2005 - Aug 2007	

achievements & capabilities

› Collaborated on various projects including Corporate, Higher Education, Restaurant, Retail, and Model Home.

› Participated in client presentations and meetings.

› Project managed and lead designer on construction adminstration for an office renovation.

› Managed and organized time for all projects and directed designers with tasks as studio manager.

› Developed interior finish palettes, furniture selections, and specifications.

› Assisted with schematic design, space planning, and design development.

› Completed Photoshop renderings to assist in developing presentation illustrations and mentored interiors staff in Photoshop.

› Maintainted Interiors Resource Library and consulted with reps on a consistent basis.

› Orchestrated the move of the Interiors library and reorganization.

education

University of Wisconsin - Stout

Menomonie, WI
Graduated: Dec 2004
Bachelor of Fine Arts - Interior Design (CIDA credited program)
› Minor in Spanish
› Pursuing LEED AP (May 13, 2009)
› Pursuing NCIDQ (October 2, 2009)

technical skills

Auto Cad, Photoshop, In Design, Word, Excel, Powerpoint, and Outlook

professional affiliation

NEWH - The Network of the Hospitality Industry

2005-present
Active Member
Past Chapter Secretary, Treasurer, and Publications
Attended NEWH leadership convention

IIDA - International Interior Design Association

2009-present
Active Member

References and project list available upon request

FIGURE 6-20 The resume of an interior designer with design experience who is seeking to move into a different segment of the design industry. ■

Laura Purcell

Permanent Address
8159 Zenith Court
Brooklyn Park, MN 55443
PH 612-716-8675
purcelll@uwstout.edu

OBJECTIVE

To obtain a full time position in a commercial firm in which I will be able to use both technical and creative skills to enhance all aspects of design in relation to the interior design field.

CAPABILITIES PROFILE

Team Oriented	Organizational Skills
Detail Oriented	Computer Proficient

EDUCATION

Bachelor of Fine Arts, Interior Design
University of Wisconsin Stout, CIDA Accredited, May 2008
GPA: 3.6/4.0

RELATED COURSEWORK

Commercial Design I & II	Lighting & Furniture Design	Architectural Design & Graphics
Residential Design I & II	Textiles	Light Construction Methods
Specifications	Presentation Techniques	Computer Assisted Design
Materials and Methods	2D Digital Imaging	Fundamentals of Speech

COMPUTER SKILLS

Adobe CS3	Photoshop	Auto CAD 2006/07
	Illustrator	Google Sketchup
	In-Design	Microsoft Office 2007

EXPERIENCE
07.07-08.07

Ellerbe Becket, Minneapolis, MN
Interior Design Intern
Preparation of presentation boards, photoshop rendering, red-line corrections, assisting with material selections, material research.

06.07-07.07

BSID, Minneapolis, MN
Interior Design Intern
Finish selections, custom furniture design, hand/Auto CAD drafting, organization.

06.05-08.05
06.06-08.06

GunkelmanFlesher Interior Design, Minneapolis, MN
Interior Design Intern
Drafting, estimating, specifications, fabric & accessory selection, researching new products, installations of projects, note taking in client meetings, marketing projects, running errands, organization of sample room.

12.02-08.04

Northwest Athletic Club, (Currently Lifetime Fitness) Maple Grove/St. Louis Park, MN
Child care provider/Summer Camp Counselor

PROFESSIONAL ORGANIZATIONS

ASID	Student Member 04-05
NEWH	Student Member 06-08
IIDA	Student Member 07-08

HONORS AND EXHIBITS

Chancellors Award
Fall 05-Spring 07
Student Gallery Sculpture Exhibit
Spring 06
Recognition of Straight "A" Average
Fall 07
BWBR Prize Finalist In Recognition of Design Excellence
Spring 07
Project Publishing
Interior Design Visual Presentation 3rd Edition By Maureen Mitton
Student Memorial Project Entry
Fall 07
Best of Design Show - Best in Show recipient, Best in Interior Design recipient
Spring 08

Portfolio and References available upon request.

FIGURE 6-21 The resume of a recent interior design graduate. ■

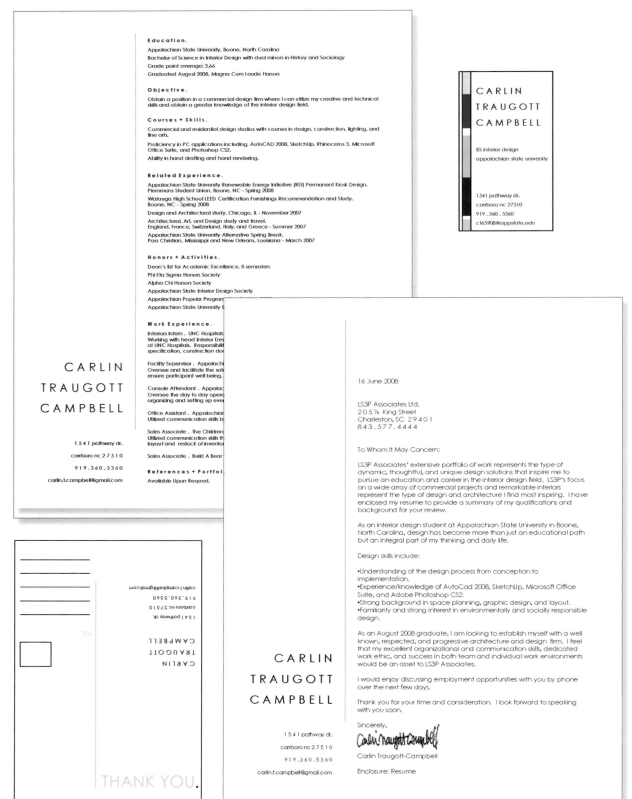

FIGURE 6-22 The cover letter, business card, thank-you note, and resume of an interior design graduate. ■

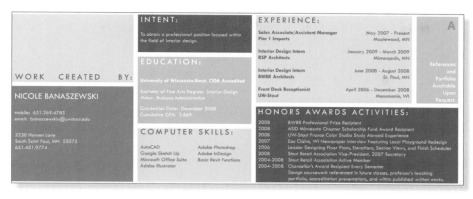

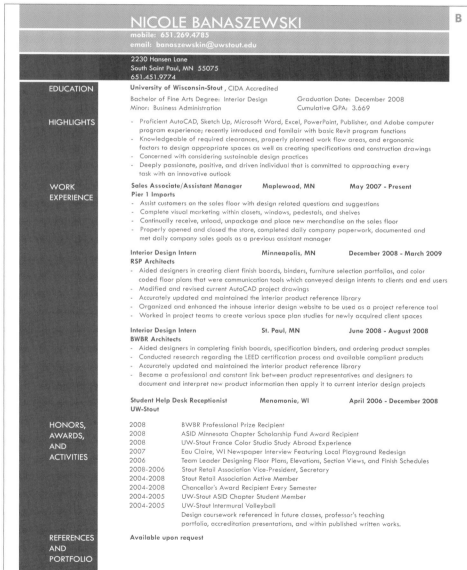

FIGURE 6-23, A,B   The resume example of a recent interior design graduate. The unusual format (a) was designed to fit into a sample portfolio mailing envelope. A standard-size resume (b) was designed to be sent separately. See Figures 7-2a through 7-2e for elements from the complete package. ■

JENNIFER IREY

Jennifer.Irey@gmail.com
2120 New Castle Ct
Davenport, IA 52807
563-343-4591

EDUCATION

BFA Interior Design, Cum Laude
Iowa State University, College of Design: 2005-2009
Rome Study Abroad Program: Fall 2008
Chinese Architecture Study Abroad: Spring 2009
Dean's List: All Semesters
3.63 Cumulative GPA

DESIGN EXPERIENCE

Paragon Commercial Interiors, Davenport, IA
Intern: Commercial and Hospitality Design
Summer 2005, Summer 2008

Phelan's Interiors, Cedar Rapids, IA
Intern: Residential, Commercial, and Retail Sales
Summer 2007

The Mad Potter, Davenport, IA
Customer Service, Sample Artist, Retail
Summer 2006

Heart of America Restaurants and Inns, Moline, IL
Intern: Hospitality Design
Summer 2004

HONORS AND EXHIBITIONS

2009 *Hospitality Design* **Magazine Awards,**
Student Finalist: May/June Issue

Outstanding Senior Interior Design Project:
2009- Iowa State University

Best Portfolio Design Award:
ISU College of Design Learning Community 2006

ISU Rome Exhibition: Spring 2009

Peer Recognition Award: "Most Computer Savvy"

RELATED COURSES

Auto-Cad
Hand Drafting and Rendering
Art History/ Design Studies
Interior Design History, Theory and Criticism
Construction and Materials
Film Studies; Set Design Emphasis
Lighting Design
Chinese Architecture and Urban Planning
Studios; Residential, Commercial, Ideation,
Retail, Hospitality, Institutional

ACTIVITIES AND MEMBERSHIPS

Interior Design Student Association: 2007 - 2009

American Society of Interior Designers: 2007 - 2009

Emerging Green Builders: 2007

Recruitment President, Alpha Delta Pi: 2007-2008

Alpha Delta Pi Sorority: 2005 - 2009

Volunteer: Relay for Life Team Captain, Relief trip to
New Orleans Katrina Disaster, Ronald McDonald
House, Weed and Read Project in Rome, Italy

SKILLS

Autodesk AutoCAD 2008
Autodesk Revit 2009
Viz Render
SketchUp with Podium Rendering
Adobe Suite CS4
Digital Photography and Editing
Currently working to obtain LEED for CI certification
Theatre, Public Speaking, French
Vocal and Piano Performance

FIGURE 6-24   The resume of a recent interior design graduate. It is a simple yet very effective design. A well-designed mini-portfolio and smaller resume designed by the same designer can be found in Figure 7-7. ■

LAURA VANDER SANDEN

Cell: (414) 803-6748
vandersandenl@uwstout.edu
6872 S. 117th Street
Franklin, WI 53132

OBJECTIVE

An Interior Design related position where I can gain experience using the skills learned through my education, towards my career goal of becoming a designer.

EDUCATION

Graduated Magna Cum Laude - May 2009
University of Wisconsin – Stout, Menomonie, Wisconsin – CIDA accredited
Bachelor of Fine Arts: Interior Design

AWARDS & ACTIVITIES

Deans List, all semesters - GPA 3.86 (Chancellors Award)
International Interior Design Association: UW – Stout Student Chapter
    Member 2006 – Present
University of Wisconsin – Stout Women's Competitive Bowling Team
    President 2007 – 2009

RELEVANT CLASSES

Residential Design 1 & 2
Commercial Design 1 & 2
Lighting Design
Materials & Methods
Construction Documentation

TECHNICAL SKILLS

AutoCAD 2007 – used abundantly on a variety of projects
Google Sketch Up – for 3D modeling of both Interior and Exterior
Adobe Products: Photoshop, Illustrator, InDesign, Dreamweaver
Microsoft Products: Word, PowerPoint, Excel, Publisher

WORK HISTORY

Intern   **June – August 2008 & January 2009**
Schroeder Solutions – New Berlin, Wisconsin
Gained knowledge in business and sales of office furniture
Assisted with color schemes and furniture selections
Assembled display boards for client viewing

Intern   **July – August 2008**
Zimmerman Architectural Studios – Milwaukee, Wisconsin
Observed and applied real life process to projects I assisted with

Summerfest Gate Attendant   **June – July 2007 & June-August 2008**
Milwaukee World Festival – Milwaukee, Wisconsin
Provided an energetic and positive attitude at entrance and exit points

Sales Associate   **May 2006 – April 2007**
Things Remembered - Greendale, Wisconsin
Offered customer assistance through sales of personalized gifts with a friendly and positive attitude

Carpenters Assistant   **June 2004 – August 2005**
VS Construction – Waterford, Wisconsin
Applied finishing skills and offered opinions throughout in-process projects

References Available Upon Request

FIGURE 6-25 The resume of a recent interior design graduate. This very simple yet effective design was done in Microsoft Word. ■

10807 Surfwood Lane
Cincinnati, Ohio 45241
Cell: (513) 659-9768
pikejl@email.uc.edu

Jennifer L. Pike

Education

Participating in the Professional Practice Co-op Program, alternating quarters of college study with quarters of work in Interior Design.

2004-Present   *Cincinnati, Ohio*
University of Cincinnati
College of Design, Architecture, Art & Planning
Major: Interior Design   Minor: Spanish
Honors Certificate in Global Studies   3.6/4.0 GPA

2000-2004   *Cincinnati, Ohio*
Princeton High School
High School Diploma

Work Experience

Autumn 2007 & Summer 2008   *Dallas, Texas*
Paul Duesing Partners
Responsibilities included conceptual sketching and space planning, design development in AutoCAD, finish and furniture selection, hand rendering and presentation board construction.

January 2007-June 2007   *Dallas, Texas*
Wilson & Associates
Responsibilities included rendering for presentations, conceptual design and construction documentation in AutoCAD, space planning, and elevations, hand drafting and detailing of custom furniture, hardware & plumbing schedules, and furniture specifications.

March 2006-June 2006   *Cincinnati, Ohio*
Champlin/ Haupt Architects Inc.
Responsibilities included library updating and maintenance, space planning and construction documentation in AutoCAD, material selection and presentation board construction.

Awards and Activities

Cincinnatus Scholarship, Member of University Honors Scholars Program, Volunteer camp counselor for seriously ill children, Volunteer ESL teacher, Study abroad in Italy and throughout South America.

Special Skills

Illustrator and Photoshop CS3, AutoCAD 2007, Sketch-Up, and Spexx, Hand drafting, rendering and 3D and physical model building skills, Fluent in Spanish & Portuguese, conversational in ASL, Italian & German, Experience designing in metric and creating detailed millwork drawings.

Portfolio and References Available Upon Request

FIGURE 6-26 The resume of a recent interior design graduate. This is also a simple, yet effective design. See Figure 7-4 for other portfolio elements. ■

SEVEN

IN THE MAIL

AND ON THE WEB

This chapter focuses on those items that serve as an introduction to an applicant's work. The sample or mini-portfolio, the CD or DVD (containing portfolio elements), and increasingly, the portfolio Web site go beyond the resume to serve as the kind of in-depth introduction required by this profession. Interior designers must share the visual qualities of their work while at the same time introduce themselves through the traditional resume. The works in this chapter are quality examples of such a visual introduction.

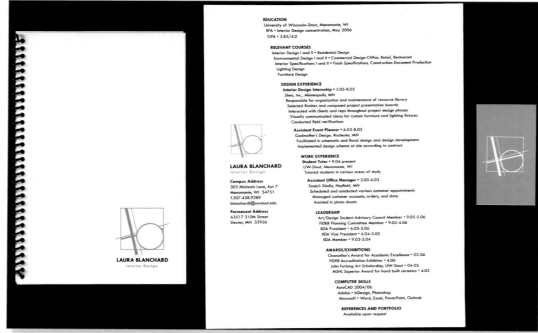

FIGURE 7-1 Mailing packet, resume, business card, sample portfolio, and sample portfolio pages. ■

FIGURE 7-2, A–E Mailing packets for a large (standard business-size) resume and a smaller resume, with sample portfolio. Notice the visual consistency between the sample portfolio (c), the resume (d), and the CD (e). ■

BY NICOLE BANASZEWSKI. PHOTOGRAPHS BY SHARON M. STICKNEY.

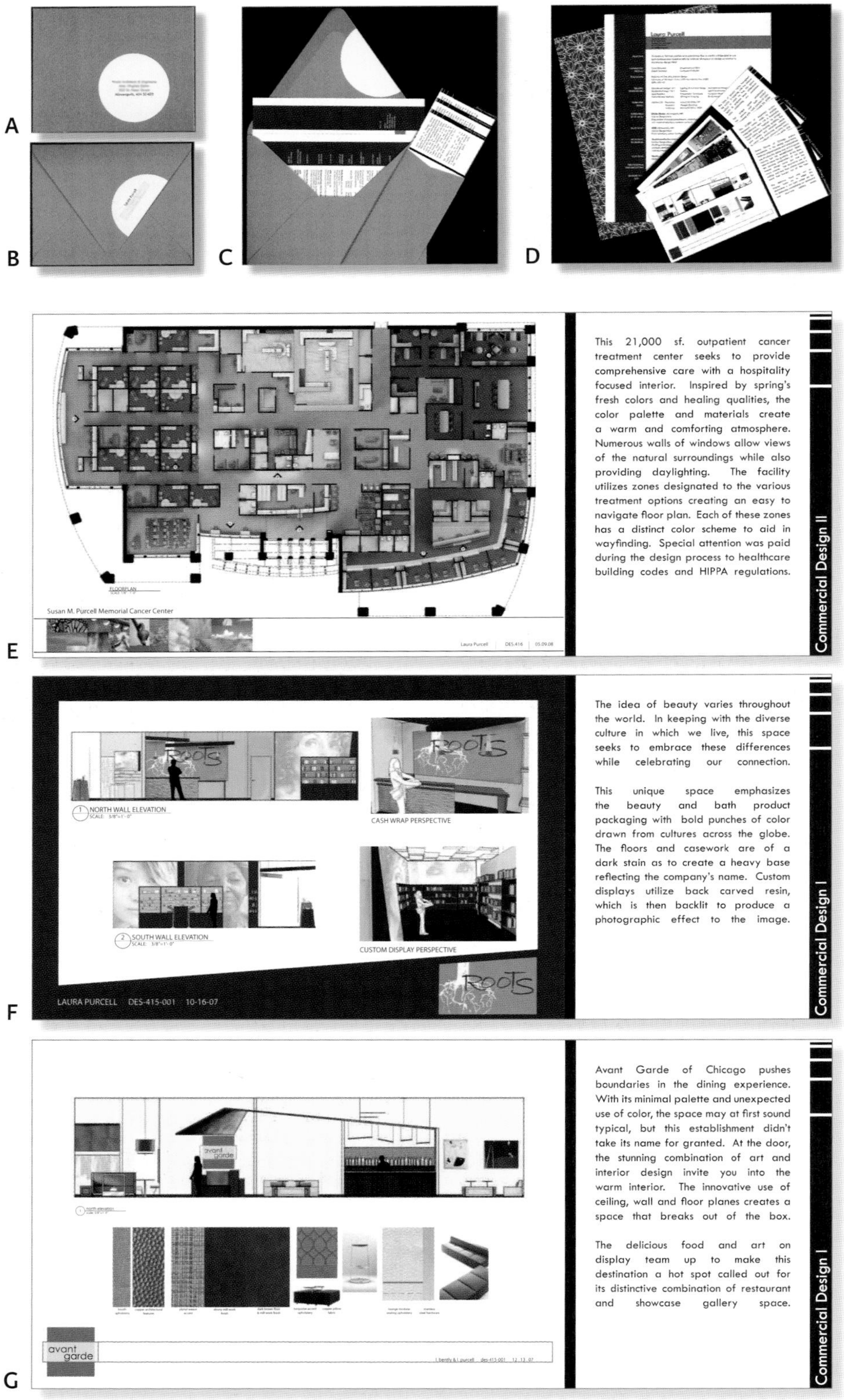

A

B

C

D

E

This 21,000 sf. outpatient cancer treatment center seeks to provide comprehensive care with a hospitality focused interior. Inspired by spring's fresh colors and healing qualities, the color palette and materials create a warm and comforting atmosphere. Numerous walls of windows allow views of the natural surroundings while also providing daylighting. The facility utilizes zones designated to the various treatment options creating an easy to navigate floor plan. Each of these zones has a distinct color scheme to aid in wayfinding. Special attention was paid during the design process to healthcare building codes and HIPPA regulations.

Susan M. Purcell Memorial Cancer Center

Commercial Design II

F

The idea of beauty varies throughout the world. In keeping with the diverse culture in which we live, this space seeks to embrace these differences while celebrating our connection.

This unique space emphasizes the beauty and bath product packaging with bold punches of color drawn from cultures across the globe. The floors and casework are of a dark stain as to create a heavy base reflecting the company's name. Custom displays utilize back carved resin, which is then backlit to produce a photographic effect to the image.

NORTH WALL ELEVATION

CASH WRAP PERSPECTIVE

SOUTH WALL ELEVATION

CUSTOM DISPLAY PERSPECTIVE

LAURA PURCELL DES-415-001 10-16-07

Commercial Design I

G

Avant Garde of Chicago pushes boundaries in the dining experience. With its minimal palette and unexpected use of color, the space may at first sound typical, but this establishment didn't take its name for granted. At the door, the stunning combination of art and interior design invite you into the warm interior. The innovative use of ceiling, wall and floor planes creates a space that breaks out of the box.

The delicious food and art on display team up to make this destination a hot spot called out for its distinctive combination of restaurant and showcase gallery space.

avant garde

Commercial Design I

BY LAURA PURCELL. PHOTOGRAPHS BY SHARON M. STICKNEY.

FIGURE 7-3 , A–G Large envelope front (a) and back (b); smaller sample portfolio and envelope (c). Standard resume shown with smaller sample portfolio (d). Images from the sample portfolio (e, f, g) include project descriptions and design drawings. ■

BY JENNIFER L. PIKE. PHOTOGRAPHS BY SHARON M. STICKNEY.

FIGURE 7-4, A–F A CD cover (a) with a matching CD, a business card, and operating instructions for the CD (b). Inside the CD case are pages with a resume (c), a project list that functions like a table of contents (d), and various project sheets with clearly written project statements (e and f). These elements reflect a clear self-assessment and distinctive visual direction. A standard resume for this individual can be found in Figure 6-26. ■

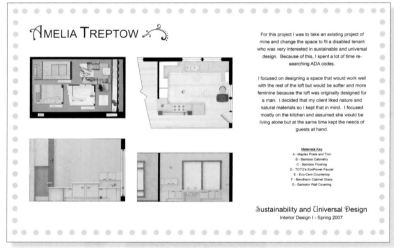

FIGURE 7-5, A–D A resume, stationery, and CD envelope (a), the matching CD and additional correspondence (b), the resume itself (c), and a portfolio page found on the CD (d). More portfolio images can be found in Figure 8-38. ■

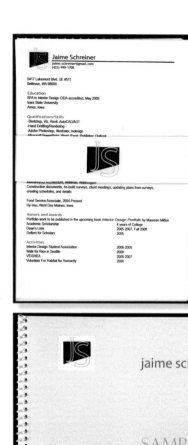

A

B

C

D

E

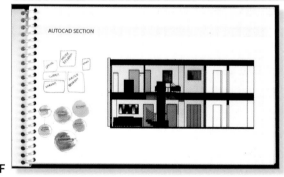

F

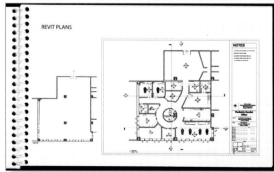

G

FIGURE 7-6, A–G A sample portfolio, bound with a resume (a); the resume and references (b); and the portfolio cover (c). The portfolio has title pages with related images (d–g). This design is very well thought out, easy to follow, and visually consistent. (Some titles and names have been obscured for publishing purposes.) This mailer is also shown in Figure 2-34. ■

A

B

JENNIFER IREY

EDUCATION
BFA Interior Design, Cum Laude
Iowa State University, College of Design: 2005-2009
Rome Study Abroad Program: Fall 2008
Chinese Architecture Study Abroad Program: Spring 2009
Dean's List: All Semesters
3.63 Cumulative GPA

DESIGN EXPERIENCE
Paragon Commercial Interiors, Davenport, IA
Intern: Commercial and Hospitality Design
Summer 2005, Summer 2008
Phelan's Interiors, Cedar Rapids, IA
Intern: Residential, Commercial, Hospital, Retail Sales
Summer 2007
The Mad Potter, Davenport, IA
Customer Service, Sample Artist, Retail
Summer 2006
Heart of America Restaurants and Inns, Moline, IL
Intern: Hospitality Design
Summer 2004

HONORS AND EXHIBITIONS
**2009 *Hospitality Design* Magazine Awards, Student
Finalist:** May/June Issue
Outstanding Senior Interior Design Project:
2009- Iowa State University
Best Portfolio Design Award: 2006 · College of Design
Learning Community, Iowa State University
ISU Rome Exhibition: Spring 2009
Peer Recognition Award: "Most Computer Savvy"

RELATED COURSES
Auto-Cad
Hand Drafting and Rendering
Art History/ Design Studies
Interior Design History, Theory and Criticism
Construction and Materials
Film Studies; Set Design Emphasis
Lighting Design
Chinese Architecture and Urban Planning
Studios; Residential, Commercial, Ideation, Retail,
Hospitality, Institutional

ACTIVITIES AND MEMBERSHIPS
Interior Design Student Association: 2007 - 2009
American Society of Interior Designers: 2007 - 2009
Emerging Green Builders: 2007
Recruitment President, Alpha Delta Pi: 2007-2008
Alpha Delta Pi Sorority: 2005 - 2009
Volunteer: Relay for Life Team Captain, Relief trip to
New Orleans Katrina Disaster, Ronald McDonald House,
Weed and Read Project in Rome, Italy

SKILLS
Autodesk AutoCAD 2008
Autodesk Revit 2009
Viz Render
SketchUp with Podium Rendering
Adobe Suite CS4
Digital Photography and Editing
Currently working to obtain LEED for CI certification
Theatre, Public Speaking, French
Vocal and Piano Performance

PLEASE VIEW MY COMPLETE PORTFOLIO
ON THE CD INSERT

C

D

PLEASE VIEW MY COMPLETE PORTFOLIO
ON THE CD INSERT

BY JENNIFER IREY. PHOTOGRAPHS BY SHARON M. STICKNEY.

FIGURE 7-7, A–D A sample portfolio, resume, and CD, all bound in a well-designed booklet. The front and back of the booklet (a, b), the resume and CD envelope (c), and the individual portfolio pages (d) work well together visually; the portfolio pages are very easy to follow. This mailer is also shown in Figure 2-35. Additional elements related to this portfolio can be found in Figure 8-1. ■

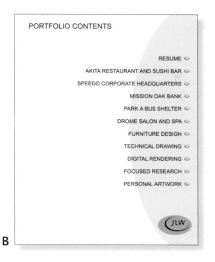

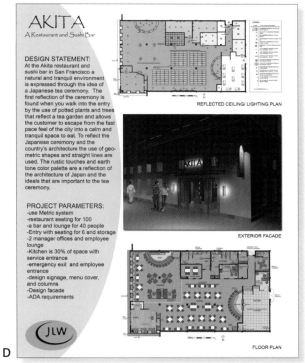

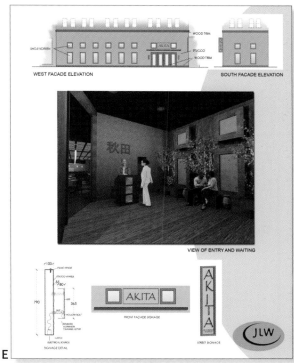

FIGURE 7-8, A–E The contents of a portfolio on a CD. The title page (a) relates well visually to the other pages, such as the table of contents (b), the resume (c), and the portfolio project pages (d, e). More of the project pages can be found in Figure 8-42. ■

A

B

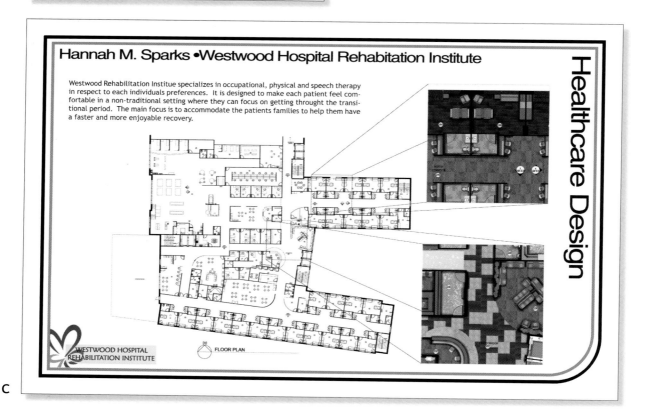

C

FIGURE 7-9, A–C The contents of a portfolio on a CD. The resume (a) relates well visually to the title page (b) and the portfolio project pages (c). More of the portfolio pages can be found in Figures 8-23 through 8-28 ■

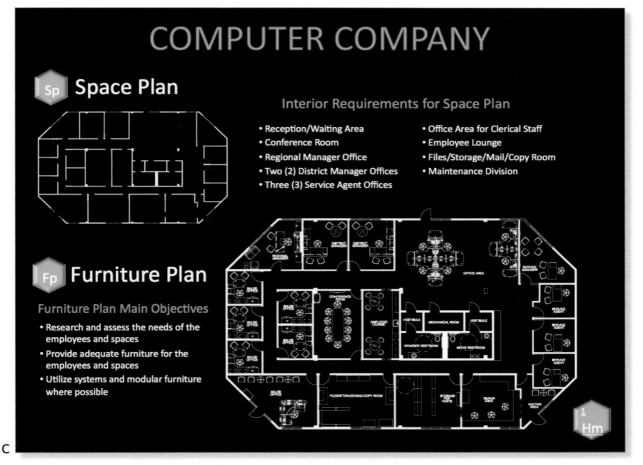

FIGURE 7-10, A–C The contents of a portfolio on a CD. The title page (a) presents a conceptual direction for the portfolio, with a resume (b) and portfolio pages (c) that follow through on the concept. ■

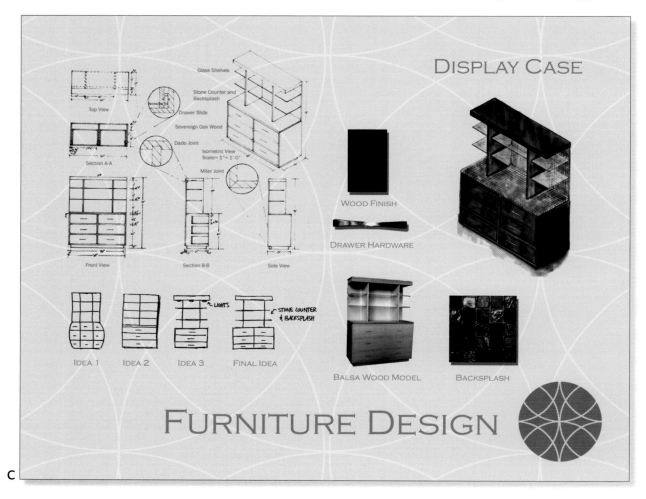

As an interior designer, I want to collaborate with clients blending their ideas with my knowledge and experience. My goal is to conceptualize and create a space that improves their quality of life and also expresses their personality. A design that is truly functional and has a timeless appeal is the basis of a successful design. When the finished product is revealed and the client loves it, that is the reward I seek as an interior designer.

FIGURE 7-11, A–C This design (a) serves as a visual anchor for other items in the portfolio, such as written statements (b) and portfolio pages (c). ■

BY MALLORY BOGACZ.

Click the image above to visit the site. If you have a "pop-up blocker" enanbled, you'll need to allow content from ambicaprakash.com to view this site.

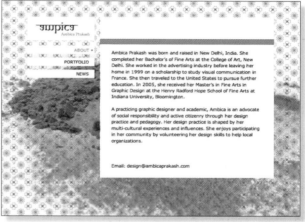

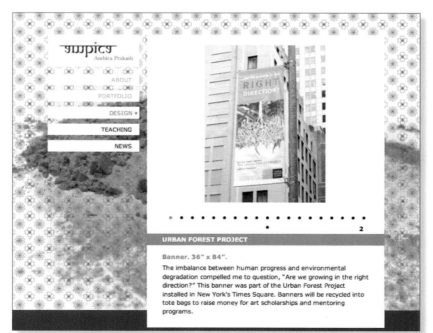

FIGURE 7-12 An example of a Web site for a graphic designer with design and teaching experience. The related resume can be found in Figure 6-17. ■

FIGURE 7-13 An example of a Web site example for a fine artist. The related resume can be found in Figure 6-18. ■

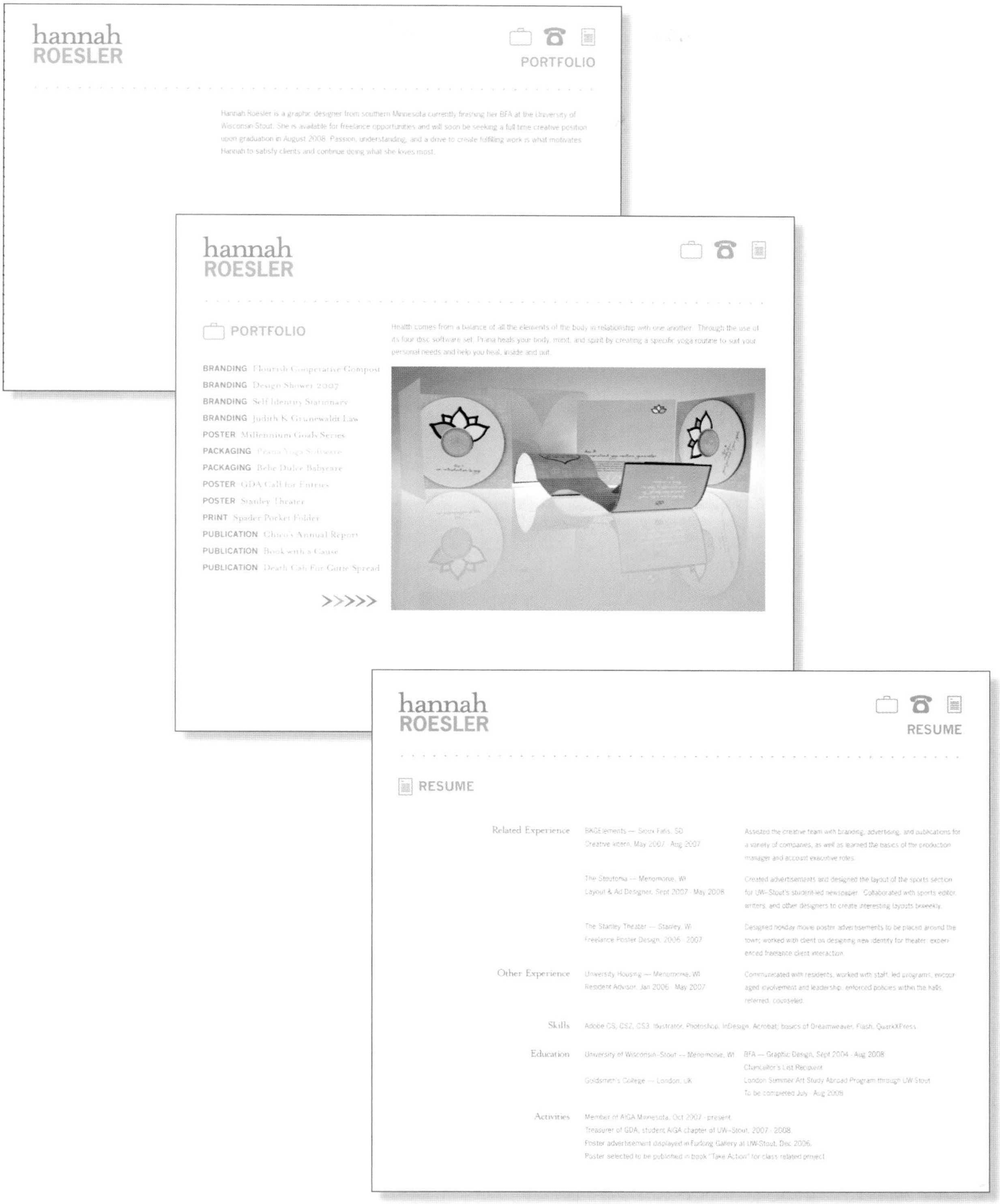

BY HANNAH ROESLER.

FIGURE 7-14 The Web site of a recent graphic design graduate. The related resume can be found in Figure 6-13. ■

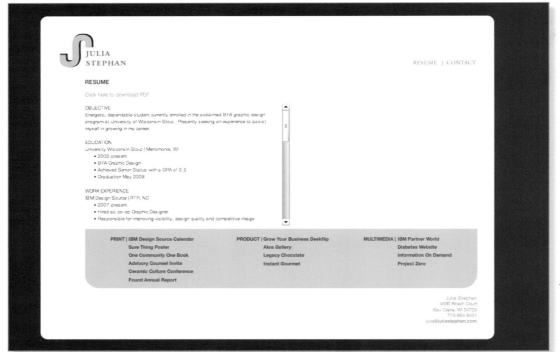

FIGURE 7-15 The Web site of a recent graphic design graduate. The related resume and other items can be found in Figure 6-9. ■

EIGHT

COMPONENTS

FROM COMPLETE PORTFOLIOS

This chapter contains high-quality examples taken directly from portfolios. The images in Figure 8-1 are from a physical portfolio.

The remaining illustrations in this chapter have been taken from a variety of portfolios. The examples were selected based on the quality of the work included, the quality of the graphic components, the clarity with which they communicate, and the strong visual direction set by the design of the portfolio pages.

A

B

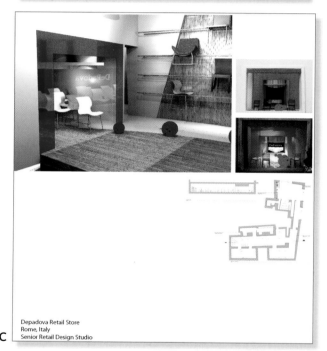

Depadova Retail Store
Rome, Italy
Senior Retail Design Studio

C

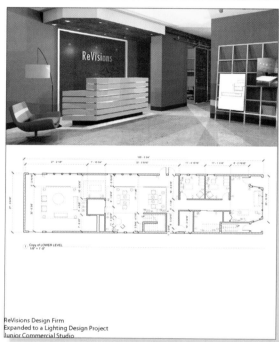

Copy of LOWER LEVEL
1/8" = 1'-0"

ReVisions Design Firm
Expanded to a Lighting Design Project
Junior Commercial Studio

D

E

F

FIGURE 8-1, A–F Figure 8-1a shows the title page from this portfolio, while 8-1b shows a project page within the portfolio; a detail of that page is shown in 8-1c. Another project is shown in 8-1d, with a detail of the project page in 8-1e. A page featuring photographic work is shown in 8-1f. The portfolio clearly sets a strong visual direction; it is both well executed and beautiful. Additional elements related to this portfolio can be found in Figure 7-7a and 7-7b. ■

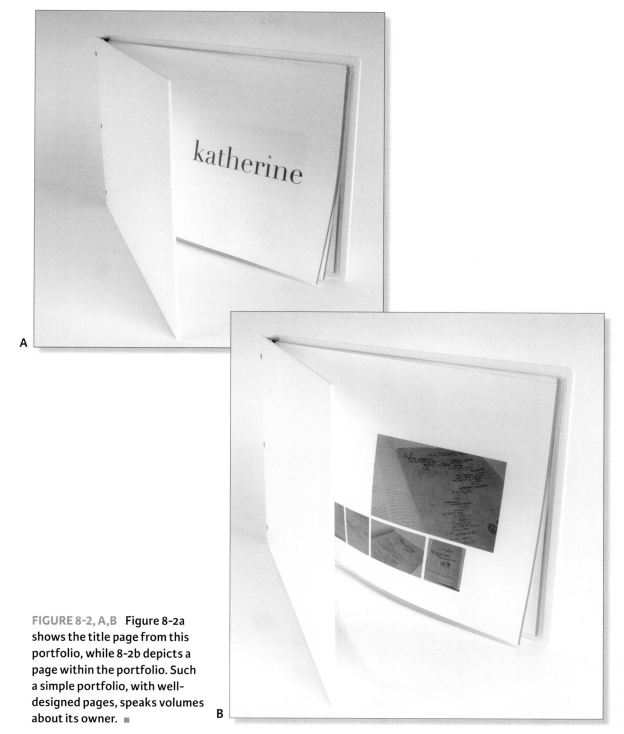

FIGURE 8-2, A,B Figure 8-2a shows the title page from this portfolio, while 8-2b depicts a page within the portfolio. Such a simple portfolio, with well-designed pages, speaks volumes about its owner. ■

Hotel in St. Martin

The Future Present

The challenge of this project was to design a "Hotel of the Future." Instead of going the obvious route by implementing loads of new technology into my hotel, I went in the other direction.

As a society, we are becoming more and more engaged with digital screens and less engaged with nature and one another—to our detriment, in my opinion. I believe that in the future, we will need increasing help staying connected with the present moment and each other, and design can help with this.

For this reason, I made the natural setting of this hotel the extreme focal point of the design. Each major area of the hotel features a direct and expansive view of the outdoors, and little else. In this way, guests are encouraged to connect with the present and each other, rather than their iPods, DVDs and laptops.

The view from the hotel's main entrance.

Looking out over the restaurant from the lobby.

A view into the lobby restaurant from outside.

8-3

Hotel in St. Martin

Looking out to sea from the pool bar.

The pool and bar from the bar patio.

The basement lounge, situated directly under the glass-bottomed pool, as seen from its entrance.

Whereas all other areas of the hotel focus the guest's attention out to nature to remind them of their physical location, the lounge's location underground and under the water of the pool made an inward focus, evoking an undersea location, more appropriate.

A detail of the lounge seating, which evokes undersea foliage.

FIGURES 8-3 THROUGH 8-5 Pages from various portfolios. While the projects are very different, common graphic elements provide visual consistency. ■

Hotel in St. Martin

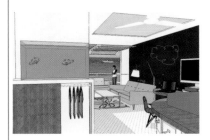

Guestrooms carry on the hotel's overall design concept of emphasizing the natural setting in order to help the guest feel rooted in the physical and temporal present.

The room can open entirely to the balcony and ocean via a windowed garage-style door.

All critical viewpoints from the room either look directly toward the outdoors, or allow for an easy view of it, from the bed to the work desk and sofa.

8-3

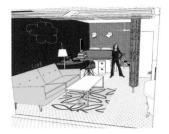

The bathroom is included among the areas with a clear view to the ocean, but can also be closed off for privacy when the room is open to the balcony, via a curtain.

In keeping with an attempt to make the hotel as sustainably furnished as possible, the decor consists of mix-and-match pieces to allow for the flexibility that sourcing second-hand furniture requires.

...le flooring allows for easy clean-
...inimal chemicals and no power-
...vacuuming, and the tiles can be
...urposed at the end of the hotel's

Dumbo Community Green Middle School

Winner, 5th Place
2008 USGBC/Urban Green Council
"Natural Talent" Competition

The challenge of this competition was to create a LEED Platinum-eligible, environmentally focused public middle school and performing arts center for Brooklyn's DUMBO (Down Under Manhattan Bridge) area using an existing pair of buildings.

The site, on the DUMBO waterfront, contains two mid-19th-century warehouses, one without a roof.

As the primary designer on a team of four other students, I cut a large courtyard into the solid larger building for greater daylighting and natural ventilation. A combination of geothermal heating and cooling, a large array of PV panels, and a passive solar tower provide HVAC and electricity. A green roof and a composting toilet system help address water conservation issues.

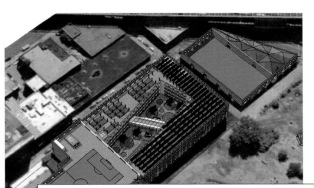

8-4

The courtyard features a vegetable garden, and a bridge not only providing a learning area in view of it, but also a shortcut from one side of the building to the other.

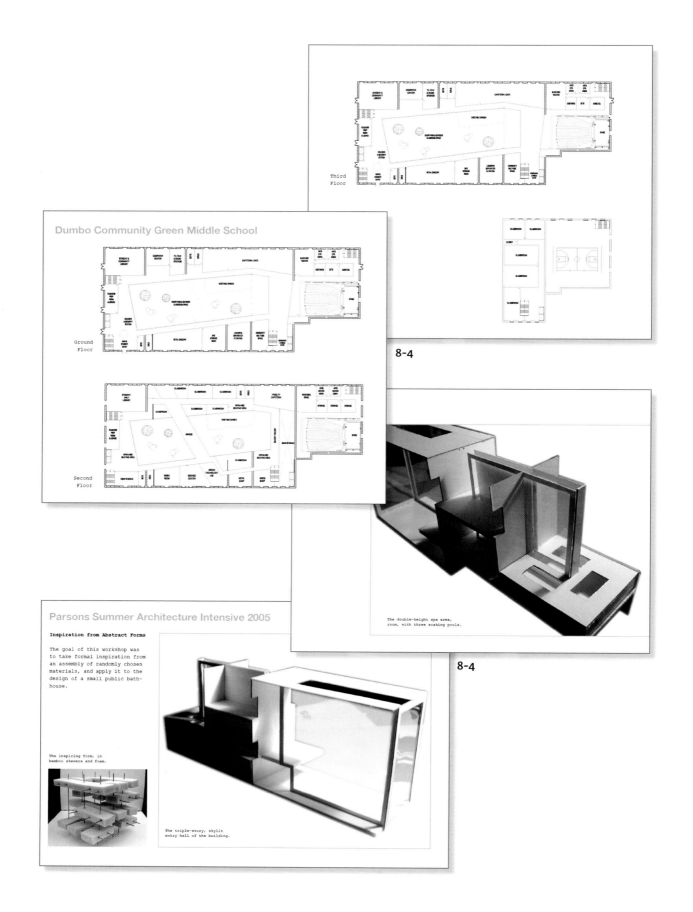

Third
Floor

8-4

Dumbo Community Green Middle School

Ground
Floor

Second
Floor

The double-height spa area,
room, with three soaking pools.

8-4

Parsons Summer Architecture Intensive 2005

Inspiration from Abstract Forms

The goal of this workshop was
to take formal inspiration from
an assembly of randomly chosen
materials, and apply it to the
design of a small public bath-
house.

The inspiring form, in
bamboo skewers and foam.

The triple-story, skylit
entry hall of the building.

Skills: **Modelmaking**

Preliminary ideas for the Asian American
Writers' Workshop space.

8-5

A live-work loft for a nature-loving musi-
cian: Monochromatic living space at one
end, and a colorful rehearsal/recording
studio at the other.

The competition boards as submitted.

8-5

Dumbo Community Green Middle School

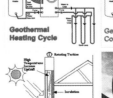

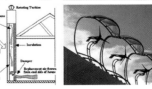

Top
Walking/cycling routes to the school from
area points of interest.

Below
A "living machine" for blackwater
filtration for reuse in the gardens.

Top
How the school's geothermal heating and
cooling systems work.

Below Left
A passive solar tower to ventilate the
auditorium and gymnasium.

Below Right
Small wind turbines that can generate
large amounts of power using the area's
slow winds line the edges of the main
building's roof parapet.

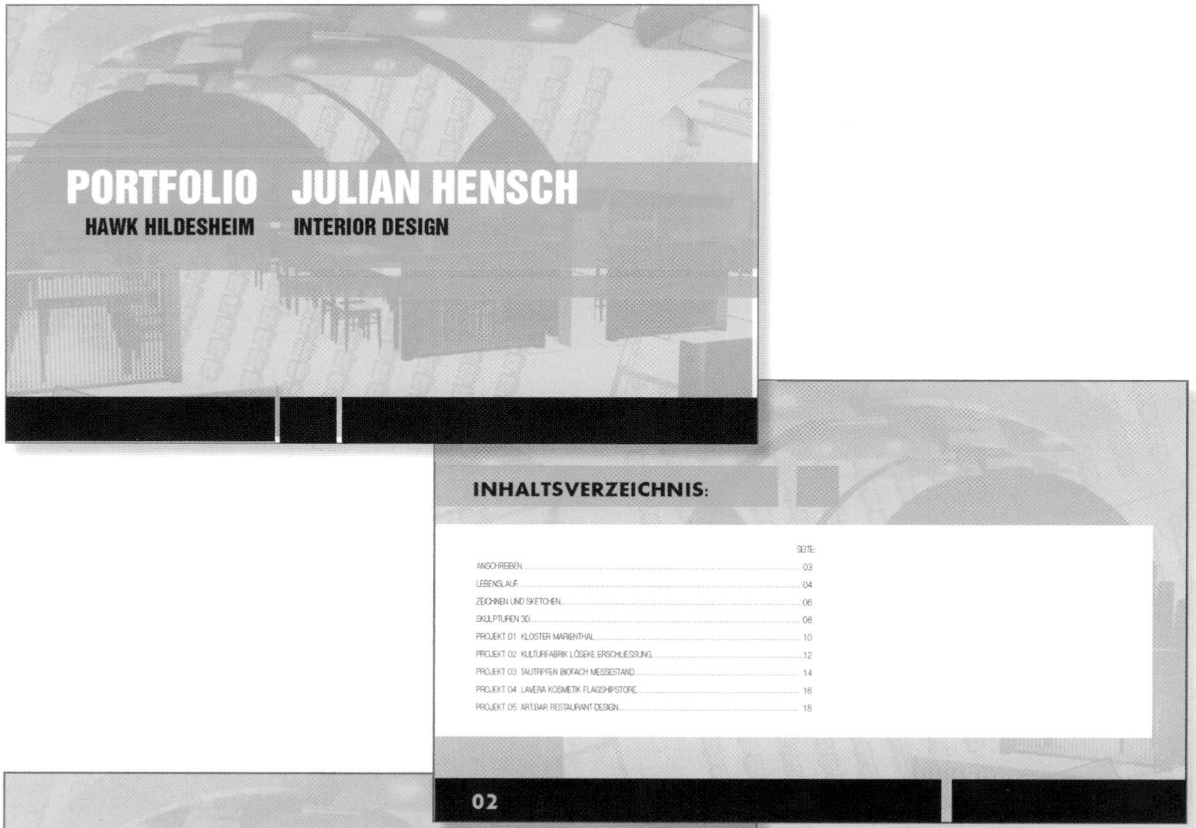

8-6

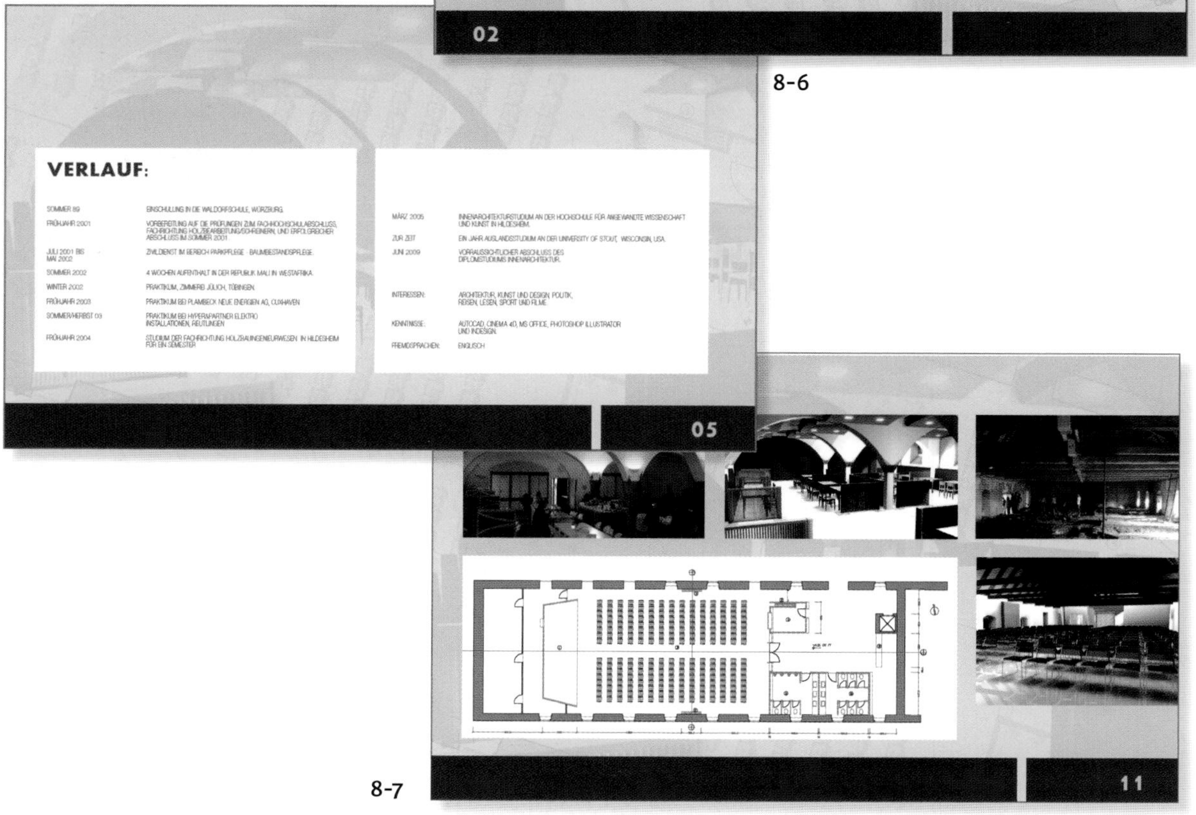

8-7

BY JULIAN HENSCH.

FIGURES 8-6 THROUGH 8-12 Several pages from a portfolio. The introduction and resume are shown in 8-6; the remaining illustrations are of different projects. Strong graphic elements provide consistency from page to page. ■

8-8

8-9

8-10

8-11

RESTAURANT DESIGN:

8-12

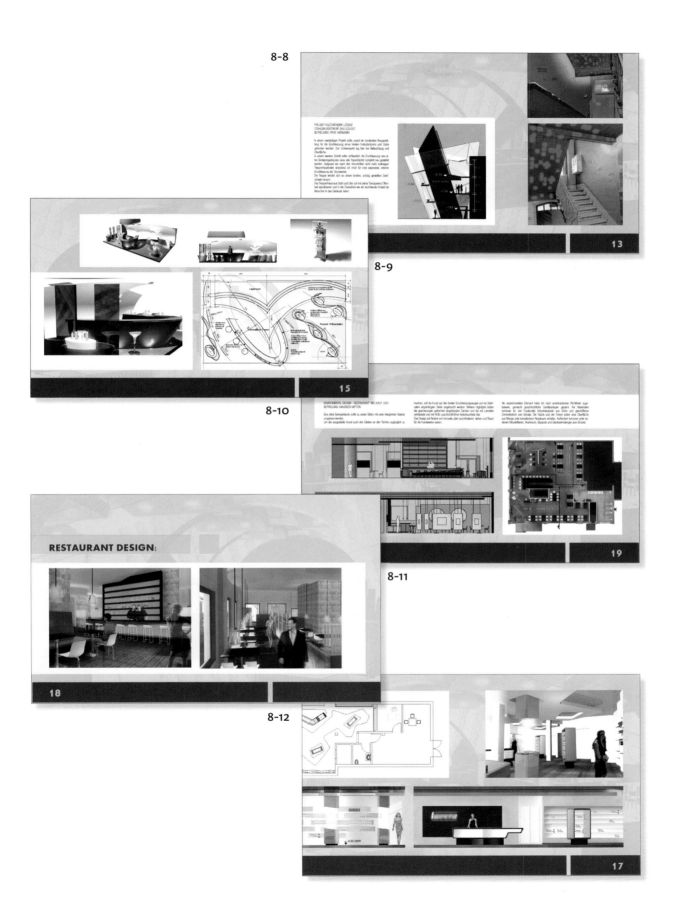

8-13

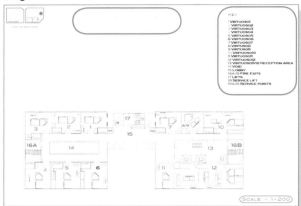

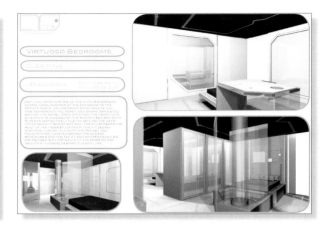

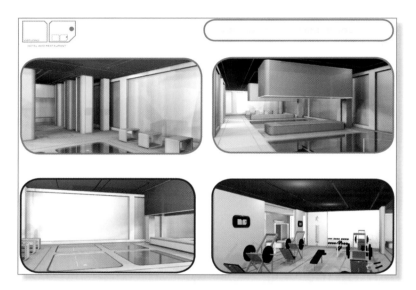

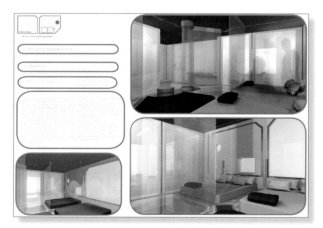

BY CLIVE WALTERS.

FIGURES 8-13 THROUGH 8-15 Several pages from a project portfolio. In 8-13, well-designed pages relate the design of a large, complex project; color is used to aid in communication. 8-14 is a resume that relates well visually to the portfolio pages. In 8-15, pages containing technical information about the same project are tied visually to the project as a whole. ■

CLIVE WALTERS
INTERIOR DESIGNER

THE HOTEL PROJECT (2008): HOTEL RENDERS

THE HOTEL PROJECT IS MY MOST ADVANCED PIECE OF WORK COMPLETED TO DATE. IT IMPLEMENTS A COMBINATION OF SKILLS AND TECHNIQUES ACQUIRED THOUGH IN THE EARLY STAGES OF MY COURSE. CONSEQUENTLY, I ACHIEVED ONE OF THE HIGHEST GRADES IN MY YEAR OWING TO AN INNOVATIVE APPROACH AND THE MANIFESTATION OF MY INTEREST IN FUTURE SYSTEMS.

OBJECTIVE

TO ACQUIRE A POSITION AS AN INTERIOR DESIGNER SO THAT A DYNAMIC FIRM THAT WILL ALLOW ME TO UTILIZE MY UNIQUE ABILITIES AND ADVANCE MY CAREER.

RELEVANT WORK EXPERIENCE – BLESSING SULE BOUTIQUE SHOP DESIGN

DURING THIS WORK PLACEMENT, I WAS ABLE TO WORK WITH AN UP AND COMING MANCHESTER BASED FASHION DESIGNER, ON THE LAUNCH OF HER FIRST BOUTIQUE CLOTHING STORE, BASED IN STOCKPORT. THROUGH THIS I WAS ABLE TO GAIN EXPERIENCE IN THE DESIGN AND CONSTRUCTION FEILD, PRODUCING PLANS, SECTIONS AND ELEVATIONS AND THEN BEING ON SITE TO SEE THE THE PROCESS COME TO LIFE.

ROLE:
- PREDOMINANTLY USING ARCHICAD 11 2008 TO MODEL THE INTERIOR OF THE BUILDING. PRODUCING PLANS, SECTIONS AND ELEVATIONS.
- WORKING CLOSELY WITH DESIGNER THROUGH THE DESIGN PROCESS AND DRAFTING TO THEIR INSTRUCTION.
- LIASSING WITH BUILDERS AND CITE MANAGING.
- SPECIFYING FIXTURE AND FITTINGS.
- WORKING TO CONTRACTUAL DEADLINES.
- WORKING TO BUILDING AND FIRE SAFETY STANDARDS.

PERSONAL PROFILE

I AM A WELL ORGANISED, PUNCTUAL PERSON WHO IS EQUALLY MOTIVATED, ENTHUSIASTIC AND DETERMINED TO BE SUCCESSFUL BY STRIVING FOR PRECISION. I AM A GOOD COMMUNICATOR AND A LISTENER AND AM ABLE TO WORK WELL INDEPENDENTLY OR AS PART OF A TEAM. MY MAIN AIM IN LIFE IS TO BECOME AN ACCOMPLISHED INTERIOR DESIGNER WITH THE INTENTION TO ESTABLISHING MY OWN COMPANY IN THE FUTURE.

HAVING ACQUIRED A WEALTH OF EXPERIENCE THROUGH MY DEDICATION TO THE JOBS I HAVE HAD, I FEEL THAT I AM A CONFIDENT AND HARD WORKING INDIVIDUAL WITH A VARIETY OF KEY SKILLS CRUCIAL TO HAVING A SUCCESSFUL CAREER WITHIN THE ARCHITECTURAL AND INTERIOR DESIGN INDUSTRY.

I HAVE A PASSION FOR INNOVATION AND AM VERY AMBITIOUS, CONSEQUENTLY SETTING MYSELF HIGH STANDARDS AND ALWAYS WORKING TO ACHIEVE NEW GOALS. CURRENTLY, MY AIM IS TO UTILISE, IMPROVE AND DEVELOP SKILLS TO THEIR FULL POTENTIAL TOWARDS TAKING THE NEXT STEP IN MY CAREER. GIVEN THESE QUALITIES THE OPPORTUNITY TO WORK WITH A COMPANY OFFERING PROSPECTS OF PROGRESSION WOULD BE MUTUALLY BENEFICIAL.

SKILLS

- THOROUGH UNDERSTANDING OF CAD SYSTEMS SUCH AS ARCHICAD.
- CAN PRODUCE HIGH QUALITY TECHNICAL DRAWINGS INCLUDING PLANS, SECTIONS AND ELEVATIONS.
- ABLE TO CREATE DESIGN AND TECHNOLOGY REPORTS TO A VERY HIGH STANDARD.
- GOOD UNDERSTANDING OF IMAGE EDITING SOFTWARE AND LAYOUT PROGRAMS INCLUDING PLOTMAKER AND IN DESIGN.
- CONFIDENT WITH ADOBE SUITE SOFTWARE.
- CAN DEVELOP PRESENTATION AND PORTFOLIO SHEETS TO A HIGH LEVEL.
- ABLE TO CREATE HIGH QUALITY SCALE MODELS OF BUILDINGS AND INTERIORS.
- CAN SUCCESSFULLY COMPLETE BUILDING LAYOUTS AND FLOOR PLANS.
- CAPABLE OF PRODUCING HIGH QUALITY SKETCHES.
- HAVE THE ABILITY TO RESEARCH TOPICS AND SUBJECTS IN DEPTH AND PRODUCE EXCELLENT ESSAYS.
- INNOVATIVE DESIGN AND CONCEPT SKILLS.

8-14

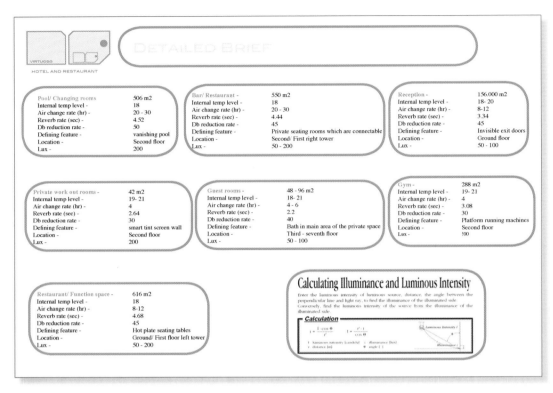

VIRTUOSO

HOTEL AND RESTAURANT

DETAILED BRIEF

Pool/ Changing rooms	506 m2
Internal temp level -	18
Air change rate (hr) -	20 - 30
Reverb rate (sec) -	4.52
Db reduction rate -	50
Defining feature -	vanishing pool
Location -	Second floor
Lux -	200

Bar/ Restaurant -	550 m2
Internal temp level -	18
Air change rate (hr) -	20 - 30
Reverb rate (sec) -	4.44
Db reduction rate -	45
Defining feature -	Private seating rooms which are connectable
Location -	Second/ First right tower
Lux -	50 - 200

Reception -	156.000 m2
Internal temp level -	18- 20
Air change rate (hr) -	8-12
Reverb rate (sec) -	3.34
Db reduction rate -	45
Defining feature -	Invisible exit doors
Location -	Ground floor
Lux -	50 - 100

Private work out rooms -	42 m2
Internal temp level -	19 - 21
Air change rate (hr) -	4
Reverb rate (sec) -	2.64
Db reduction rate -	30
Defining feature -	smart tint screen wall
Location -	Second floor
Lux -	200

Guest rooms -	48 - 96 m2
Internal temp level -	18- 21
Air change rate (hr) -	4 - 6
Reverb rate (sec) -	2.2
Db reduction rate -	40
Defining feature -	Bath in main area of the private space
Location -	Third - seventh floor
Lux -	50 - 100

Gym -	288 m2
Internal temp level -	19- 21
Air change rate (hr) -	4
Reverb rate (sec) -	3.08
Db reduction rate -	30
Defining feature -	Platform running machines
Location -	Second floor
Lux -	!00

Restaurant/ Function space -	616 m2
Internal temp level -	18
Air change rate (hr) -	8-12
Reverb rate (sec) -	4.68
Db reduction rate -	45
Defining feature -	Hot plate seating tables
Location -	Ground/ First floor left tower
Lux -	50 - 200

Calculating Illuminance and Luminous Intensity

Enter the luminous intensity of luminous source, distance, the angle between the perpendicular line and light ray, to find the illuminance of the illuminated side. Conversely, find the luminous intensity of the source from the illuminance of the illuminated side.

Calculation

$$I = \frac{I \cdot \cos \theta}{r^2} \qquad I = \frac{r^2 \cdot I}{\cos \theta}$$

I luminous intensity [candela]   I illuminance [lux]
r distance [m]   θ angle [°]

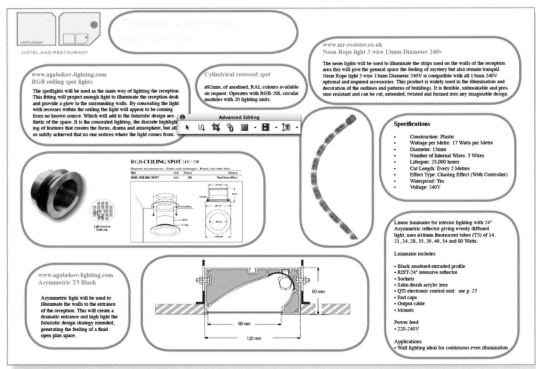

VIRTUOSO

HOTEL AND RESTAURANT

PUBLIC LIGHTING - RECEPTION

www.agabekov-lighting.com
RGB ceiling spot lights

The spotlights will be used as the main way of lighting the reception. This fitting will project enough light to illuminate the reception desk and provide a glow to the surrounding walls. By concealing the light with recesses within the ceiling the light will appear to be coming from no known source. Which will add to the futuristic design aesthetic of the space. It is the concealed lighting, the discrete highlighting of features that creates the focus, drama and atmosphere, but all so subtly achieved that no one notices where the light comes from.

Cylindrical recessed spot

ø92mm, of anodised, RAL colours available on request. Operates with RGB-20L circular modules with 20 lighting units.

www.mr-resistor.co.uk
Neon Rope light 3 wire 13mm Diameter 240v

The neon lights will be used to illuminate the strips used on the walls of the reception area this will give the general space the feeling of mystery but also remain tranquil. Neon Rope light 3 wire 13mm Diameter 240V is compatible with all 13mm 240V optional and required accessories. This product is widely used in the illumination and decoration of the outlines and patterns of buildings. It is flexible, unbreakable and pressure resistant and can be cut, extended, twisted and formed into any imaginable design.

Advanced Editing

RGB-CEILING SPOT 24V / 5W

	Volt	Power	Source
RGB-CEILING SPOT	24V	5W	Red/Green/Blue

Light source RGB 20L

Specifications

- Construction: Plastic
- Wattage per Metre: 17 Watts per Metre
- Diameter: 13mm
- Number of Internal Wires: 3 Wires
- Lifespan: 25,000 hours
- Cut Length: Every 2 Metres
- Effect Type: Chasing Effect (With Controller)
- Waterproof: Yes
- Voltage: 240V

Linear luminaire for interior lighting with 24° Asymmetric reflector giving evenly diffused light, uses ø16mm fluorescent tubes (T5) of 14, 21, 24, 28, 35, 39, 49, 54 and 80 Watts.

Luminaire includes

- Black anodised extruded profile
- RIST-24° intensive reflector.
- Sockets
- Satin-finish acrylic lens
- QTi electronic control unit: see p. 27
- End caps
- Output cable
- Mounts

Power feed
- 220-240V

Applications
- Wall lighting ideal for continuous even illumination

www.agabekov-lighting.com
Asymmetric T5 Black

Asymmetric light will be used to illuminate the walls to the entrance of the reception. This will create a dramatic entrance and high light the futuristic design strategy intended, generating the feeling of a fluid open plan space.

60 mm

90 mm

120 mm

8-16

facade elevation
not to scale

floor plan- ground floor
not to scale

reflected ceiling plan- ground floor
not to scale

interior elevation 3
not to scale

reception table

floor plan- mezzanine
not to scale

reflected ceiling plan- mezzanine
not to scale

BY KATARZYNA BOROWY.

FIGURES 8-16 THROUGH 8-18 Several pages from a portfolio; a different project is depicted in each figure. Each project is treated quite differently; consistency is primarily created by the orientation of the pages, which works well because the projects are varied and sophisticated. ■

view of the 'bob cut' area

stylist table
scale: 1/2"=1'-0"

view of the 'beehive' area

the 'beehive' area is where your Locks would be shampooed and massa

8-16

view of the 'bangs' area

this is the lounge area, where clients can have a drink or a small snack
before their hair treatment. it is meant to be relaxed and fun area.
also, client's guests may rest here while waiting for their friends.
there are two staircases and one elevator leading to this area, which
is located in an upper level of the salon.

right before entering Locks

reception desk
not to scale

piggy serves as a money pot for all the tips that hair stylists receive from
their clients. envelopes are provided at the reception desk.

view of the facade

the building is located on west broadway and spring street. most of the stores
in that area have high ceilings. the look of the store also goes with the theme
of the buildings in the area.

view of the 'bun bun' area

Locks

8-16

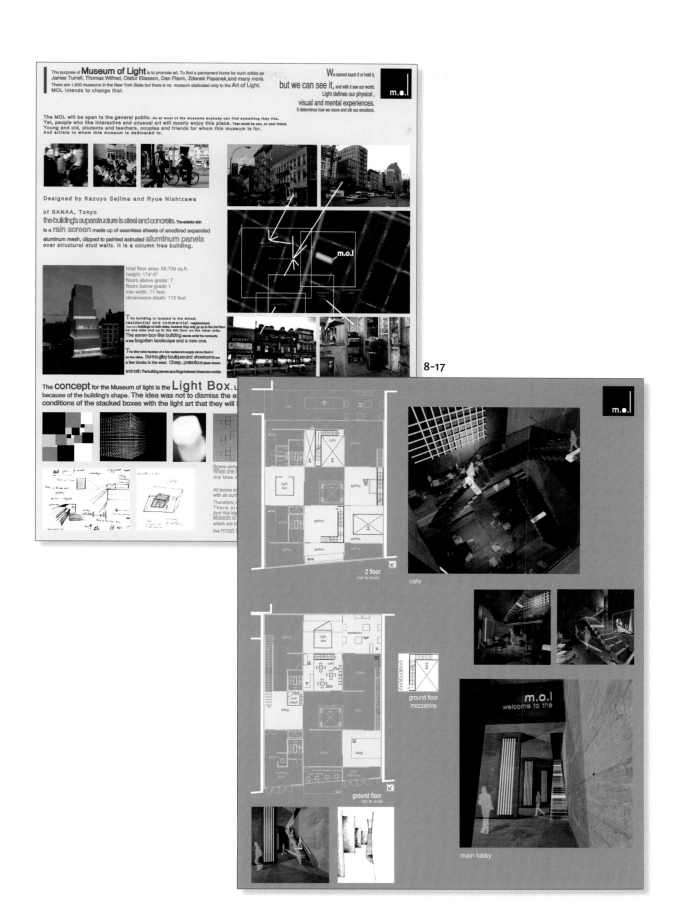

8-17

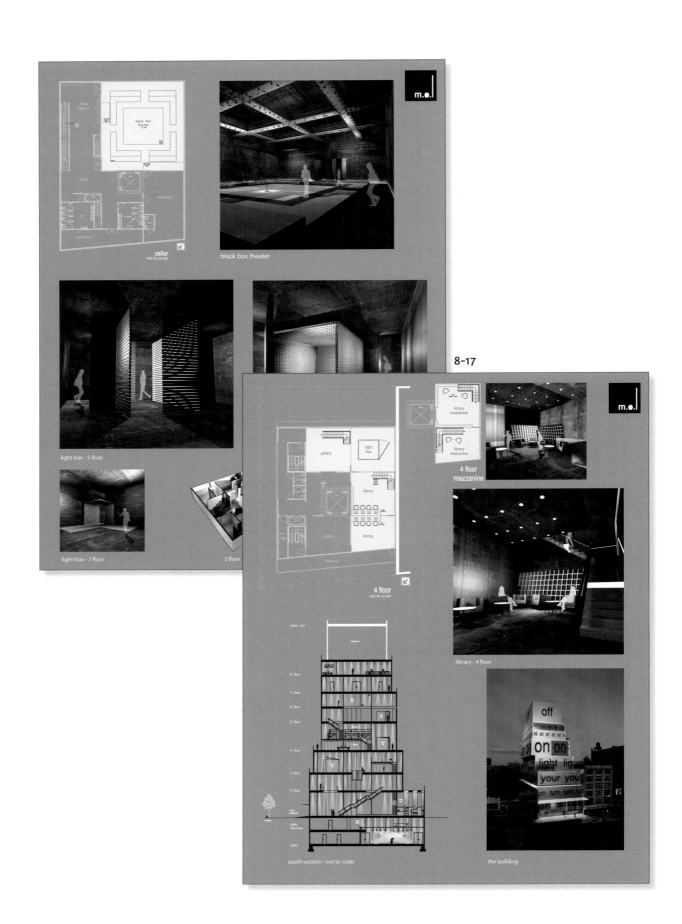

8-17

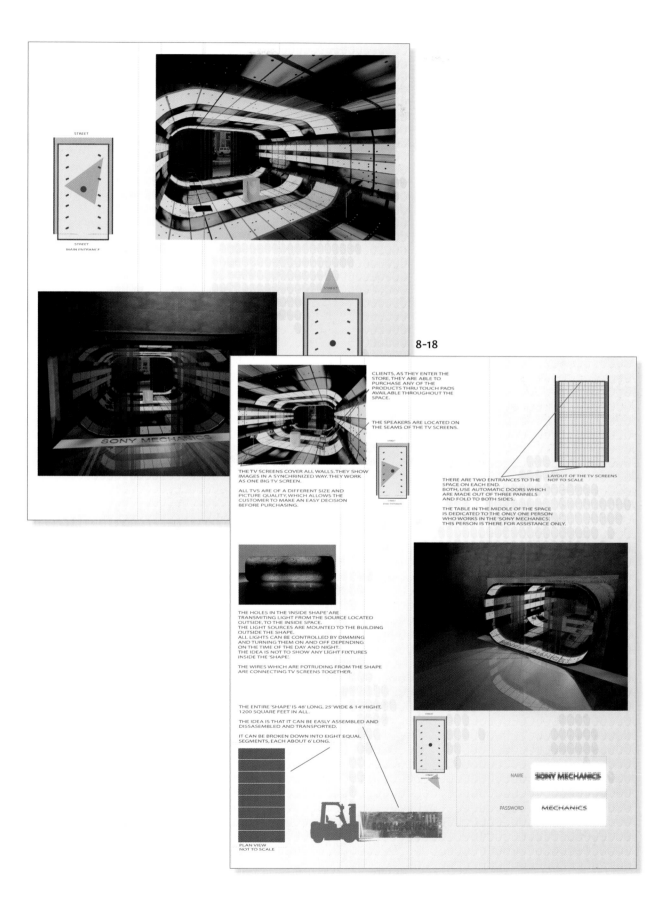

8-18

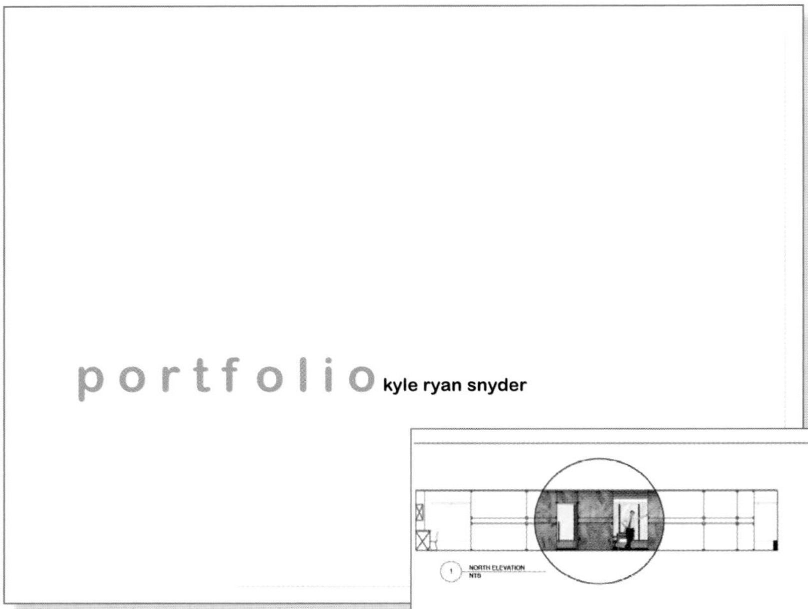

portfolio kyle ryan snyder

8-19

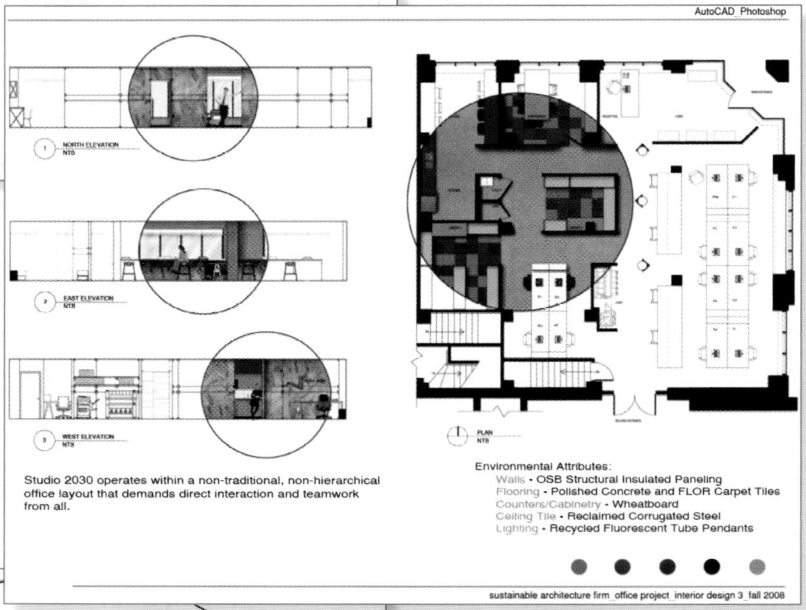

AutoCAD_Photoshop

1 NORTH ELEVATION
NTS

2 EAST ELEVATION
NTS

3 WEST ELEVATION
NTS

1 PLAN
NTS

Studio 2030 operates within a non-traditional, non-hierarchical
office layout that demands direct interaction and teamwork
from all.

Environmental Attributes:
Walls - OSB Structural Insulated Paneling
Flooring - Polished Concrete and FLOR Carpet Tiles
Counters/Cabinetry - Wheatboard
Ceiling Tile - Reclaimed Corrugated Steel
Lighting - Recycled Fluorescent Tube Pendants

sustainable architecture firm_office project_interior design 3_fall 2008

8-20

PERSPECTIVE
NTS

sustainable architecture firm_office project_interior design 3_fall 2008

FIGURES 8-19 THROUGH 8-22
Pages from this portfolio include the
cover (8-19), an office design project
(8-20), a retail project (8-21), and
a furniture design concept (8-22).
Although the projects' presentation
styles vary, they are tied together by
title and border locations. ■

BY KYLE SNYDER.

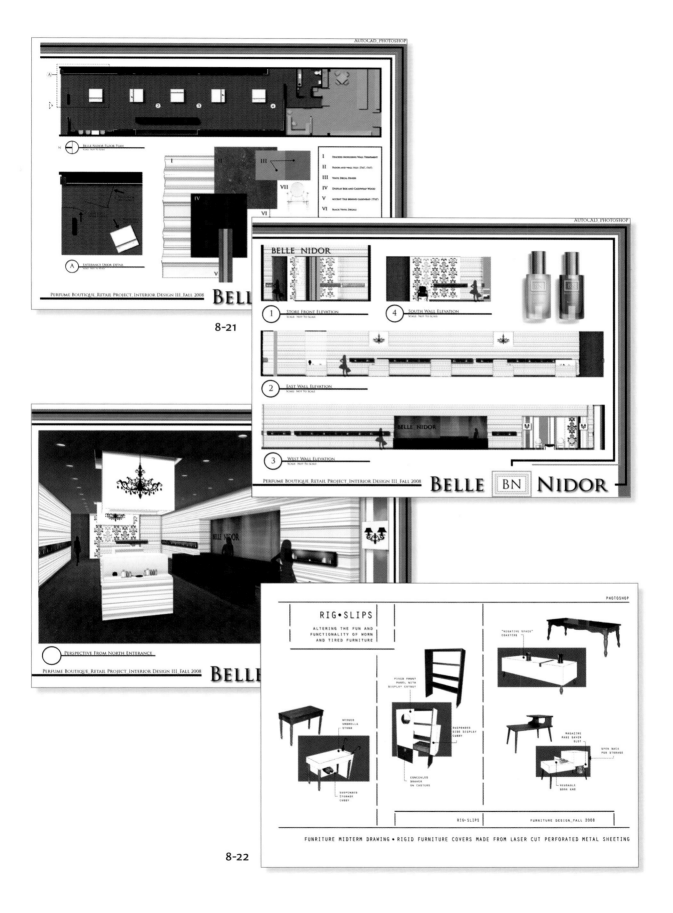

8-21

8-22

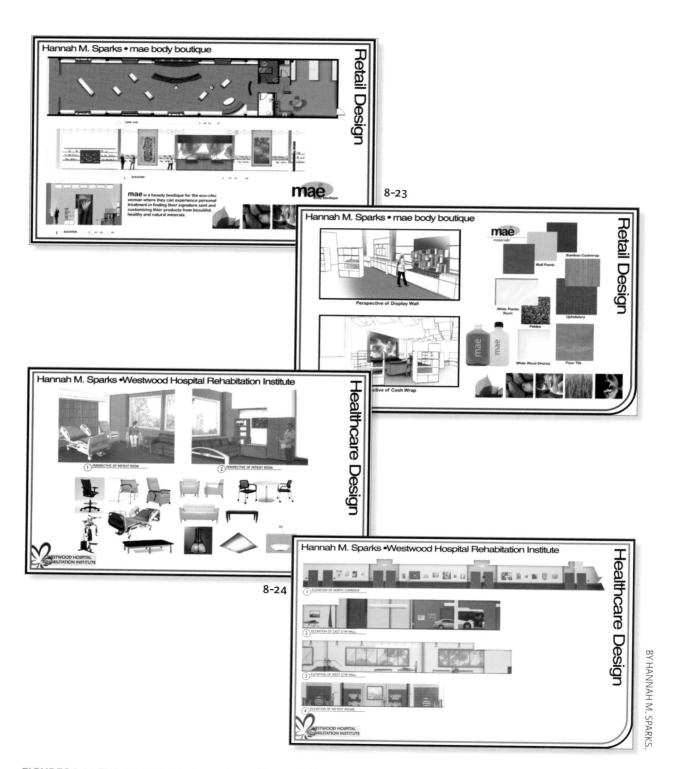

8-23

8-24

FIGURES 8-23 THROUGH 8-28 Pages from this portfolio include a retail project (8-23), selected pages from a larger healthcare design project (8-24), and a restaurant design project (8-25). Additional project pages include furniture design (8-26), a cafe design project (8-27), and fine arts and presentation projects (8-28). While all of the projects shown are very different in scope, design, and presentation style, they are unified by a consistent page layout and use of type. Note that 8-27 and 8-28 contain images that were generated by hand, photographed, and incorporated into the digital file for the portfolio. ■

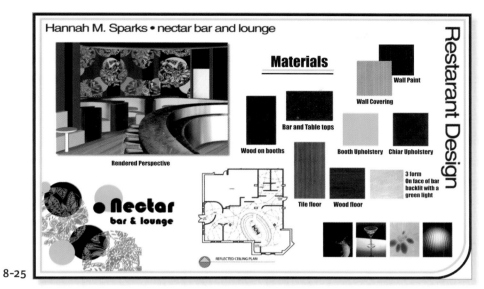

8-25

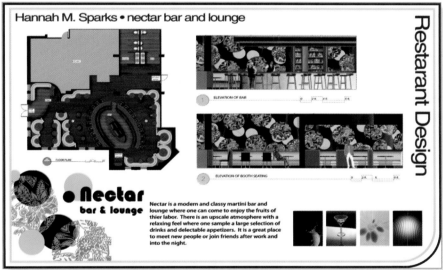

8-26

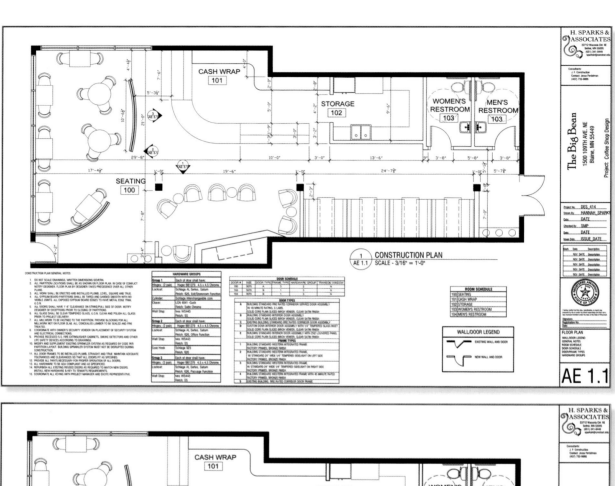

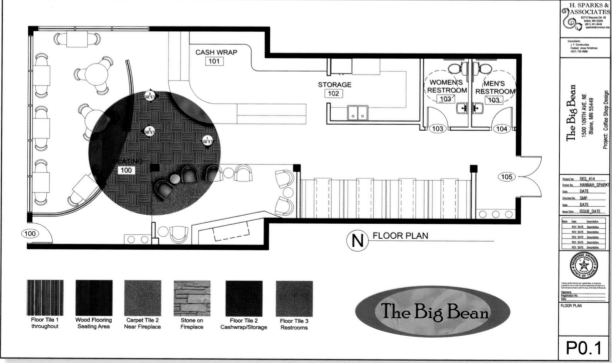

Hannah M. Sparks • 3D Studio and Art Metals II, III

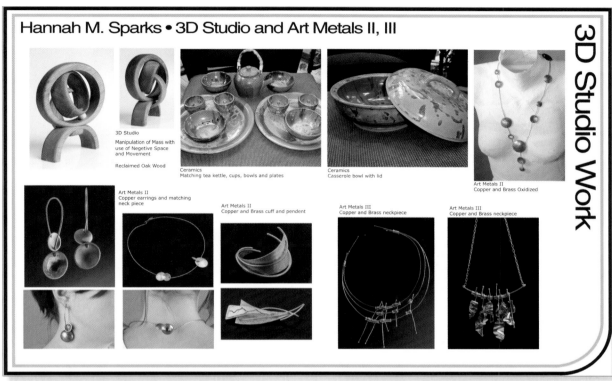

3D Studio
Manipulation of Mass with use of Negetive Space and Movement

Reclaimed Oak Wood

Ceramics
Matching tea kettle, cups, bowls and plates

Ceramics
Casserole bowl with lid

Art Metals II
Copper and Brass Oxidized

Art Metals II
Copper earrings and matching neck piece

Art Metals II
Copper and Brass cuff and pendent

Art Metals III
Copper and Brass neckpiece

Art Metals III
Copper and Brass neckpiece

3D Studio Work

Hannah M. Sparks • Presentation Techniques and Drawing II

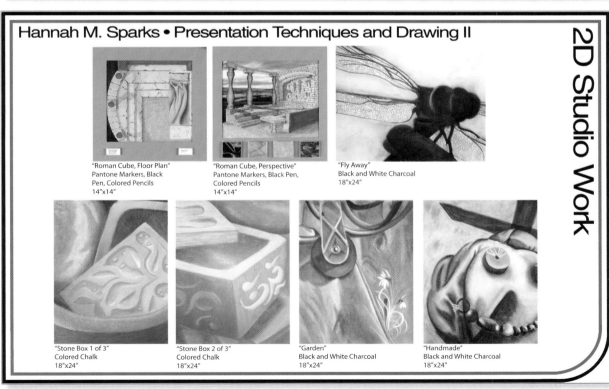

"Roman Cube, Floor Plan"
Pantone Markers, Black Pen, Colored Pencils
14"x14"

"Roman Cube, Perspective"
Pantone Markers, Black Pen, Colored Pencils
14"x14"

"Fly Away"
Black and White Charcoal
18"x24"

"Stone Box 1 of 3"
Colored Chalk
18"x24"

"Stone Box 2 of 3"
Colored Chalk
18"x24"

"Garden"
Black and White Charcoal
18"x24"

"Handmade"
Black and White Charcoal
18"x24"

2D Studio Work

8-28

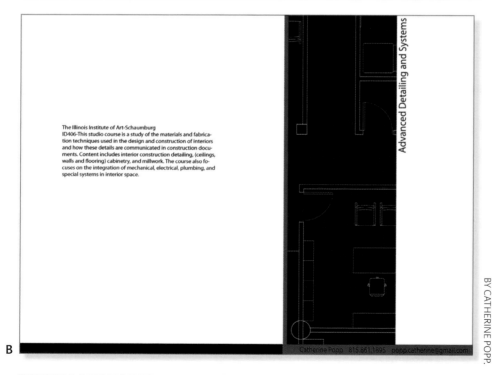

8-29

A — Catherine Popp
815.861.1895
popp.catherine@gmail.com

Interior Design Portfolio

The Illinois Institute of Art-Schaumburg

B — Advanced Detailing and Systems

The Illinois Institute of Art-Schaumburg
ID406-This studio course is a study of the materials and fabrication techniques used in the design and construction of interiors and how these details are communicated in construction documents. Content includes interior construction detailing, (ceilings, walls and flooring) cabinetry, and millwork. The course also focuses on the integration of mechanical, electrical, plumbing, and special systems in interior space.

Catherine Popp   815.861.1895   popp.catherine@gmail.com

BY CATHERINE POPP.

FIGURES 8-29 THROUGH 8-32 Pages from this portfolio include the main cover page (8-29a) as well as title pages for each section (8-29b). Project pages include project information and in-process design sketches (8-30a) and the refined design (8-30b) for several projects. Projects are identified by border colors (8-31 and 8-32) and unified by consistent graphic elements despite containing a range of drawing types, including construction documents (8-32). Additional elements related to this portfolio can be found in Figure 2-29. ■

8-30

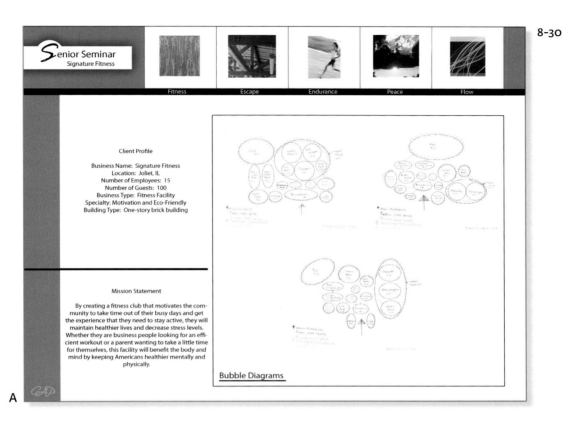

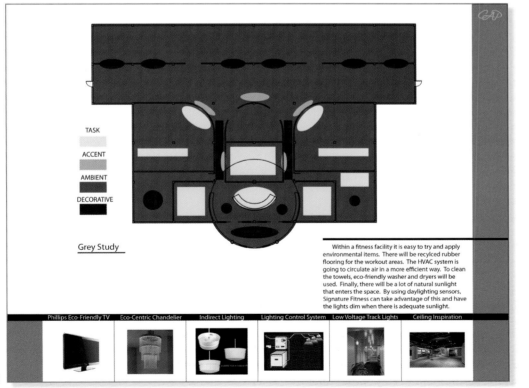

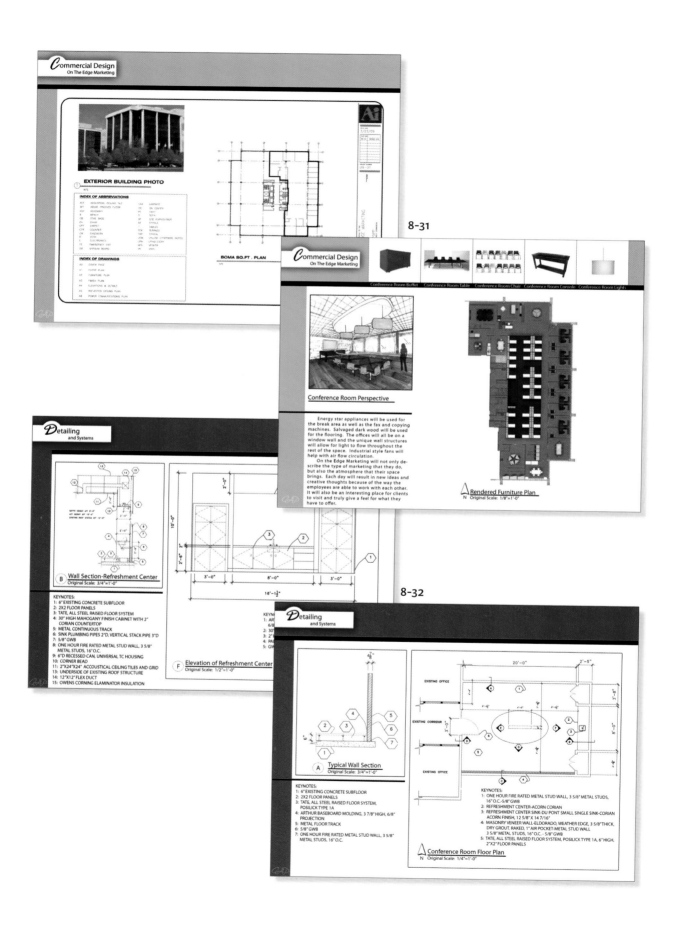

8-31

8-32

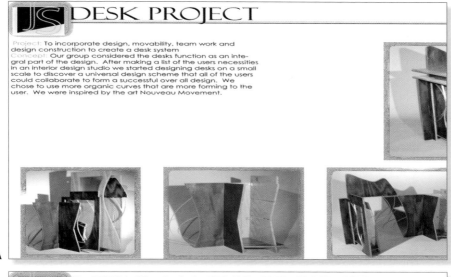

A

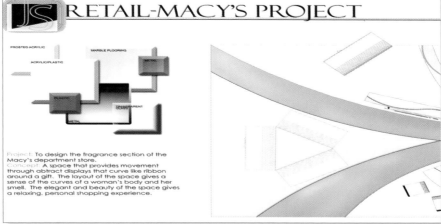

B

C

BY JAMIE SCHREINER.

FIGURE 8-33, A–C Portfolio pages from three very different projects are tied together visually by consistent graphic elements. Photographs of three-dimensional work (a) are nicely integrated into the portfolio page, as are digital models (c). Additional elements related to this portfolio can be found in Figure 2-34. ■

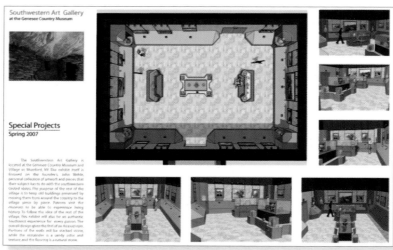

FIGURE 8-34, A–C Portfolio pages from two very different projects. Figure 8-34a and 8-34b use photographs of scale models, while 8-34c employs models created digitally. Both projects are tied together visually through the use of consistent graphic elements.

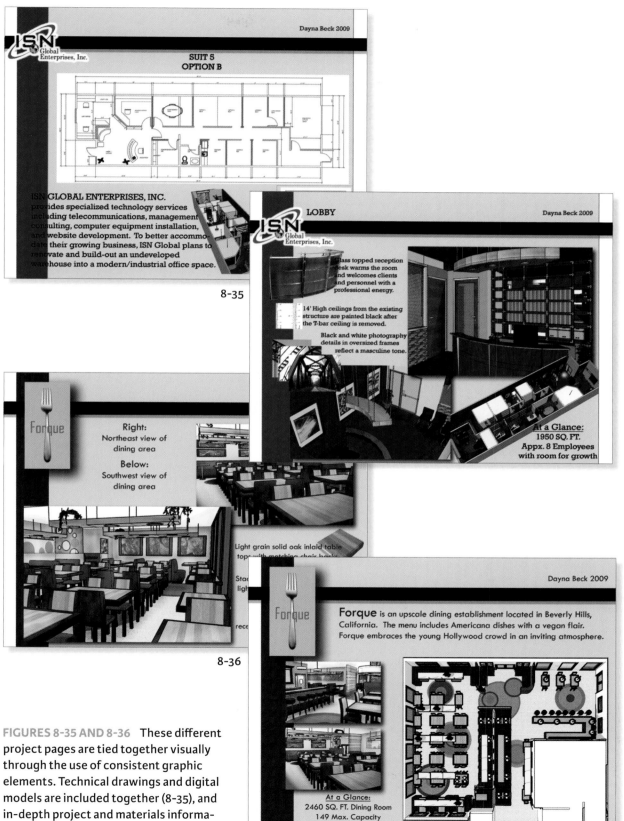

8-35

8-36

FIGURES 8-35 AND 8-36 These different project pages are tied together visually through the use of consistent graphic elements. Technical drawings and digital models are included together (8-35), and in-depth project and materials information is provided for each project. ■

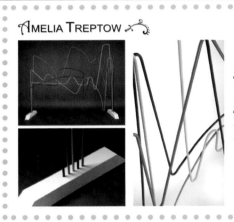

Senior Studio is used to showcase the talents of students in their final semester. I choose to design a residence hall because Housing and Student Affairs is something that is very important to me and has shaped much of my collegiate experience and many aspects of my life. I wanted to create a space for architecture students where they had studio space in their living environment. I feel that because of the numerous hours that are typically spent in the studio these students weren't always making the healthiest lifestyle choice. I figured that by providing them a space where they could live and work that they would not only be able to live healthier lives but possibly be inspired by the surroundings.

I started the project be researching all aspects of academic housing design and toured numerous campuses to see examples. From there several phases of design and presentations occurred. Materials were selected, analyzed and decided upon. The presentation of all of my drawings and research was presented in a manner as if it were the work of an architectural student, who perhaps lived in Sims Architectural Residence Hall.

8-37

Sims Achitectural Residence Hall
Environmental Design II - Fall 2008

As my interests turned to architecture and form I decided to take a sculpture class which taught me about contemporary artists and the many uses of engaging space. This particular piece is one of my favorite pieces measuring approximately 7 ft wide by 5 1/2 ft tall and 2 feet deep. It was an expression of identity and reflected on my life line. I also have a fascination with color and color identification so I used the different color to reflect on different areas of my life, which the colors represented. (Purple for religion, blue for health, yellow for education, green for work, and pink representing relationships.)

8-38

FIGURES 8-37 AND 8-38 Portfolio pages for a range of projects. Figure 8-37 is for a thesis project and shows the large floor plan, elevations, three-dimensional models, and the exhibition of the project. Figure 8-38 shows fine art projects. Clear project descriptions define the projects, and graphics tie the various pages together. ■

The final examples are from a mono-type printmaking class. It was a subject matter that had never drawn my interest but after taking the class was truly one of the most enjoyable experiences. The first print is a modern interpretation of a seascape. I focused a lot on the use of fabrics and material to create unique textures. I was also creating transitional skies. The second print was a part of my final portfolio and focused on my use of color and replicating a scene.

As a Fine Arts major I had the opportunity to really explore numerous types of media. One of my first loves was the use of charcoal. I created several pieces using that media and even sold a few and was commission for others. This particular piece is one of the first in a series of still life drawings. I love the blending of the charcoal and think that my perfectionist behavior allowed me to keep the paper particularly clean and crisp which attributed to my love of the media.

Monotype Print Making
Studio - Summer 2008

Charcoal Drawing
Drawing I - Fall 2005

BY AMELIA TREPTOW.

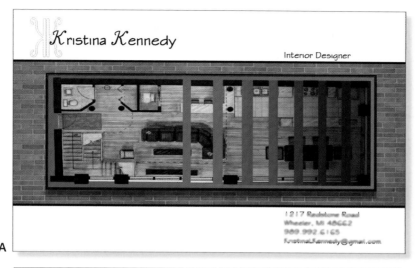

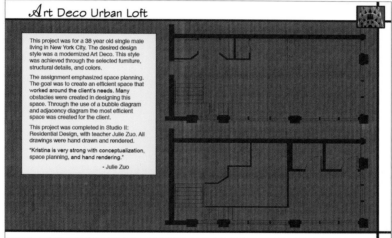

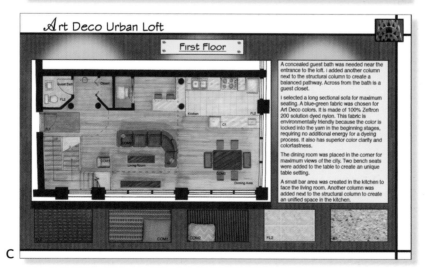

FIGURE 8-39, A–C These pages use a project for the portfolio title page (a) and show the architectural parameters (b) and the refined floor plan (c). This series provides a sense of the design process and includes a critique statement by the course instructor (b). ■

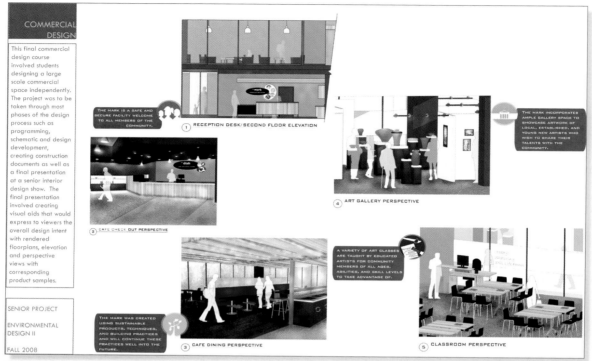

COMMERCIAL DESIGN

This final commercial design course involved students designing a large scale commercial space independently. The project was to be taken through most phases of the design process such as programming, schematic and design development, creating construction documents as well as a final presentation at a senior interior design show. The final presentation involved creating visual aids that would express to viewers the overall design intent with rendered floorplans, elevation and perspective views with corresponding product samples.

SENIOR PROJECT

ENVIRONMENTAL DESIGN II

FALL 2008

THE MARK IS A SAFE AND SECURE FACILITY WELCOME TO ALL MEMBERS OF THE COMMUNITY.

① RECEPTION DESK/SECOND FLOOR ELEVATION

② CAFE CHECK OUT PERSPECTIVE

THE MARK WAS CREATED USING SUSTAINABLE PRODUCTS, TECHNIQUES, AND BUILDING PRACTICES AND WILL CONTINUE THESE PRACTICES WELL INTO THE FUTURE.

③ CAFE DINING PERSPECTIVE

THE MARK INCORPORATES AMPLE GALLERY SPACE TO SHOWCASE ARTWORK OF LOCAL, ESTABLISHED, AND YOUNG NEW ARTISTS WHO WISH TO SHARE THEIR TALENTS WITH THE COMMUNITY.

④ ART GALLERY PERSPECTIVE

A VARIETY OF ART CLASSES ARE TAUGHT BY EDUCATED ARTISTS FOR COMMUNITY MEMBERS OF ALL AGES, ABILITIES, AND SKILL LEVELS TO TAKE ADVANTAGE OF.

⑤ CLASSROOM PERSPECTIVE

8-40

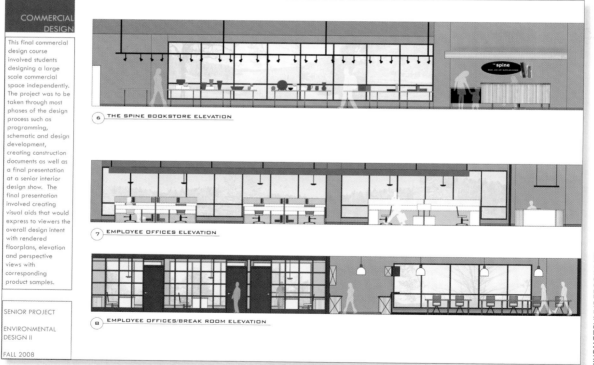

COMMERCIAL DESIGN

This final commercial design course involved students designing a large scale commercial space independently. The project was to be taken through most phases of the design process such as programming, schematic and design development, creating construction documents as well as a final presentation at a senior interior design show. The final presentation involved creating visual aids that would express to viewers the overall design intent with rendered floorplans, elevation and perspective views with corresponding product samples.

SENIOR PROJECT

ENVIRONMENTAL DESIGN II

FALL 2008

⑥ THE SPINE BOOKSTORE ELEVATION

⑦ EMPLOYEE OFFICES ELEVATION

⑧ EMPLOYEE OFFICES/BREAK ROOM ELEVATION

BY NICOLE BANASZEWSKI.

FIGURES 8-40 AND 8-41 Portfolio pages for one project (8-40) and pages for a range of different projects (8-41). The page design is used to unify the different types of projects shown—from color study sketches (8-41a) to technical drawings (8-41b). Additional descriptive statements have been added to the statement found in the left column on all the sheets. A related resume can be found in Figure 6-23. ■

8-41

A

ART STUDIO

This study abroad experience involved a traveling studio course in France. Each student carried with them a sketchbook that was filled with drawings, collages, notes, and more as the class traveled to different destinations across the country. The main focus was to view how color was depicted in the French environment and how it differed in various parts of the country. Students were able to create their sketchbook submissions and assigments using any medium or technique they wished. I chose to use colored pencil to depict how color appeared in different lighting environments.

COLOR STUDIO

FRANCE STUDY ABROAD EXPERIENCE

SUMMER 2008

B

CONSTRUCTION DOCUMENTS

This Interior Specifications II course involved learning how to create accurate interior specifications and construction documents that are consistent with those created in professional practice. Relationships of space planning, interior mechanical and electrical systems, furnishings, materials, finishes that abide to safety standards, building codes and ADA regulations were to be incorporated. Time keeping procedures and other administrative documentation was also learned.

CONSTRUCTION DOCUMENTS

INTERIOR SPECIFICATIONS II

SPRING 2008

C

RESIDENTIAL DESIGN

For this final project, students were asked to create a sustainable/universal kitchen space. The professor also stressed how the presentation should be carefully considered and consistent with a proposed design concept. For the presentation of this project, sustainable and unused materials from previous projects were incorporated. Also a unique way of using line drawing overlays over the rendered depictions were also used.

SUSTAINABLE/ UNIVERSAL DESIGN

INTERIOR DESIGN I

SPRING 2007

A

DIGITAL RENDERING

AUTODESK AUTOCAD 3-D PERSPECTIVES

JORDAN MOSER
EAST HOTEL
HAMBURG, GERMANY

PROJECT PARAMETERS:
Take an existing space and create a 3-D rendering using
Autodesk AutoCAD and VIZ. Animation available

VIZ PHOTOREALISTIC RENDERING

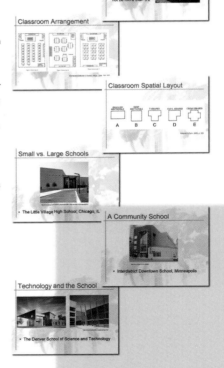

FOCUSED RESEARCH

SCHOOL FACILITIES:
THE INFLUENCE OF DESIGN ON
LEARNING AND PRODUCTIVITY

Today's schools are under intense pressure to produce successful students. With governmental programs such as No Child Left Behind and state voucher programs, schools are in high stakes competition to prove they are providing the highest level of education. With this increased competition, schools are developing ways to improve students' learning and productivity through new teaching techniques and technology. One aspect that must also be considered is the learning environment. The environment in which students learn can not only have implications on the students' performance but also on their ability to process information as well. The issue of learning environments and the affect on student success is bringing a need for a closer look at the school facility. With the increased number of students and the advances of technology, the design of the school facility is becoming a vital part of improving educational standards. There are many factors to consider when examining a school facility including the current building age, air quality, acoustics, and the classroom design. This paper will examine these factors as well as future trends and how they can be incorporated into designing a school facility.

Classroom Features
Classroom Arrangement
Classroom Spatial Layout
Small vs. Large Schools
A Community School
Technology and the School

JLW

B

FIGURE 8-42, A–C Portfolio pages for a range of projects, from digital rendering (a) to focused research (b) to an in-depth exploration of restaurant design (c). This portfolio is unified through the use of a consistent, appealing page design. It includes an example of the successful visual documentation of in-depth research (b). Additional elements from this portfolio can be found in Figure 7-8. ■

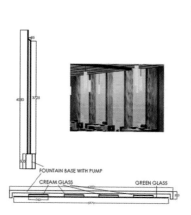

DINING AREA FOUNTAIN DETAIL

FOUNTAIN BASE WITH PUMP

CREAM GLASS   GREEN GLASS

VIEW OF MAIN DINING AND FOUNTAIN

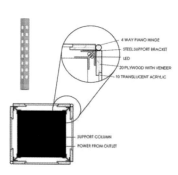

4 WAY PIANO HINGE

STEEL SUPPORT BRACKET

LED

20 PLYWOOD WITH VENEER

10 TRANSLUCENT ACRYLIC

SUPPORT COLUMN

POWER FROM OUTLET

COLUMN DETAIL

VIEW OF SUSHI BAR AND DINING

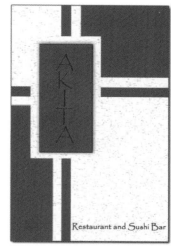

MENU DESIGN

C

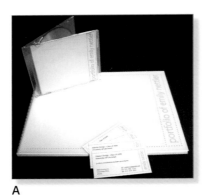

A

B

Co-op Experience:
Interbrand Design Forum
Dayton, Ohio
Fall Quarter 2008
Environmental Designer - Intern
Worked on drawing perspectives by hand quickly and accurately while mastering rendering skills: product fills, perspective/elevation alterations, photo transformations, and line drawing color addition.

Susan Butcher Design
Santa Fe, New Mexico
Spring Quarter 2008
Design Intern
Head of a residential design project located in the British West Indies and aided for other projects. Worked with Microsoft Office and Adobe Suite programs. In communication with design representatives daily.

Huntsman Architectural Group
San Francisco, California
Spring/Fall Quarters 2007
Junior Design Intern
Responsibilities included: creating and editing construction documents, site verification, obtaining building permits, space planning and finish selection.

Design Forum
Dayton, Ohio
Spring/Fall 2006
Environmental Designer - Intern
Enhanced hand drawing skills and rendering skills in Photoshop with a Wacom Pen used on-screen. Also worked in the Materials Library and with product reps/vendors.

Travel Quarter Abroad:
Summer 2007
8 week tour throughout Europe
Studied and have credit with:
Ecole Speciale D'Architecture in Paris, France and Architettura de Alghero in Sardinia, Italy

Special Knowledge:
Trained in: AutoCad 2007, Adobe Photoshop CS3, Adobe Illustrator CS3, Adobe InDesign CS3, Sketch Up, Form-Z, Microsoft Office and Visual CADD 4.0.3.

Education:
University of Cincinnati
Cincinnati, Ohio
2004 – Present
College of Design, Architecture, Art and Planning
Major: Interior Design
Class of 2009
G.P.A.: 3.3/4.0
Deans List: 3 consecutive school quarters

Anderson High School
Cincinnati, Ohio
2000-2004
G.P.A.: 3.88/4.0
Class Rank: 53/347 – Top 15%

Work Experience:
Henry N.
Santa Fe, New Mexico
April-June 2008
Freelance Designer
Created two photo portfolios of his work that is distributed to magazines, galleries and future employers. Used Adobe Photoshop and Adobe InDesign for composition.

Professional Business Services, Inc.
Cincinnati, Ohio
Summer 2004
Design Consultant
Individually developed a scheme then re-painted and re-decorated the entire office complex.

Special Interests:
Graphic design, identity and branding, marketing and advertising, millwork and fixture design, painting, photography, glass blowing, jewelry making.

Achievements and Awards:
College:
IBDF Holiday Card Design Competition Winner
U.C. Global Studies Scholarship Recipient
Elsie Minnick Scholarship Recipient

High School:
Academic Excellence Award 2000-2001
Top Scholar Athlete 2000-2001
Honor Roll Student Athlete 2000-2004
Anderson Achiever 2000-2004
Academic Letter Award 2000-2004
Choraliers Certificate and Letter 2002-2004
Two-Year Varsity Letter 2002-2004
National Honor Society Member 2002-2004
"Just Say No" Team Leader 2002-2004

Volunteer Experience:
College:
LEAP '07 Nature Rocks - Sand Castle Competition
WE CARE '07 - Christmas Celebration
IHM Batahola Child Sponsor
Member of Organization of Student Interior Designers
Various brochure, invitation, and company logo designs

High School:
Immaculate Heart of Mary
Cincinnati, Ohio
1999-2004
Teaching assistant for religion classes. Worked with second grade students for five years and first grade students for one year. Received a Certificate of Appreciation from IHM 1999-2004

Contact Info:
Email:
nettleee@email.uc.edu
nettleee2@gmail.com

Telephone:
House: (513) 474-3942
Cell: (513) 266-1328

School Address:
521 W. McMillan St.
Cincinnati, OH 45219

Permanent Address:
8648 Toronto Ct.
Cincinnati, OH 45255

resume of emily nettler

C

The final step in a four part urban mixed-use center studio project was to create a retail store, both inside and out. We were challenged to come up with an exciting new brand experience that engages every customer. Working individually, each person came up with their own narrative, name of a store, design for the store, materials and finishes, and storefront design. The concept for a 2-D graphic store called Graphically Expressed was produced.

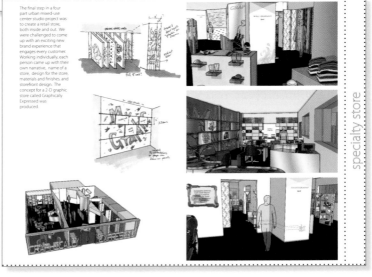

specialty store

D

FIGURE 8-43, A–D Consistent portfolio elements, including the portfolio itself, business cards, and a CD (a). The portfolio cover (b), the resume included in the portfolio (c), and a project page from the portfolio (d) illustrate how a simple yet consistent design can create unity. ■

BY EMILY NETTLER.

PROFESSIONAL VOICES

I have been working with designers and design students for over twenty-five years. During that time, I have had many discussions with professionals about creating effective portfolios, handling interviews successfully, and the job search in general.

The following are things I have heard from people who work at top design firms, teachers from a range of programs, and designers doing good work across the United States.

WHAT TO DO

Resumes and Cover Letters

List special things about your program of study, and whether the program you graduated from is accredited by the Council for Interior Design Accreditation (CIDA).

Mention any qualifying exam that you have passed, such as National Council for Interior Design Qualification (NCIDQ) or Leadership in Energy and Environmental Design (LEED).

Clearly indicate any internships that you have had (having one may be essential prior to being hired).

Include specialized skills (like software).

The resume and cover letter should stand out. These should set you apart, yet be polished and professional.

Portfolios

Show process items to indicate how you think. Demonstrating a creative thought process is important; it indicates logical, productive thinking. The sketches don't have to be perfect, but they should indicate an understanding of process.

While the portfolio does not have to be completely consistent (in terms of formatting), there should be some element(s) that tie it together, and it should demonstrate care and forethought.

Show freehand drawing skills as well as quick drawing skills, to indicate that you can convey ideas quickly.

Show complete, in-depth projects as well as some fine art (or other related items).

Craftsmanship is important in all elements of the portfolio. It should reflect creativity and yet be simple and straightforward.

Include only top-notch work.

Entry-level employees will help with rendering and making boards, so include examples of such work.

Show examples of your use of AutoCAD, Autodesk Revit, Adobe Photoshop, and other software. Revit and/or AutoCAD skills are fundamental, and new hires are often expected to be able to use Photoshop.

Make sure you *and* your portfolio are well organized.

Interviews

Being enthusiastic about the profession—and about your work—is essential.

Those hiring get a feel for how you will fit into the firm's culture based upon the attitude you convey during an interview, so always convey motivation. Even with the very best portfolio, you will not be hired if you have a poor attitude.

Speech, attire, and grooming are all important. Speak and dress appropriately.

Listen!

WHAT NOT TO DO

Don't make your resume too lengthy; pick and chose the most important information.

Don't make grammatical or spelling errors on your resume or in your portfolio.

Don't convey a bad attitude:

Never appear snobby at an interview, no matter how good your work or how well-known your university.

Don't project that you believe some tasks and jobs are beneath you. (This has been described as "the kiss of death" in one top firm looking for "team players".)

Never convey a general disregard for the thoughts or work of others.

Don't demonstrate an inability to take constructive criticism.

Don't appear unenthusiastic. Appearing unexcited about what you do is very worrisome for many employers.

Never arrive late to an interview.

Never appear disorganized.

PERSONAL
NARRATIVE EXERCISE

This is an ideation or brainstorming exercise.

STEP 1

Select a minimum of twenty images from a variety of sources. They should represent what inspires you as a person and as a designer. Think in terms of the following in selecting the images:

1. How you see yourself

2. What you value (e.g., hard work, spirituality, money, fame, etc.)

3. What inspires you (e.g., nature, music, art, color, architecture, etc.)

4. One more area that is of interest to you (such as music, science, engineering).

The images need not make any particular sense or relate specifically to design. For example, selecting a picture of a cloud-filled sky or an open field is just as reasonable as are images of your favorite design projects or designers. There is no right answer or wrong image. For the first part of the exercise, don't worry about selecting things based on beauty; select them because you connect with them.

STEP 2

Sort the images into two piles. One pile will be those that you really connect or identify with (and do not want to part with); the second pile is for those images that don't make the cut. Use the items from the "keep" pile to make a collage, focusing the composition on what is most meaningful to you. (Alternatively, treat the overall composition as a graphic exercise and focus on the images whose graphic qualities work best together.)

STEP 3

Select three words descriptive of your design personality, interests, or sensibility, and at least two additional random words that speak to you. After reading chapter 3, select typefaces that relate to the content of each word, print these, and post them in your work area with the collage generated in step 2.

At the conclusion of this exercise, you will have a personal visual narrative and list of words that have been translated into type. These two items will help you set the tone of your portfolio's visual direction. The portfolio need not include any of the images or the specific typeface or words selected: these are meant to inspire you as you move forward in the process. You may find that using one or two of the images from the collage helpful when creating thumbnails for the portfolio design (see Figure 2-10). Or simply using colors, or compositional elements from the collage may be helpful in generating thumbnails and/or generating compositional elements for the portfolio.

PORTFOLIO PROJECT
REVIEW AND INVENTORY WORKSHEET

Photocopy and fill out a worksheet for each project. For entry-level employment, consider and review each major school project using this sheet. Any supporting work, such as fine art or major research projects, should be reviewed using this sheet as well.

For those with professional experience, recent projects should be reviewed, along with those older projects that were particularly successful or challenging.

PORTFOLIO PROJECT REVIEW SHEET

What is the project's name?

What type of work was involved?

Is it an individual or team project?

Is this project similar to other project types (e.g., residential, hospitality, etc.)?

Is this project a unique project type?

Does this project employ a similar solution/aesthetic/concept to another?

Rate the project's quality (1 = bad, 10 = perfect).

What is required to improve it?

How much time is needed to fix any problems?

Does including this project support my goals to some degree?

Other comments.

Use the worksheets, when completed, to form a list of projects and priorities. This is accomplished by determining which projects require the least additional work or refinement for inclusion in the portfolio and which projects require the most additional work. Sort the worksheets, with those requiring the least work in the first positions. Create a list of the best projects inventoried that can be presented in thirty minutes as discussed in chapter 2. Use the list of projects to generate portfolio thumbnails (see Figure 2-10) and to create an action plan for improving projects as required.

THE PAMPHLET STITCH:
INSTRUCTIONS

The outer cover can be made of card stock, heavy decorative paper, or something of similar weight. Both the cover and the paper signatures (the folded sheets of paper making up the interior of the book) should be cut to the same size. The interior pages must be full sheets folded in half for the desired page size rather than individual sheets. Fold the cover and the pages in half separately so that they have perfectly creased edges. Use a bonefolder (a special tool) or the handle of a kitchen knife to make the perfectly folded creases.

A Punch holes using an awl or large needle. The illustration shows three holes, which should be equally spaced. (It is also possible to create a five-hole binding.) Punch through the cover and signatures at the same time (be careful not to punch your finger). N.B.: Do not try to punch holes or stitch through too many pages simultaneously; instead, limit the number of pages or use another binding method for booklets with many pages.

B Use special waxed binding thread, embroidery thread, or string to bind the book. If you choose to use embroidery thread or string, run it through a wax block or a wax candle to wax the thread so that it is easier to work with. Cut the thread at least three times the length of the book.

C After threading a large needle, make the first stitch through the middle hole. If you want to tie off the final stitch on the outside of the book, begin the first stitch on the outside. If you want the final tie-off on the inside, make the first stitch on the inside.

D and E The second stitch can go through the top hole (D shows the interior of the book). Make a loop from the top hole on the outside to the bottom hole, creating one long stitch on the outside of the booklet (shown dashed to indicate that it's on the outside of drawing D). N.B.: When pulling each stitch, keep the thread and needle parallel to the booklet rather than pulling upward, as you would with standard sewing stitches; pulling upward can cut the paper.

F Tie off the stitch by tying on top of the long loop created in D and E. Either a square knot or bow can be used. In this example, the stitch is tied and visible on the outside of the book because the first stitch was made on the outside.

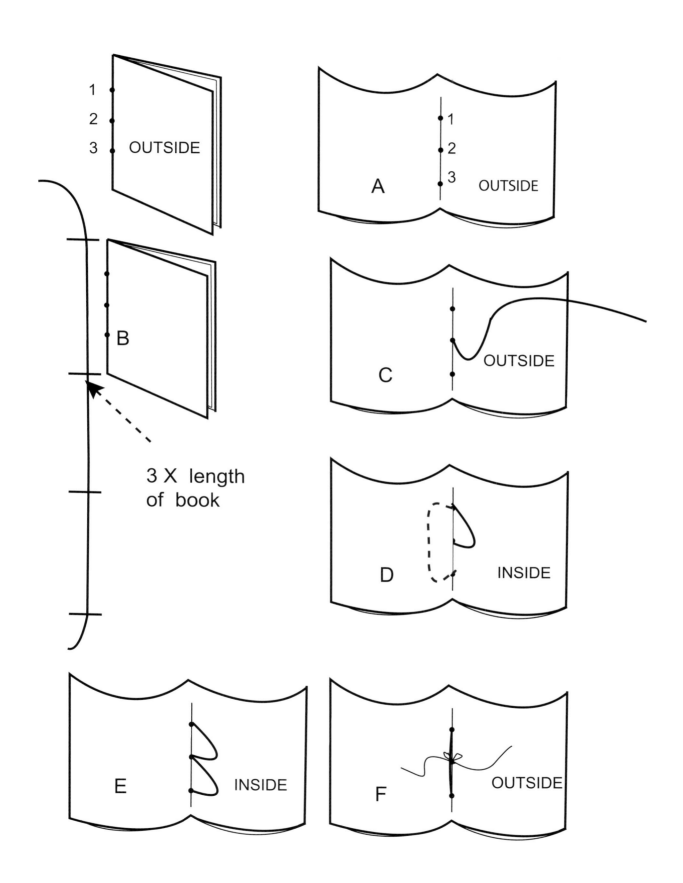

1
2
3 OUTSIDE

A OUTSIDE
1
2
3

B

3 X length of book

C OUTSIDE

D INSIDE

E INSIDE

F OUTSIDE

INDEX